ISBN 978-1-5284-5336-3
PIBN 10923694

English
Français
Deutsche
Italiano
Español
Português

www.forgottenbooks.com

Mythology Photography **Fiction**
Fishing Christianity **Art** Cooking
Essays Buddhism Freemasonry
Medicine **Biology** Music **Ancient
Egypt** Evolution Carpentry Physics
Dance Geology **Mathematics** Fitness
Shakespeare **Folklore** Yoga Marketing
Confidence Immortality Biographies
Poetry **Psychology** Witchcraft
Electronics Chemistry History **Law**
Accounting **Philosophy** Anthropology
Alchemy Drama Quantum Mechanics
Atheism Sexual Health **Ancient History**
Entrepreneurship Languages Sport
Paleontology Needlework Islam
Metaphysics Investment Archaeology
Parenting Statistics Criminology
Motivational

THE

GOVERNMENT OF PENNSYLVANIA

AND

THE NATION

BY

CLINTON D. HIGBY, Ph.D.

"If we would preserve our government, we must
endear it to the people." — WILLIAM PENN.

REVISED

D. C. HEATH & CO., PUBLISHERS

BOSTON   NEW YORK   CHICAGO

PREFACE

SOME years ago I prepared a small book, "A General Outline of Civil Government," for use in schools, and after its publication my associate teachers and friends suggested that I should write a book describing the government under which the people of Pennsylvania live. It should be a book giving the whole of their government, the part conducted by the State and the part administered by the nation, so that students in schools and others who used the book would have before them the complete fabric of their government.

So many of the elements of good citizenship depend upon the conduct of the citizen toward the things of his government that are near him — the public schools, care of the poor, public roads, elections, taxation, expenditure of public money, administration of justice, and other public affairs in the local districts — that the study of civil government would indeed be barren without them. These subjects I have placed first in the book, and have proceeded to them along the path of history which shaped them. In describing the government I have told how the townships are erected and classified; how the school districts, poor districts, and election districts are formed, and how the government is conducted in them; how the counties supervise the local affairs of the State, taking a larger part in the fiscal and judicial affairs than the townships; how the boroughs and cities are incorporated, and their legal relation to the State; how the central government of the State proceeded from the early provincial government; and how the national government developed from the united action of the colonies, remaining everywhere within reach of the people, so that the government of the people of the State, both State and federal, is in every part their own government.

The actual workings of the government are given, and the numerous details are so arranged as to illumine the subject rather than to obscure it. Any detail may easily be found, and the references to correlated sections of the text will help the student to proceed from page to page with a clear knowledge of the subject. I have taken great pains to be accurate, and to put the student in possession of the right knowledge of the principles involved.

To know one's government is to love it, and to find pleasure in the support of its authority and its interests. I have placed a high value on this knowledge. I believe it will lead one to take a larger part in the government, in·the affairs of the home, the township, the borough, the city, and the county. It is here that the good citizen finds the opportunity of taking part in his government, and it is here that good citizenship is worth most to the State, for if the local life of the State is not of high character, the State is not well governed.

CLINTON D. HIGBY.

ERIE, PENNSYLVANIA,
May 1, 1908.

CONTENTS

THE GOVERNMENT OF PENNSYLVANIA AND THE NATION

CHAPTER I

COLONIAL BEGINNINGS OF PENNSYLVANIA

1. Penn obtains land for a free commonwealth. — Pennsylvania was founded by William Penn. He desired to provide a home for persecuted Quakers and to establish for them a free commonwealth. Therefore he petitioned Charles II, King of England, to grant him land in America in which to make settlements. The king favored the request. Penn's father had rendered the English government great service and had lent Charles II a large amount of money. In payment of this debt, the king granted William Penn, March 4, 1681, the tract of land lying north of Maryland, extending west from the Delaware River as far as the western limit of Maryland, and north as far as the State now extends. In drawing up the deed, the secretary left a blank space for the king to fill in the name of the province. Penn suggested the name New Wales, as the country was hilly like Wales; but the king did not like the name. Then Penn suggested Sylvania, the country being wooded. This name pleased the king; and, putting the word Penn before it, he called the country Pennsylvania, in honor of Penn's father, Sir William Penn.

Penn's
deputy takes
possession,
1681.

2. William Markham takes possession for Penn. — The
king issued a proclamation commanding the people living
in the province to obey the new proprietor; and Penn sent
William Markham, his cousin, to take possession. He gave
Markham authority to announce the king's proclamation,
appoint officers, establish courts, call a council, and to do
whatever he found necessary for the peace and safety of
the country. Markham embarked in May, and arrived in
the province July 1, 1681. Immediately on his arrival he
established his authority. Out of respect for the different
nationalities represented in the population, Markham named
two Swedes to sit in the Council, and chose the Dutch
village of Upland as capital. The place is now Chester,
about fifteen miles down the river from Philadelphia.
Markham appointed also a number of justices of the peace.
They met at Upland, and held court for all of Upland
County, as the country about Upland was called. Some of
the records of this early court may be seen at West Chester.
At the second session of the court Markham sat with the
justices. Penn had given him authority to do so.

Penn per-
fects his
title.

3. Penn prepares the way for his government. — Penn
remained in England until the autumn of 1682. He was
engaged in perfecting his title to the province, and in
informing his followers of the opportunity for settlement
in Pennsylvania. At the time England came into control
of the settlements on the Delaware River and the Bay,
Charles II gave his brother James, Duke of York, the
right to direct the government of the settlements. Penn
took the precaution to obtain from the duke a deed
releasing any claim he might have to Pennsylvania.
Penn also published a description of the country, and
explained the government which he proposed to establish.
The plan of the government consisted of a Charter of

Privileges and a number of laws approved by the king. The Penn Papers in possession of the Historical Society of Pennsylvania show that Penn made twenty drafts of the Charter of Privileges before he was satisfied with the result. Every freeman was given the right to vote for a representative in the Assembly, and to be elected to that body ; and no law could be made without the approval of the representatives at a session of the Assembly. The only requirement as to religion was that the people should acknowledge God, and live just and peaceable lives. *Penn's plan of government.*

4. Penn arrives in his province. — William Penn arrived in the Delaware River and landed at New Castle, October 27, 1682. In addition to the papers showing his title to the province, he had two deeds from the Duke of York for the land farther down the river, which is now the State of Delaware. One deed gave him the town of New Castle and a district of twelve miles around it,[1] and the other gave the land now embraced in the Delaware counties of Kent and Sussex. These Lower Counties, as they were called, were obtained by Penn so that he might control the way for ships to his province. After showing the people the deeds for the Lower Counties, Penn took formal possession of the town of New Castle. The key of the fort was delivered to him; and to signify the passing of the land the people gave him " one turf with a twig upon it, and a porringer of river water and soil." This is the way possession of land was delivered at that time. Then the people assembled at the court-house and Penn made a speech to them. He .explained his plan of government, and assured the people that they should be protected in their religious freedom and civil liberty. All *Penn arrives in his province, 1682.* *The Lower Counties.*

---

[1] This circular district around New Castle accounts for the northern boundary of Delaware being a curved line.

he asked of them was sobriety and good conduct toward one another.

The first Council.

5. Provincial Council and Assembly. — As soon as Penn had taken possession of the province, he ordered an election to be held in each county to choose twelve members for the Council. The province had three counties (§ 48) and the three Lower Counties joined with them, so that the Council consisted of seventy-two members. The Council acted as advisor to the proprietor and represented his interests. Its duties were to originate bills;[1] execute the laws; care for the safety of the province; fix the location of ports, cities, and roads; inspect the public treasury; establish courts, appoint judges, and organize schools; and summon and dissolve the General Assembly. The Assembly represented the people. In accordance with Penn's desire, all the freemen met the first year as members of the Assembly to adopt the plan of government. After the first year the Assembly was to have two hundred members. It was soon found that both bodies were too large and their membership was reduced.

The Assembly.

The first General Assembly, 1682.

6. Meeting of the first Assembly. — The first Assembly met, December 4, 1682, at Chester. The members of the Council met with the Assembly. Nicholas Moore was chosen president, rules were adopted, and committees appointed to assist in bringing matters before the General Assembly. Two important bills were passed, one annexing the Lower Counties and the other making the alien freemen citizens. The freemen who were citizens of England were considered citizens of the province, but all aliens — those who came from foreign countries — had to be made citizens by law, that is, naturalized.

---

[1] A form or draft of a proposed law is called a *bill*. If it is accepted by the law-making body, it becomes a *law*.

7. Plan of government adopted. — The General Assembly then sent a committee to William Penn to inquire if he had anything to present. This committee received from him the Charter of Privileges and the laws agreed upon in England. Taken together they were the constitution, or Frame of Government, as Penn called it. The laws consisted of forty carefully drawn rules of government, and the Charter of Privileges was a declaration of the rights of the people. A statement of these inalienable rights is usually made the first part of every constitution. Penn submitted also a number of bills which he thought should be made into laws. The General Assembly adopted the Charter of Privileges and the laws without alteration ; but the bills proposed by Penn did not fare so well. Several of them were changed, and some of them were wholly rejected.

Constitution adopted, 1682.

8. Changes in the constitution. — At the meeting of the second General Assembly it was agreed that seventy-two members would be enough for both the Council and the Assembly — three from each county for the Council, and nine from each county for the Assembly. The constitution was amended to this effect. Penn's constitution was not an unalterable document; it was the first constitution in force in America that could be amended. The next year the Assembly was reduced to six members from each county. Another amendment was much desired by the Assembly. The members insisted that the Assembly should have the right to introduce legislation; according to the constitution, only the Council could frame the proposed laws, and the Assembly merely accepted or rejected the bills sent to it. An effort was made to pass an amendment giving the Assembly the right to originate bills, but Penn would not consent to it.

Amendments.

Conflict over legislation.

9. The Assembly contests for its rights. — Just at this time Penn had to go back to England. A dispute there over the boundary line between Pennsylvania and Maryland was threatening his interests. He sailed in August, 1684, leaving Markham deputy-governor in his absence. The members of the General Assembly at once renewed the contest for the right to introduce legislation. They refused to approve many of the bills introduced by the Council. Markham would not grant them the power they asked, and the members of the Assembly kept on rejecting bills. The contest lasted for some time. Finally Markham had to yield, and a new constitution was adopted.

Penn annuls the Markham constitution, 1699.

10. Penn annuls the Markham constitution. — William Penn, accompanied by his wife and daughter, returned to the province in November, 1699, after an absence of fifteen years. He was not altogether pleased with the way affairs had been managed by his governor. He annulled the Markham constitution; it had not received his approval and was not legally in force. The people still insisted very strongly that the Assembly should not only have the right to introduce bills, but that it should be given all the rights of a free, law-making body. Penn told them, finally, to prepare a constitution, and embody in it whatever they wanted. The free commonwealth which he had promised the people was now to be established. The General Assembly soon met and the members undertook to frame a new constitution; but they found it difficult, and adjourned without accomplishing it. They tried again at the next session, and were still unable to complete the work.

Constitution of 1701.

11. Constitution of 1701 adopted. — A bill to annex to the crown all the proprietary governments in America was presented to Parliament at this time, and Penn must hasten to England. Before going, he called an extra session of the General Assembly to settle the matter of adopting a constitution. It met in September, 1701. The members proceeded with earnestness, and framed what is known as the constitution of 1701. This constitution gave the Assembly the right to introduce bills, to choose its own officers, to appoint committees, to fix the time of its adjournment, and to have the general powers and privileges of a free legislature. The power of establishing the courts was also given to the Assembly; but the proprietor continued to appoint the judges, and it was one hundred and fifty years before they were elected. The Council no longer met with the Assembly; its legislative powers were all given to the Assembly. Liberty of conscience, recognized in the constitution, could not be taken away by any power; but any other part of the constitution could be amended. So complete and just was this constitution that in only one thing did the Assembly increase its power in the next seventy-five years; before 1740 it became a fixed principle that to the people, through their representatives in the Assembly, belongs the right to expend public money, and to determine the manner of raising it. *Important changes.*

12. The Lower Counties withdraw. — The Lower Counties — New Castle, Kent, and Sussex — did not unite closely with the province. The people living in them wanted to withdraw from the government of Pennsylvania and to have a government of their own. This question came before the General Assembly in 1701. The Lower Counties were joined to the province by an act of the General Assembly, and it was only proper that the separation should be by the same authority. It was agreed that they might withdraw any time after three years, and in 1704 *Lower Counties withdraw, 1704.*

they withdrew. Immediately they organized a government with an Assembly chosen by the people and a
governor appointed by the proprietor of Pennsylvania.
This form of government continued in Delaware until
the Revolution.

End of pro-
prietary con-
trol, 1776.

13. End of proprietary control. — It was late in 1701
when Penn embarked for England. He never came again
to the province, and his interests were in the care of
deputies till his death in 1718, at the age of seventy-four
years. Trustees of his estate, and later his widow and
sons, conducted the proprietary affairs until the Revolution. Then the Assembly of the State of Pennsylvania
abolished the power of the Penns and their title to the
land. They were permitted, however, to keep their private
estates and the rents reserved in the sale of lands; but
the right to conduct the government no longer remained
to them. The Assembly voted the Penns a large sum of
money (£130,000), the final payment of which was provided for by the State in 1781. England also paid them
an annuity (£4000) for the losses occasioned by the Revolution. The annuity was later commuted by the payment
of a fixed sum (£67,000) by the British government.

14. **Summary.** — In 1681 William Penn obtained from Charles II
land in America for a home for persecuted Quakers. He prepared the
frame of a free government, to which the king consented, and came to
the province of Pennsylvania in the autumn of 1682 and organized the
government. He permitted all the freemen to take part in adopting the
plan of government and made such changes in the laws as they desired.
The affairs of the province were managed by the proprietor, or a governor
appointed by him, and by a Council and an Assembly; the members of
these two bodies were elected by vote of the people. The people con-
tended strongly for the right to make the laws in the Assembly, instead
of only accepting or rejecting them, and Penn finally granted this right.

QUESTIONS

What events led to William Penn's becoming proprietor of Pennsylvania? How did William Markham assist Penn? Why did Penn delay going to his province? How did Penn take possession when he arrived in the territory? How is possession of land passed now?

What interest did James, Duke of York, have in the lands granted to Penn? How did Penn acquire this interest?

What part did Charles II take in shaping the government of Pennsylvania? How did Penn try to perfect his Frame of Government? Explain the Charter of Privileges and the laws agreed upon in England.

Distinguish between Council and General Assembly. Who composed the first General Assembly? Why?

What powers did the Assembly have at first? What additional powers did it obtain? How did it get them? What right did the Assembly come to have later in raising and expending public money?

Did Penn make his province a "free commonwealth" in 1682 or in 1701? What became of the Lower Counties?

What right had the people later to set up an independent State government? Should the Penns have been paid for the land? What right had Charles II to grant the land to Penn? Under what circumstances does the State of Pennsylvania now take land from private owners (§ 55)?

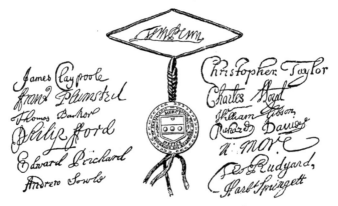

SEAL AND SIGNATURE TO THE FRAME OF GOVERNMENT.

CHAPTER II

LOCAL DISTRICTS

First
settlements. **15. The first settlements.** — At the time William Penn arrived in the province, in 1682, about two thousand people were living in small settlements on the shores of the Delaware Bay and up the river as far as the falls where Trenton now stands. They were mainly Swedes, Dutch, and English. The Swedes came in 1638 and settled near the mouth of a stream which they named Christina Creek, in honor of their queen. This stream is in Delaware and still bears the name — now spelled Christiana — and Wilmington occupies the site of the settlement. Other Swedes joined them at Christina Creek, and the settlement remained under the control of Sweden seventeen years. Then the Dutch came and captured it from the Swedes, and held all the Delaware lands nine years as Dutch settlements, until the English in turn took them away from the Dutch.

Early local
government. **16. Their government.** — The settlers were too far from home to return, so they remained in the settlements, even though the authority over them had changed. England encouraged them to stay by permitting them to continue their government much as they had been conducting it. The people continued to meet and make rules to regulate the local affairs, and they had a voice in choosing the local officers. They also had courts in the different settlements to punish offenders and to correct private wrongs.

In 1664, when the English came into control, Charles II gave his brother, Duke of York, the right to direct the government. For twelve years the duke made few changes, but in 1676 he ordered the government he had prepared put into force. The territory was divided into three parts, Counties like English counties; the names of many of the offices established. were changed; and the county was given control of local affairs. This manner of government was only begun, however, when William Penn, five years later, took possession of the country. Penn's government did not deprive the people of the right to conduct the affairs of government near their homes, but it rather fostered this right. The same general plan of dividing the whole country into counties (§ 48), and giving each county the supervision of the local affairs, was followed. The small settlements within the county retained a part in the government; to them were left the details and the control of matters belonging to the immediate localities. Thus the local government came to be administered partly by the township, and partly by the county.

The Township

17. The settlements become townships. — At first there The first were no political lines bounding the settlements; they townships were divided only by the unsettled portions of the country. Each settlement, however, was a distinct division, and its government was in a large degree separate from that of the other settlements. The settlements had their local officers, such as were needed. These primitive divisions came to be more completely organized, and their boundaries more definitely fixed, as the population increased. They were first called towns; later they were called townships. Penn continued the name township.

Organiza-
tion of new
townships.

18. Additional townships. — The first townships were erected near Philadelphia, and as fast as the country was settled other townships were organized. After a time the whole of Pennsylvania became settled, and all the territory was divided into townships. They were irregular in size and shape;[1] some were very large and had only a small population. As the population increased, the townships were divided and new ones were organized. Large townships are even now subdivided. There is no limit to the number the State may have. Whenever the people want a new township erected, they petition the court of quarter sessions to erect it. Persons who are interested may be heard by the court. If the conditions favor the petition, the court orders an election so that the people may vote on the question. If the vote is favorable, the erection of the new township is ordered by the court. The papers and a map showing the boundaries are preserved by the clerk of the court, and officers are chosen to conduct the affairs of the new township.

19. Classification of townships. — Prior to 1899 all the townships of Pennsylvania had the same government. In that year they were divided into two classes, and the more populous ones were given a more elaborate government. Those having a population of 300 or more to the square mile are now townships of the first class; all the others are townships of the second class. Townships of the second class, which form much the larger part, continue to have the same government that all the townships had before the classification. The townships of the first class, few in number, have a government somewhat like

Townships
of the first
class; the
second class.

[1] In many of the Western States the townships are uniform and regular, each six miles square.

that of a borough, but the legislature did not go so far as to give them borough government.

20. Government and duties of townships. — The govern- Government of townships. ment of the township is in the hands of officers elected by the people. The citizens do not hold township meetings to discuss local matters and vote on them, as is done in the New England towns. The decision is intrusted to the local officers and their choice is binding. The only way to change their decision is to elect a different set of offi- cers. This takes time and affords an opportunity for the people to consider the question at issue before they act on it. This method, by which the people regulate the policy of government through periodic election of officers, is an important principle of government in both the State and the nation.

In the administration of local government the township Local districts. is chiefly concerned with the care of public roads, the levy- ing and collecting of taxes, and the administering of justice in the local courts. The care of paupers and the manage- ment of public schools have become separated from the township. Each of these duties falls to a special district — the poor district and the school district. Still another local district is the election district, a division of territory for the convenience of voters. The township, school dis- trict, and poor district are corporate bodies, that is, they have power to do business as one man would.

The township is responsible for the condition of the pub- Township roads. lic roads and the small bridges — the county usually cares for the large bridges. The township supervisors have charge of keeping the roads in good condition and build- ing new roads. In townships of the first class the town- ship commissioners care for the roads. The old custom of working out the road tax no longer exists. The road tax is now all paid in money and the officers who care for the roads employ men to keep them in good condition. They hire the work done by the day or let it by contract. The State helps keep up the roads. This it does by furnishing part of the money used on them and by giving the local officers information about building roads and caring for them. New roads are opened by order of the court of quarter sessions. The people living in the vicinity petition the court for a road, and viewers are appointed to go to the locality and see if the road is needed. If they report to the court that the road should be opened, an order is made, directing the township supervisors to open the road. Private roads are opened in the same way, but at the expense of those who ask to have the roads opened.

THE POOR DISTRICT

Care of paupers.

21. Care of the poor. — At first each township[1] and borough provided for its own poor. But larger districts have grown in favor, because it is convenient in providing a home for paupers to bring together a considerable number of them. Whenever an almshouse is provided for the paupers of the entire county, the care of the poor becomes a part of the county government. The county officials appoint agents in different parts of the county to assist them in giving personal attention to paupers. A residence of one year entitles paupers to public aid from the district. If they wander from one district to another, they must be sent back. The needy, sick, and injured poor must be provided with food, shelter, and care, — and in case of death, with burial, — whether they reside in the district or not; the

[1] Philadelphia and some of the adjoining townships, however, were from the first united to form one large poor district.

county bears this expense. William Penn taught that the public purse should be opened to help those who put forth their honest endeavors to earn a living, and fail; but able-bodied persons who try to earn a living do not become paupers.

THE SCHOOL DISTRICT [1]

22. Local management of schools. — The immediate management of the public schools is in the care of officers elected by the people in small districts. Each township, borough, and city is a school district. The meetings of the school directors are open to the people of the district; but the school directors decide all questions of local management of the schools. The people do not vote on these questions; they elect the school directors to act for them, and the school directors control the schools. For this reason it is always important that the best-fitted persons should be chosen school directors.

School management.

23. Formation of school districts. — The territory comprised in each township, borough, and city is by law made a school district; and whenever a new township, borough, or city is organized, it becomes also a school district. The administration of the school affairs of the new district begins on the first Monday in July; this is the time the school year begins.

School districts.

School districts are classified. Those having a population of 500,000 or over are districts of the first class; those

[1] Penn provided in his Frame of Government that all the children of the province should be taught some useful employment. He realized that a necessary part of education is that which fits each one to earn his own living, and to provide for those who may be dependent upon him. Penn desired that the poor should have the means of earning a living, and that the rich, if they became poor, might not come to want. Instruction of this kind is indeed a wise equipment for life; and Penn added a dignity to it by placing it in his Frame of Government.

30,000 or over, but less than 500,000, second class; those 5000 or over, but less than 30,000, third class; and those less than 5000, fourth class.

THE ELECTION DISTRICT

Election districts.

24. The people vote near their homes. — Townships and boroughs having a small population are each an election district; those having a large population, and the cities, are divided in forming election districts. It is a rule that when the number of voters in an election district become 250, the district is divided and a new one formed. This rule is a legal requirement in cities. A voter cannot vote outside the district in which he resides; for this reason the districts must be small enough so that all the votes may be cast in the time given for voting.

Municipal election.

25. The elections. — Two elections are held — the municipal election and the general election. The municipal election, at which are chosen city, ward, borough, township, and county officers, is held on the Tuesday next after

General election.

the first Monday in November in the odd year. The general election, at which are chosen state and national officers, is held on the same day in November in the even year. The same election officers conduct both elections. The polls open at seven o'clock A.M., and close at seven o'clock P.M.

Primaries.

Two primaries, or meetings of voters in the election district, are held to choose candidates for the offices to be filled. The spring primary is held on the second Saturday in April in the even year at which candidates for State and national offices are nominated. The fall primary is held on the last Saturday in September in the odd year, at which candidates for the local offices are nominated. The members of all political parties meet at the same primary. Each voter has the right to receive the ballot of the party for which he asks, unless some one objects to his receiving it on the ground that he is not a member of that party. To entitle him then to receive the ballot, he must make oath or affirmation that at the last general election in which he took part he voted for a majority of the candi- dates of that party. The primaries are held from two o'clock to eight o'clock P.M.

26. The voter. — The right to vote is limited to male citizens twenty-one years of age and upward. A resi- dence in the State for one year immediately preceding the election is required. But if a man has once been a voter in the State and establishes a residence outside, a residence of only six months is required on his return. For the last two months, in every case, he must live in the election dis- trict where he offers to vote. Men who come from other countries must be naturalized at least one month before they can vote; and to be naturalized requires a residence of five years in the United States. Young men of legal age may vote until they are twenty-two years old without paying a tax. After that age (which gives time to levy and collect a tax), all voters are required to pay a State or county tax before they can vote. The tax must have been levied at least two months before the election, and paid not later than one month before that date.

Qualification of the voter.

Voters are registered before each election. The lists are sent to the county commissioners, who copy the names and send them to the election officers to use as voting lists. In the cities each man is required to register in person. Those who claim the right to vote go to the polling places on certain days, the registrars examine them, and if they are legal voters their names are put on the lists. Voters absent from the city or ill on registration day, may have their names added to the lists later. In the election dis-

Registra- tion.

tricts outside the cities, assessors register the voters
(§ 34).

Only about one fifth of the population are voters. The
right to vote is given by the people of the State; and
every voter is by duty bound to the State to accept the
privilege and to exercise it to the best of his ability. It is
his civil duty, and is as important to the State as his military duty.

27. **Summary.** — The government of the State began in a number of
small settlements. The independence of these settlements has not been
wholly lost; it is still present in the local divisions of the State. The
people elect the officers in the local districts, and these officers apply
the laws of government as they think best. The people must abide by
their judgment, or at the next election choose new officers, who have the
same freedom of judgment in conducting local affairs. The township is
the road district, and it is also the division for the levy and collection
of taxes, and for the administration of justice in the lowest court. The
management of the public schools and the care of the poor are separate
from township affairs; each has its own district, which is a corporate
body similar to a township. Elections are held in small divisions of
territory, called election districts. They have no corporate powers,
being mere divisions for convenience in voting.

QUESTIONS

How many settlers were living on the Delaware River and Bay when
Penn arrived? Of what nationalities, mainly?

What had the Duke of York to do with the government of the settlements?

What is a township? What affairs belong to the township? To the
school-district? To the poor district?

How many townships may be erected? How is a township erected?
How are townships classified? How does the government of the two
classes differ?

Do the supervisors in repairing the roads have to go beyond the
limits of their township? Could a tax collector go from his township
into another and collect taxes? Could a justice of the peace sit and
hear a lawsuit for some other justice of the peace in another township?

Are school directors officers of the school district or of the township? Which is liable for the care of a pauper, the poor district or the township?

What is a pauper? Should an able-bodied man out of work be given public aid? What was Penn's rule?

What provision did Penn put in the first constitution of the province as to education? How does the number of school districts increase? How are school districts classified?

What is an election district? When are new election districts created? Can a man vote in the election district where he happens to be at the time of an election? What officers are elected at the municipal election? At the general election? When are these elections held? When is the fall primary held? The spring primary? Give all of the qualifications of a voter.

THE FIRST TOWN HALL AND COURT-HOUSE, PHILADELPHIA.

CHAPTER III

OFFICERS IN THE LOCAL DISTRICTS

28. Election and term of office. — The officers of the local districts are elected by the voters of the districts at the municipal election (§ 25). At this election general political questions do not enter, and the people are free to consider the needs peculiar to the districts. The term of local officers begins, with some exceptions, on the first Monday in March. Magistrates and constables in Philadelphia take their offices on the first Monday in April; justices of the peace and aldermen in cities, on the first Monday in May; and school directors, on the first Monday in June. The term of office is four years, except for school directors and officers holding local courts, who are elected for six years, and constables in Philadelphia for five years.

Term of local officers.

29. Vacancies in office. — In most cases the court of quarter sessions fills a vacancy in office in a local district, usually for the remainder of the term. A vacancy in the office of justice of the peace, alderman, or magistrate is filled by the governor until the next municipal election; in the office of school director, by the remainder of the school board until the next municipal election; in the office of assessor, by the county commissioners; and in the offices of judge of election and inspector of election, by the court of common pleas for the cities, and by the court of quarter sessions for the townships and boroughs.

Filling vacancies.

OFFICERS IN CHARGE OF PUBLIC ROADS

30. Township supervisors. — The roads and small bridges in townships of the second class are in the care of three township supervisors, chosen, one at the first election, and two at the next. They meet annually on the first Monday in December, and levy the road tax and divide the township into road districts. They hire a superintendent for the whole township or appoint a roadmaster in each district to direct the work of men employed to work on the roads. It is their duty to take care of the roads, and to see that such necessary conveniences as watering-troughs and guideboards are provided. Landowners may build sidewalks in front of their property, and the law protects the walks. They may also erect watering-troughs and plant trees along the roadside. For these services, and also for using wide-tired wagons, the taxpayers receive a small credit on their road tax. Road supervisors are paid for work done.

Township supervisors in townships of second class.

31. Township commissioners. — In townships of the first class (§ 19) the duties of the former road supervisors are now performed by township commissioners, who are given much larger duties. One township commissioner is elected every two years in each election district in the township. If the township does not have as many as five election districts, — the smallest number of commissioners a township of this class may have, — one township commissioner is elected in each election district, and the remainder of the number from the township at large. They not only keep the roads in good condition, but they may provide curbstones, pavements, and sidewalks. They may construct sewers and make the owners of adjacent land use them to preserve the public health, and also regulate or abate places harmful to health. They may also maintain a police

Commissioners in townships of first class.

force and a fire department, and supply the people with water.   In regulating these matters they pass ordinances[1] at their monthly meetings.   Any breach of these ordinances may be punished by fine and imprisonment.   Township commissioners have power to levy a tax, borrow money, and issue bonds; but these powers are carefully limited.   They receive no pay.

Town clerk.

32. Town clerk and secretary. — The board of township commissioners elect a town clerk who acts as secretary of the board, keeping the official minutes of the board and performing other clerical duties.   He also keeps a record of all the transfers of land in the township, showing the number of acres conveyed, the location of the land, and the price it sold for, if given.   The purpose of keeping this record is to enable the township assessors to put the true value on the land and to assess it in the name of the real owners.   The board of township commissioners fix his salary by ordinance.

Secretary.

In townships of the second class the township supervisors appoint a secretary annually.   He keeps the official minutes of their meetings and performs other minor duties.   His pay is fixed by the township auditors.

OVERSEERS OF THE POOR

Overseers of the poor.

33. Overseers of the poor. — The local poor districts that still exist elect each two overseers of the poor, one of whom may be a woman.   They are elected for four years.   It is their duty to furnish public relief to persons who are entitled to it (§ 21).   Assistance may be given such paupers in their own homes, or they may be cared for in

[1] Ordinance is the term applied to local laws and regulations passed by the local governing body.

other places.   An order from two justices of the peace is
necessary in ordinary instances to put a pauper on the
public charge.   In some parts of Pennsylvania, however, Care of the
an order from one justice is enough.   In cases of emer- poor.
gency, relief may precede the order.   Poor persons who are
able to work, but are without employment, may be put to
work at whatever the overseers provide.   The overseers
may put them to work on the roads, with the consent
of the road supervisors.   Those not able to work must
be cared for without laboring.   Indigent orphan children
may be put out as apprentices — girls till they are
eighteen, and boys till they are twenty-one.   Overseers
of the poor have power to levy a tax for the relief of
paupers.   They are paid by the day.

OFFICERS IN CHARGE OF FISCAL AFFAIRS

34. Assessors. — Taxes are apportioned according to the Assessors.
value of property of various kinds.   This value is determined by officials called assessors.   Every three years
assessors receive notice from the county commissioners to
make a true list of all taxable persons and taxable property
in their districts, with a just valuation of the property.
Each township has an assessor, and boroughs have
assessors,— one in each ward, if the borough is divided.
Cities and some large counties have several assessors,
organized as a board of assessment.   Philadelphia has two
assessors in each assessment district, appointed by the
board of revision of taxes of the city.   Assessors are paid
by the day.

The property assessed consists of land and the buildings Property
thereon ; horses, mules, and cattle, over four years old ; that is assessed.
offices and positions of profit, professions, and trades,
except farming.   The number of dogs in each district

is recorded, for the county commissioners lay a tax on them, which goes into a fund to pay for sheep killed or injured by dogs. A valuation is also put on cabs, stages, coaches, and other vehicles used in transporting passengers for hire, except street and steam railway cars. Vehicles used for hire are taxed four mills on the dollar, if the income from the business exceeds $200 a year, and the money goes to the State. The State also taxes mortgages and certain other legal papers four mills on the dollar. The amount of such property is ascertained by the assessors from the sworn statement of each taxable person.

The tax levy.   The county commissioners examine the lists returned by the assessors, and correct any errors. Upon the valuation given in these lists they levy the annual county tax.[1] Copies of the assessments are then given to the assessors, who give the taxables in their respective districts notice of the valuation put on their property and of the rate of the levy. Persons who claim that errors have been made in the valuation of their property may appeal to the commissioners. The county commissioners sit as a board of tax revision after each triennial assessment for the purpose of correcting, revising, and equalizing the valuation of property.

This valuation is also the basis on which are laid the taxes levied in the local districts. The county commissioners furnish copies of the valuation to the local officers who levy taxes.

School tax.   All resident men of twenty-one years or older are assessed, in addition to the tax on property, a per capita

---

[1] The amount of money to be raised by taxation is determined, and that sum, divided by the total assessed value of the district, fixes the rate of tax to be charged.

tax of one dollar, for school purposes; and a similar tax
is laid in townships and boroughs for the improvement of Road tax.
roads. In order to encourage the growth of trees a small
rebate in taxes on timber land is given to owners of land
having on it young trees.

In addition to their duties in assessing property, assess- Registry of
ors make lists of voters in the election districts outside voters.
the cities (§ 26). If there is more than one election district
in the local division, assistant assessors are appointed to
register the voters.

35. Collector.— A collector of taxes is elected in each Collectors of
township of the second class and in each borough. In taxes.
townships of the first class the treasurer or his deputy
collects the tax. In cities the collectors are appointed by
the county commissioners. They collect the State, the
county, and the dog tax on an order, or warrant, from
the county commissioners; and the township, borough,
city, school, and road taxes on warrants from officers who
levy the taxes in these different divisions. The road tax
may be collected by township supervisors themselves, or
by any person whom they authorize; but all the other
taxes, except in townships of the first class, must be collected by the collector. There is, however, an occasional
instance where a local law provides otherwise.

Each tax list given the collector is copied into a small The process
book, called a duplicate, in which is stated his authority of collecting
to collect the tax. After receiving the duplicate, the taxes.
collector in a township or in a borough posts notices
informing the taxpayers that he is ready to receive the
tax. Those who pay their tax within ninety days receive
a reduction of five per cent. If payment is delayed six
months after the notice is given, a charge of five per cent
is added to the tax. If a taxable does not pay his tax,

his goods may be seized and sold by the collector; and if this proceeding fails to get the tax, an order may be had from a justice of the peace to put him in jail. Duplicate stubs of tax receipts are sent to the county commissioners, who keep them to prevent the use of false tax receipts in voting (§ 26).

A collector receives for his services three per cent on the money paid him within the sixty days from his notice, unless such payment would exceed $1000; if that is the case, he has only two per cent. On all money collected afterward he receives five per cent.

Treasurers.

36. Treasurer. — All the townships and boroughs now have treasurers. In townships of the first class, and boroughs, treasurers are elected for a term of four years. In townships of the second class treasurers are appointed by the township supervisors each year at the time the supervisors organize the board. The treasurer receives the money collected for the township and pays it out on warrants drawn by the township officers who have authority to expend the money. He keeps distinct accounts of the funds in his care, and his books are open to the public. He is required to give a bond[1] with sureties for the performance of his duties. The pay of the treasurer in the boroughs and townships of the second class is only a small percentage of the money received and paid out by them. In townships of the first class, treasurers are also paid for collecting the taxes.

Auditors.

37. Auditors. — The townships and boroughs have each three auditors who are elected for a term of four years.

---

[1] The *bond* is a document which the official signs binding himself to perform fully and honestly the duties of his office. Some person or company, as *surety*, becomes responsible for the performance of the obligations stated in the bond and for the payment of a specified sum in case of failure or loss.

Independent school districts also have three auditors. It is the duty of auditors to audit the public accounts; that is, to examine the accounts of the persons who keep the public funds to see if the money has been expended according to the law, and that no mistakes have been made. If the auditors disapprove of an expenditure, the officer who paid out the money must either return it or take the matter to the court of common pleas for a higher decision.

How the auditors protect the public money.

After auditing the accounts, the auditors report the result of their examination by filing one copy of the accounts with the local clerk — or the auditor longest in office, if there is no clerk — and another copy with the clerk of the court of quarter sessions. They also post itemized statements of the accounts for the inspection of the public. If an officer or any citizen is not satisfied with the report, he may have the matter reviewed by the court of common pleas.

Auditors are sometimes required to act as fence viewers in disputes over line fences, and to adjust damages for opening public roads. They may also be called upon by a justice of the peace to appraise damage done to sheep by dogs. They are paid by the day.

ELECTION OFFICERS

38. Election officers. — A board of election officers, consisting of one judge and two inspectors, holds the elections (§ 25). They are elected for two years. In choosing the inspectors, only one is voted for by each voter. This gives the choice of one of them to a political party in minority. Each inspector appoints a clerk. Questions as to qualifications of persons offering to vote are submitted to the inspectors. If they cannot agree, the judge of election

Judge and inspectors of election.

The ballot. must decide. The ballots, which are furnished by the county commissioners, are kept sealed by the judge of election until the polls (*i.e.* the voting place) are open. Each voter then receives a ballot, which he marks and folds in a private voting booth, and passing out puts into the ballot-box. If a voter is unable to mark his ballot by reason of disability, he may choose some voter to assist him; but soliciting votes is not permitted in the voting room.

The result of an election. As soon as the polls close, the election officers begin counting the votes. When they are counted, the result is fully and publicly declared, and a statement showing the number of votes cast for each candidate is posted on the outide of the door of the polling place. A similar report is delivered personally by the judge of election to the clerk of the court of quarter sessions, if the election is held to choose township or borough officers — or to the prothonotary of the court of common pleas, if county, State, or national officers are being elected.[1] The records

The ballot-box. of the election are put in the ballot-box, which is securely locked and sealed. It is then delivered by the judge of election and minority inspector to such person as the court of common pleas has designated — except that in Philadelphia and some other cities the mayor is custodian of the ballot-boxes. In the country districts justices of the peace are usually designated as custodians. Unless the ballot-boxes are opened to investigate some charge of fraud or mistake, they are kept sealed until the next election. Then the election officers, when ready to use the ballot-boxes, open them and burn the former ballots and other papers in them.

[1] Officers holding the local courts who are commissioned by the governor, are in that sense State officers, and their election is therefore reported to the prothonotary.

The election officers receive a fixed amount of pay for
their services in holding each election, and one half of that
amount for holding primaries (§ 25).

OFFICERS OF LOCAL COURTS

39. Justices of the peace. — In each of the townships
and boroughs the law provides for the election of two
justices of the peace, but sometimes, if there is little
business, only one of them qualifies for office.   More than
two may be elected, if a majority of the voters so decide.
Boroughs that are divided into wards have usually two
justices of the peace in each ward, but in some boroughs
there is only one in each ward.   In many of the cities
(except Philadelphia) one alderman having the same duties
as a justice of the peace, is elected in each ward.   Philadelphia is divided into districts for each 30,000 inhabitants,
and one magistrate is elected for each district.   His duties,
too, are practically the same as those of a justice of the
peace, except that he cannot hear cases involving more
than $100.   Justices of the peace and aldermen have juris-
diction of cases involving as much as $300.

A man who is elected justice of the peace or alderman,
if he wishes to take the office, delivers to the prothonotary within thirty days of his election his acceptance of
the office.   The acceptance is sent to the secretary of the
State, and the governor issues a commission to the person elected.   The commission is sent to the recorder, from
whom the officer-elect receives it, after he has taken the
oath of office and given the required bond, and the commission has been recorded.

Justices of the peace represent the government as guardians of the peace.   They have final jurisdiction of certain
petty criminal offenses, but give only a preliminary hear-

Justices of the peace.

Justices' jurisdiction in criminal cases.

ing to persons charged with serious crimes. If they find no ground for the charge of a serious crime, they may set the accused person free. But if there is ground for the charge, they may send the accused to the county jail to await trial; or they may release him on bail[1] with surety. In the most serious cases bail cannot be taken by a justice of the peace, the higher courts having control of such matters.

Civil jurisdiction.

Justices of the peace have also civil jurisdiction — that is, authority to decide disputes between citizens. A justice of the peace, alderman, or magistrate may perform the marriage ceremony for persons who have procured a marriage license (§ 68). They may also administer oaths or affirmations to persons making affidavits, and take acknowledgments of deeds, mortgages, and other papers to be recorded.

Justices of the peace and aldermen hold their offices in their local districts, but cases may come to them from any part of the county. The pay consists of fixed fees for services rendered; magistrates in Philadelphia receive a salary.

40. Civil suit before a justice of the peace. — If a person wishes to sue another in a justice's court, he goes to the justice of the peace for a summons. This is a writ directing the constable to summon the person against whom the suit is brought to appear before the justice at a certain time, to answer the demand of the plaintiff. The person or party that begins a civil suit is called the plaintiff, and the one against whom it is brought is the defendant.

At the time fixed for the defendant to appear, the trial

---

[1] In giving *bail*, the accused guarantees that he will appear for the trial whenever the court orders, or forfeit the sum named as his bail. His *surety* is some person or persons who take the responsibility for his appearance in court or for the payment of the forfeiture.

of the case begins, unless it is adjourned to some other Trial of a . day for some reason, such as the sickness of an important civil suit. witness. The plaintiff makes a concise statement of his demand, which must be accompanied by the evidences of debt, or copies, such as notes, contracts, book entries, and the like. The defendant must then say whether he denies all or any part of the claim, or admits it. If he admits the plaintiff's claim, the justice gives the plaintiff judgment for the amount of the claim, with costs; but if he denies the claim, or any part of it, the matter in dispute is heard by the justice. Written documents having a bearing upon the matter may be put in evidence, and persons who know about the disputed matter may be examined. After the evidence is given, the parties to the suit, or their attorneys, may address the justice, calling attention to the evidence produced and the law that bears upon the questions to be decided. The justice then gives his decision publicly, or he may take time to decide, but not longer than ten days.

If either party believes that injustice has been done Appeal. him, he may take an appeal[1] to the county court within twenty days. If the amount passed upon by the justice does not exceed $5.33, no appeal can be taken; the case is too trifling.

Immediately after judgment is given, the plaintiff may have a writ, called an execution, authorizing the constable to seize property of the defendant and sell it in due course of law to pay the judgment. But the usual course is to wait until the time for taking an appeal has expired, unless the property of the defendant is about to be removed or

---

[1] In taking an appeal, the appellant must make affidavit that the appeal is not taken for the purpose of delay, pay the costs as the law directs, and give security for the payment of costs that will be made in the higher court.

otherwise disposed of.   An immediate procedure, however, does not deprive the defendant of his right to take an appeal or to have the time allowed by law in which to pay the judgment upon his giving security for its payment.

Criminal prosecution.

41. Criminal prosecution before a justice of the peace. — A criminal prosecution is begun before a justice of the peace by making a written information that some designated person has committed an offense against the law and — as runs the required endings of such complaints — against the peace and dignity of the commonwealth of Pennsylvania.   The offense must be specially set forth. On this complaint the justice issues a warrant, which is directed to a constable or other proper officer, commanding him to arrest the person named therein and bring him before some police or justice court for trial or examination.

Function of the justice.

If the offense alleged is of a petty nature and within the power of the justice to try, the matter is disposed of very much as a civil case is tried : the information is read to the prisoner and he is given an opportunity to plead, that is, to say whether he is guilty of the offense charged or not.   If he pleads guilty, there is nothing for the justice to do but sentence him according to law, provided the offense is one that does not require the sentence to be given by a higher court.   If he pleads not guilty, the question of his guilt must be settled before the case can proceed.   If the case must go to the higher court because it legally belongs there, it may be sent there on the plea of guilty, or after the preliminary hearing at which good grounds for the charge are found.   If the charge is not supported before the justice by such testimony as would convict, the accused is discharged.

Criminal offenses are wrongs committed against all the

people of the State, and the commonwealth of Pennsylvania seeks to prevent crimes by punishing those who commit them. For this reason the commonwealth is always one party to a criminal case, and the accused person is the other — the defendant. The person who makes the complaint is called the prosecutor. He is the principal witness for the commonwealth, and gives in evidence the facts which led him to make the complaint. *The commonwealth is a party in criminal cases.*

Every person is in duty bound to help keep the laws inviolate. Even a private person may make an arrest without a warrant, if a breach of the peace or other criminal offense is committed in his view, — it is his duty to do so, if a felony[1] is committed in his view. Justices of the peace, constables, and policemen, and also the sheriff and other high officers, must arrest persons committing a breach of the peace or other criminal offense in their view, and they must arrest any person who they have good reason to believe has committed a felony. If it were always necessary to have papers drawn before criminals could be arrested, many of them would escape. *The duty to arrest.*

42. Constable. — The peace and safety of a community are in the care of the constable. It is his duty to preserve order and enforce the law. He must arrest persons who break the law, and bring them before the court to answer for their conduct. He serves writs issued by justices of the peace, — summonses, warrants, and executions. He also posts notices of township elections, and attends the voting places on election day to see that voters are free to go to and from the polls without hindrance. The constable must visit once a month places where *Duties of the constable.*

[1] Felony includes the gravest crimes, usually punishable by imprisonment or death.

liquors are sold and report any violations of the law to the court of quarter sessions. This report is made the first week of each term of the court, at which time he reports other breaches of law in his district. He is also fire, game, and fish warden. As fire warden he has authority to arrest any person wantonly starting a fire in a forest and to take means to extinguish such fire. As game and fish warden he may arrest any person killing game or taking fish out of season.

Aid to constable.

In the execution of the duties of his office a constable has the right to call upon bystanders to help him. If any one refuses to assist a constable or other peace officer who is being resisted, when asked by him to do so, he may be punished for not helping the officer. Not only must the citizen assent to the laws, but he must give aid, if necessary, in their execution.

High constable.

One constable is elected in each township. A borough may elect a constable and a high constable, or one person to act as both. The duties of a high constable are usually confined to serving papers issued by the burgess or other officers of the borough. Both boroughs and cities have this office of high constable, but it is frequently filled by the same person who is constable. The boroughs divided into wards, and the cities, have a constable in each ward. Constables receive fixed fees for each item of business.

LOCAL MANAGERS OF THE PUBLIC SCHOOLS

School directors.

43. School directors. — School districts of the fourth class (23) — nearly all the townships, and the small boroughs — have each a board of five school directors; school districts of the third class — thickly populated townships, large boroughs, and small cities — have each a board of seven school directors; school districts of the second class — large cities, except Philadelphia and Pittsburg — have each a board of nine school directors; and school districts of the first class — Philadelphia and Pittsburg — have each a board of fifteen school directors.

In all school districts, except those of the first class, the school directors are elected at large, part of the board at a time — that is, all voters take part in choosing each director. The term of office is six years, and begins on the first Monday in December. In districts of the first class the school directors are appointed in the month of October, five every two years, by the judges of the courts of common pleas, for a term of six years, which begins on the second Monday in November. The school year (23) in districts of the first class begins on the first day of January. *Elected at large. Appointed.*

The school directors are required to establish schools for the education of all children of school age residing in the school district, and to keep the schools open as required by law. The school term must be not less than seven months in the year and not more than ten months. The school directors may grade the schools, decide what branches shall be taught in addition to the elementary course of study (§ 46), which must be taught, and suspend or expel pupils. They may also give directions as to the way in which the work shall be done, but they are not permitted to teach. They hire the teachers, and adopt and purchase school books and supplies. In purchasing books or supplies they may not act as agents for them or promote their sale in any way; and in hiring teachers family, political, or church influence is not to enter into the selection. Teachers are not permitted to wear while teaching any dress or other thing indicating that they *Duties and powers.*

belong to any particular church denomination. School directors may adopt measures to prevent the spreading of contagious diseases in the schools, and to protect schools from danger by fire. They receive no pay.

Common
schools.

44. Public schools. — Elementary common schools are established in every school district. The city and the borough districts, and many of the township districts, have also public high schools. A special appropriation is

High
schools.

given high schools by the State, provided the board of school directors of the district adopts a course of study approved by the state superintendent of public instruction and employs teachers qualified to teach the course. There are three grades of high schools: those having a course of study extending four years beyond the common school course are of the first class; those three years beyond, of the second class; and those two years beyond, of the third class.

Special
schools.

For boys and girls employed during the day, school directors may provide an evening school. It is controlled and supported the same as a day school. Schools are also provided for deaf mutes, blind children, feeble-minded children, and soldiers' orphans; and kindergartens for children between the ages of three and six years may be established.

Libraries.

Also, in connection with public schools, a school library and a district library may be provided. The school library is for the use of the pupils of a school only; the district library is a public library for the use of the residents of the district. A small tax may be laid by the board of school directors to support the district library, but the school library is supported by the pupils and persons interested in the school.

Pennsylvania now appropriates annually the sum of $7,500,000 to its public schools.

45. Compulsory attendance. — Since the attendance law of 1895 was passed, parents who do not of their own accord send their children to school are compelled to do so. Children between the ages of eight and sixteen years must attend the public school, or some other school where the elementary English branches are taught, or must be taught the same studies by a private tutor during the time the public school is in session. The school directors may reduce the time of compulsory attendance, if they see fit. An exception is made in the law so that the requirements do not apply to children who reside more than two miles from a public school, and to those above fourteen years of age who are employed in some useful service, provided they have learned to read and write English.

46. Teachers of public schools. — A teacher of a public school must have a teacher's certificate. To obtain the lowest grade certificate requires a fair knowledge of the elementary branches[1] taught in the public schools. Good moral character is required, and the applicant for a certificate must not be addicted to the use of intoxicating drinks as a beverage, or to the habit of taking opium. Superintendents of schools hold public examinations in the elementary branches once a year, and issue provisional certificates to those who qualify under them. They mark on the certificates the branches in which the person has

---

[1] In Pennsylvania the elementary school subjects required to be taught are spelling, reading, writing, arithmetic, geography, English grammar, history of the United States and of Pennsylvania, including the elements of civil government, physiology and hygiene. The lowest grade certificates include also elementary algebra, school management, and methods of teaching.

been found proficient, and indicate the degree of proficiency. Higher certificates are given to persons of experience in teaching, and to those who complete the courses of study in normal schools and in other institutions of learning.

Term and pay of teachers.

Teachers are hired for the annual term of school, but those who hold the higher grade certificates may be hired for a longer period. They are paid by the month. A school district must pay its teachers at least forty dollars a month in order to share the appropriation to the public schools made by the State. Twenty days of teaching constitute a month. Public schools are not kept open on Saturdays or on legal holidays; and they are closed during the week of the county teachers' institute. The teachers attend the institute and are paid three dollars a day.

47. Summary. — The officers in the local districts are: —

The officers in charge of the public roads, — three township supervisors in townships of the second class; five or more township commissioners in townships of the first class, who may also construct sewers, regulate places injurious to health, maintain a police force and a fire department, and supply the people with water; and a secretary of the board of supervisors and clerk to the township commissioners, called town clerk.

The officers in care of the paupers, where the paupers are in the care of the township, — two overseers of the poor.

The officers who have to do with the funds of the school district, the poor district, and the township, — one assessor, one collector, one treasurer, and three auditors.

The officers who hold the elections, — one judge of election and two inspectors of election, and a clerk appointed by each inspector.

The officers of the local courts, — two justices of the peace and one constable.

The officers in charge of the public schools, — five or more school directors.

QUESTIONS

When are officers in local districts elected? For how long a term? When do they take office? How are vacancies in local offices filled?

Compare township supervisors and township commissioners, — as to manner of election ; number of officers ; meetings ; powers. What are the duties of the town clerk?

When does a poor person become a public charge? Can he be put to work? Where? How may indigent orphan children be employed? How is money obtained for use in caring for paupers?

How is property assessed for purposes of taxation? Give all the proceedings from the assessment of property to the collection of county tax on land, of tax on dogs, of state tax on mortgages. How is the valuation of property obtained on which to levy a road tax; a poor tax; a school tax? Who levies each tax? If a township officer makes a wrong use of township funds, how is it found out? What two courses only are open to the officer?

Tell all the steps in the course of a ballot from its printing by direction of the county commissioners till it is burned by the election officers. What election returns go to the clerk of the court of quarter sessions, and what to the prothonotary of the court of common pleas?

Tell where justices of the peace, aldermen, and magistrates hold office ; and compare them. Give the ordinary steps in a civil suit before a justice of the peace by A to collect $65 from B, balance due on a written contract to build a fence. Give the usual steps in criminal proceedings before a justice of the peace to punish X for stealing a garden hose worth less than $10 from Y, the theft of property to that value being punishable in the local court. Give the steps, if X had broken into Y's house in the night time and stolen $100, that being a felony.

How many school directors are there in the school district in which you reside? Name their duties. How many public schools are there? In what branches would one have to be examined to teach the lowest school in the district? Who would give the examination?

CHAPTER IV

THE COUNTY AND THE COUNTY COURTS

Origin of counties.

48. The first counties. — Soon after Penn arrived in Pennsylvania, in 1682, the Assembly divided nearly all the province into the counties of Chester, Bucks, and Philadelphia. Chester County embraced the southern half of the province, west almost as far as where Pittsburg now stands; Bucks, the northern half, west to the Allegheny River; and Philadelphia embraced what is now Montgomery County and part of Berks, in addition to its present territory. The western end of the State was added to Westmoreland County in 1785. The province contained only the three original counties for nearly half a century. During the next fifty years ten more were added, and in the fifty years following the Revolution the interior and western portion of the State was settled rapidly, and forty additional counties were erected. Since 1836 fourteen more have been organized. A new county can be organized only from a county having a population of not less than 150,000, with the consent of the voters of the part proposed for the new county. A county is a corporate body.

Early government by court.

49. Their organization. — From the first the county has been the district over which the local court has jurisdiction; in which taxes are levied; and in which representatives of the people in the government are elected. The primitive counties did not have the complete sets of officers that counties now have. All the authority of the county

40

was for a time centered in the court of quarter sessions of the peace. This court not only tried all the smaller cases in the county, both civil and criminal, but it had wide powers in carrying on the local government. The justices of the peace held the court. These county justices (§ 16) superintended the laying out of roads, took acknowledgments of deeds, levied the county tax, contracted for the erection of public buildings, directed the expenditure of public money, and had numerous other duties that are now obsolete.

50. The present county. — These administrative powers soon passed to officers chosen in the counties and in the townships to perform these duties. The county commissioners were given most of these powers. The court of quarter sessions of the peace now retains supervisory power in only a few things, — in opening roads, fixing the boundaries of local districts when changes are made, passing on the report of bridge viewers, and recommending the purchase of land by the county, or the erection or improvement of buildings after the same has been recommended by the grand jury. In practically every division of the local government, the county conducts one part of the government and the township, or other local district, the other. The part taken by the county makes the local government more uniform, and gives it the advantages of centralization without removing its control far from the localities affected. *{Present organization of the county.}*

51. Courts in the county. — In each county there are four courts: two for the trial of criminal cases, one for the trial of civil cases, and one for the settlement of the estates of orphans and of deceased persons. The two criminal courts are the time-honored court of quarter sessions of the peace and the court of oyer and terminer and gen- *{The four county courts.}*

eral jail delivery. The court of oyer and terminer, as it is commonly called, has power to try persons charged with the more serious criminal offenses. It may try all the criminal offenses committed in the county, but in practice, it tries only those cases beyond the jurisdiction of the court of quarter sessions. The court that tries the civil cases is the court of common pleas; and the court having jurisdiction of estates is the orphans' court.

Court of quarter sessions.

52. Court of quarter sessions. — The court of quarter sessions [1] is an old-time English county court, held by the justices of the peace. It was so held in Pennsylvania until 1838, at which time judges learned in the law were required to hold the county courts. It never had jurisdiction beyond the smaller misdemeanors which do not amount to felonies. Its present jurisdiction, as defined by law, extends to the inquiry, trial, and punishment of all crimes, misdemeanors, and offenses against the law that have been committed within the county, except the serious offenses which may be tried only in the court of oyer and terminer. Nearly all the trials are before a jury upon an indictment [2] accepted by the grand jury; but some small matters are tried by the judge alone, just as cases are tried by a justice of the peace. The sessions of the court are held in most counties four times in a year, but in some counties, owing to the amount of business, more than four sessions are held annually. In Philadelphia county, sessions of the court are held every month.

[1] The court of quarter sessions takes its name from the fact that the court originally met once in each quarter of the year.

[2] An indictment is a written accusation of the crime. It is drawn up by the district attorney and is termed a *bill* of indictment until sanctioned by the grand jury.

53. Court of oyer and terminer. — Prior to 1790 felonies were tried by the supreme court judges, who went circuit spring and fall into the counties for that purpose. In that year a court of oyer and terminer and general jail delivery was established in each county. It was to be held by the judge learned in the law who held the county courts. If, however, a judge of the supreme court was holding court in the county, this higher judge should hold the court of oyer and terminer. This is still the law. The offenses tried exclusively by the court of oyer and terminer are murder, arson, robbery, burglary, and the like. There are three somewhat distinct parts in a criminal case, — the inquiry, the trial, and the punishment. When the law says that a court shall have power to inquire of, hear, and determine certain offenses, it means that the court has authority to conduct these different parts in the trial of the criminal case. The words *oyer* and *terminer* mean "to hear" and "to determine." The inquiry is intrusted to the grand jury ; the trial is conducted before a trial jury ; and the punishment is the execution of the sentence pronounced by the judge. After the inquiry by the grand jury, the cases go to the court having power to try them.

Court of oyer and terminer.

54. The grand jury. — All the cases in which persons are charged with offenses of any gravity must be investigated by the grand jury before the defendants can be put on trial, and must be found to be supported by such testimony as would convict, if not contradicted or explained away. Certain small offenses are given a summary trial; that is, the cases are heard and sentence is passed by the judge without the delay of an indictment and jury trial. The men who sit as grand jury are drawn by lot (§ 71). Twenty-four are summoned to attend the court. If they all

Grand jury.

attend, one is excused from serving so that twelve will be a majority of the body; twelve is the number that must concur to find a true bill of indictment.

Method of procedure. When they assemble in court, they are sworn, one member is appointed foreman, and they are instructed by the judge in their duties. Then they go to the grand-jury room, attended by a constable, who remains outside the room and protects their sessions, which are secret, from any intrusion. The district attorney or his assistant presents the bills of indictment. On the back of each bill are the names of the witnesses to be heard by the grand jury. These witnesses are called separately, sworn, and examined by the foreman. After all have been examined — unless the grand jury is satisfied that the bill is "true"[1] without calling them all — the district attorney retires, and the grand jury votes on the question whether the bill of indictment is a true bill or not. Unless twelve jurors vote in favor of finding a true bill, the prisoner goes free. The grand jury may impose the costs on the prosecutor or on the county in certain minor cases when they find not a true bill. In all other cases the county must pay the costs.

Reports of the Grand Jury. After passing on a number of bills, the grand jury goes into court and reports its findings. Returning to the room, they continue the grand inquest, as their sitting is called, until they have passed on the bills presented to them. They must then examine the county buildings. Finally they make a written report to the court, saying that they have performed the duties to which the court called their attention, and making such recommendations concerning the county buildings and the preservation of peace as they think proper.

[1] Each case is reported either "A true bill" or "Not a true bill."

55. Court of common pleas. — The name of the court of common pleas is taken from the English civil court. It is called the court of common pleas to distinguish it from the criminal court. In the criminal court are tried the pleas of the people as a whole — the commonwealth; but in the civil court the pleas may be between any of the people, that is, common. This court has power to try all the civil cases brought within the county, no matter what kind of property is involved. The action is always brought to enforce the rights or redress the wrongs of an individual, and does not include any criminal proceeding. Some powers which are not of the ordinary judicial nature are exercised by the court. It appoints election officers to fill vacancies, and inspectors to examine schoolhouses to see if they accommodate the pupils as required by law. It also appoints viewers to assess damages in cases where private property is taken by the State by right of eminent domain,[1] or by some corporation to whom the State has given the right. More than one court of common pleas is established in a county, if the business requires it.

Court of common pleas.

56. The law. — The law governing cases in the courts of Pennsylvania consists of the federal law (the Constitution, statutes, and treaties of the United States) and the State law (the Constitution, statutes, and common law adopted by the State). By common law is meant the will of the people as it is gathered from long-established custom and expression of legislative power. It derives its force and authority from the universal consent and immemorial practice of the people. The law of the federal government,

State and federal law.

[1] The right of *eminent domain* is the supreme authority which the State has over all property within its limits. By this right the State may take private property upon paying for it, whenever the public good demands it.

owing to its national character, applies to but few cases tried in the courts of the State; but when it does apply, the courts observe it as a part of the law.

In criminal trials the law presumes the defendant to be innocent. He must be counted innocent until the commonwealth produces sufficient evidence to prove his guilt. Before a verdict of guilty can be brought against him, the entire jury must agree, and moreover each juror, before agreeing to such a verdict, must be satisfied from the evidence, beyond a reasonable doubt, that the defendant is guilty. If there is a doubt that arises fairly out of the evidence, the defendant must be given the benefit of the doubt, and acquitted, so careful is the law not to punish an innocent person. Until recently a person charged with a crime could not be a witness in his own behalf; his interest in the outcome of the trial was thought to disqualify him. Now, at his own request, but not otherwise, he may testify, and the jury gives his testimony the credence they think it deserves. If a defendant is too poor to hire a lawyer, the judge appoints some member of the bar to defend him. This is done without pay.

57. The trial jury. — The jury in both civil and criminal courts is spoken of as the trial jury. It is sometimes called the travers jury to indicate that it is the jury which tries a matter that has been traversed, that is, alleged by one side of the case and denied by the other. It is frequently called also the petit[1] jury, which means little jury, to distinguish it from the large or grand jury. The whole number summoned as jurors is usually not less than thirty-six nor more than sixty, but the judge directs the number to be summoned in each court. When a case is ready for trial,

[1] Pronounced " petty."

the clerk of the court takes from a box one after another slips of paper bearing each the name of a juror attending the court, and calls these jurors into "the box" — as the inclosure containing their seats is called. The lawyers for each side of the case may challenge (*i.e.* reject) any juror as permitted by law until a satisfactory jury is obtained. When the necessary twelve jurors have been called and accepted, they are sworn to try the case well and truly and give a verdict according to the evidence, and the trial begins.

Each side in its turn outlines briefly to the jury what it proposes to prove, and proceeds with its evidence. When the evidence is all in, and questions as to the law are decided by the court, the attorneys make their pleas to the jury. The judge then charges the jury — that is, explains to them the law of the case and goes over the evidence sufficiently to help them get at the matter they must decide. The jury then retires to a jury room, attended by a constable, who permits no one to speak to them or in any way interfere with their deliberation. When they have agreed upon a verdict, they return to the court room, their names are called over to see that all are present, and the verdict is taken. The clerk records it and then reads it aloud, and the jury is discharged from the case. *Method of procedure.*

Sometimes the jury fails to agree. Then they are discharged and the case is tried again with a new jury, except in capital[1] offenses. A person charged with a capital offense can be tried only once. He is in jeopardy when a jury has been impaneled and sworn to try him for such an offense; and the Constitution does not permit the putting of any one in jeopardy of life twice for the same offense. The judge does not discharge the jury in such a case, without the consent of the accused, until they have agreed,

[1] A capital crime is one for which death is the penalty.

except in case of great necessity, as the serious illness of a juror.

58. Orphans' court. — The authority of the orphans' court embraces the care of the persons and property of orphans; the administration of estates of deceased persons; and the guardianship of minors. It has full control of matters connected with such estates, and power to settle the accounts of persons acting as guardians, administrators, or executors.

A guardian is a person intrusted by law with the interests of one who does not have legal capacity to act for himself, such as a child under age whose father is dead, or whose father, from drunkenness or other cause, does not care for his child; and such as a person of age who is so weak of mind that he is unable to care for his property.

An administrator is a person appointed by the register of wills to collect the debts due the estate of a deceased person, to pay the debts owing by the estate, and to distribute what is left among those entitled to it, under the direction of the orphans' court.

An executor is a person whom the maker of a will names in his will to see that its provisions are carried into effect after his death. His duties are the same as those of an administrator, except that after the debts are paid the property goes to the persons named in the will.

59. Judges of county courts. — If a county has a population of 40,000, it is made a separate judicial district; smaller counties are joined together in districts. The State is thus divided into judicial districts, to the number of fifty-six at present. In each district is elected a district judge learned in the law — more than one may be elected if the business requires. This judge is judge of the

court of common pleas, with power also to hold the other
courts in the county.   Large districts have separate judges
for the orphans' courts.   The office of judge became elective in 1851.   In districts consisting of more than one
county, each county elects two associate judges, not re-   Associate
quired to be learned in the law. They act with the law   judges.
judge of the district when he holds court in their county.
In his absence in another county, they act alone in
matters that will not admit of delay and which are not at
variance with his orders.   These local judges are a remnant
of the system when three or more justices of the peace
held the county courts (§ 52), and will continue only until
each county becomes a separate judicial district.

It is the duty of judges to administer justice according   Term and
to law.   District judges hold office ten years, and may be   pay of
reëlected.   The associate judges hold office five years.   judges.
District judges in districts having a population of less than
90,000 receive an annual salary of $6000, and higher
salaries in more populous districts; the highest is $11,000.
They are paid monthly by the State treasurer.   Associate
judges receive a small salary.

60. Attorneys-at-law. — One of the laws agreed upon   Attorneys in
in England before William Penn came to America (§ 7)   the court.
gave the people the right to appear in court and plead their
own cases, or to have their friends plead for them.   Any
person may still appear in court and plead his own case;
but in the county courts, and in the higher courts, no one
but a person admitted to practice law before the court
may appear for another and plead his case.   In the local
courts, any person whose service a litigant engages may
appear for him.   The admission of attorneys is a matter in
control of the judges of the respective courts; they make

rules governing the matter. Persons of either sex may be admitted, but women very seldom enter the legal profession.

61. The county seat. — The place in each county where the courts meet is the county seat of justice, commonly called the county seat. Here the county commissioners erect a court-house and a county jail. The court-house must be a convenient place to hold the courts, and have suitable office rooms for the county officials. The papers and documents of each office are either copied into books or filed in such order as to be easily found, and persons interested in them may examine them. In the different offices are kept the records of the courts ; records of taxation and expenditure of public money by the county ; books in which are recorded sales of land, agreements concerning land and liens against land ; and numerous other records of a public nature.

62. Summary. — Counties were organized as rapidly as the local government required. For a time all important local affairs were under the supervisory control of the court of quarter sessions of the county. This court was held by the justices of the peace, who met once in each quarter of the year, and tried both the civil and the criminal suits, except the felonies. Felonies were tried by judges of the supreme court who came into the counties for that purpose, until 1790. In that year the judges learned in the law who held the county courts were given authority to hold the court of oyer and terminer which tried the felonies. In some counties justices of the peace sat as judges of the county courts until 1838 ; after that date all the district judges were required to be learned in the law. In 1851 the office of judge became elective. The court of quarter sessions still sits four times a year in the counties, but it may be held oftener if the amount of business requires it. The court of oyer and terminer continues to try the felonies. The civil cases are tried in the court of common pleas, and the orphans' court cares for the estates of orphans and of deceased persons. All the courts are held at the county seat.

QUESTIONS

How many counties has the State? How rapidly were they organized? Can more be organized? Is it right for A to sue B before a justice of the peace in the farther end of the county? What makes the county taxes in each county uniform?

What was the court of quarter sessions in the primitive counties more than a place where justice was administered? Explain. Who performs these administrative duties now? Name all the non-judicial duties that the court still performs.

Name all the county courts. How did the county come to have two criminal courts? Who first held the court of quarter sessions? The court of oyer and terminer? Who holds them now?

Explain the three parts of a criminal trial. Give the duties of the grand jury. What are some of the reasons for keeping the inquest of the grand jury secret? Tell all you can about the trial jury. Why are trials always public? What becomes of a case if the jury is unable to agree on a verdict? May a jury be discharged because it cannot agree in a murder case? Why is it right to start in a criminal case with the presumption that the defendant is innocent? Can a person be tried in a State court under federal law for robbing the mails?

What is the business of the orphans' court? Define guardian, administrator, and executor.

Why are judges who hold the county courts called district judges? May a person plead his own case in court? Would you advise him to? What is the county seat?

CHAPTER V

COUNTY OFFICERS

Election of
county
officers.

63. The election of county officers. — The officers of the county are elected by the voters of the county (§ 25) for a term of four years. A voter who has resided one year in the county is eligible to any county office, except that a district attorney must be a lawyer of two years' practice; a county surveyor, a person qualified in surveying; and a county superintendent of schools, a person of special attainments in teaching. Neither a sheriff nor a treasurer can succeed himself in office; and a treasurer cannot hold the office of county auditor within two years from the expiration of his term of office as treasurer — if he could, he would be auditing his own accounts. In the election of county commissioners and of county auditors only two of the three elected are voted for by each voter, and of the two jury commissioners only one is voted for by each voter. This gives an opportunity for the party in minority to elect one member of each of these boards.

Filling va-
cancies.

64. Vacancies in office. — The same requirements as to eligibility are observed in filling a vacancy in a county office as govern in the election to the office; and the same rules are followed as to succession in office, and also in securing minority representation.

Vacancies are filled as follows:

Judge, county controller, treasurer, clerk of courts, prothonotary, sheriff, coroner, register of wills, and recorder of deeds: By appointment of the governor, with the advice and consent of the Senate, if the Senate is in session, until the next election. If the vacancy happens within three months immediately preceding a general election, the governor's appointment holds until the second succeeding general election. Filling vacancies.

County commissioner, jury commissioner, and county auditor: By appointment of the court of common pleas of a voter of ·the same political party for the remainder of the term.

Surveyor: By appointment of the court of quarter sessions until the next general election.

District attorney: By appointment of the court of common pleas until the next general election, if the vacancy occurs thirty days or more before the general election; but if not, until the second succeeding general election.

Director of the poor: By appointment of the board of directors of the poor, or the court, as determined by law, until the next general election.

Superintendent of schools: By appointment of the State superintendent of public instruction until the next quadrennial convention of the school directors.

OFFICERS OF THE COUNTY COURTS

65. Sheriff. — The sheriff is the chief conservator of the peace within the county. It is his duty to arrest on view persons breaking, or attempting to break, the peace; also to pursue and arrest criminals, when authorized to do so by a warrant issued by the court. He may call on the people of the county to assist him in the performance of these duties (§ 42), if necessary. He serves and executes within the county the processes,[1] writs, and orders Sheriff.

[1] A *process* is a command by which a person or a matter requiring action is brought before a court. A *writ* is a command that the person addressed

Duties of
the sheriff.

of the courts above the justice's court. He is custodian of the county jail, having charge of the prisoners in jail awaiting trial. It is his duty to execute the sentences of the courts by keeping prisoners in jail, conveying them to prison, or executing them, if the death penalty has been pronounced upon them and a death warrant issued by the governor. His authority is usually confined to the county, but in some instances he may go into other parts of the State. He has a chief deputy, who may act in his place upon order of the court of common pleas, if the sheriff is ill or otherwise temporarily unable to act. The sheriff also gives notice of the general election by proclamation. He assists the jury commissioners in drawing the panels of jurors from the jury wheel (§ 70), and afterward keeps the key to the jury wheel, while the commissioners keep the jury wheel; neither they nor the sheriff, in the absence of the other, may have both the key and the jury wheel at the same time.

Clerk of
courts.

66. Clerk of court of quarter sessions. — The clerk of the court of quarter sessions is also clerk of the court of oyer and terminer; he is called briefly the clerk of courts. He keeps his office open in vacation as well as during term time of the courts. His chief duties are to enter upon the records of his office the official acts of the courts, and the papers connected with such matters; administer oaths and affirmations in conducting the business of the courts; and affix the seal of the court to all papers and copies of the records issued from the office. When the court is in session, the clerk is present in court and keeps

---

should do, or refrain from doing, some specified act. The sheriff *serves* any of the various forms of command when he delivers it to the person to whom it is addressed.

a record of the proceedings. He calls the jurors for the trials, administers the oath or affirmation to the jurymen after the jury is selected, and to witnesses whose testimony is about to be taken. If the judge is absent from the county seat, or unable to attend to the duties of his office, the clerk may take bail and recognizances [1] in all cases, except treason, felonious homicide, and voluntary manslaughter — these crimes are bailable only by a judge. The applications, bonds, and other papers in connection with liquor licenses are filed in his office. He keeps a record of the returns made to his office after township and borough elections (§ 38), and issues to persons elected certificates of their election.

67. Prothonotary of the court of common pleas. — The name prothonotary is the former English name of the chief clerk of the court of common pleas. The word means chief clerk. The prothonotary issues the summonses and other papers in suits brought in the court of common pleas; and records the official acts of the court, the papers filed, and the legal steps taken by the parties to suits. At the request of the plaintiff he makes record of judgments authorized by the defendants to be confessed against them either by the prothonotary or by an attorney of record, provided the plaintiff files with him the judgment note or bond. When judgments are paid and properly receipted, he makes record of that fact. He takes bail in civil cases, administers oaths or affirmations in conducting the business of the office, and issues certified copies of the record. When the court is

Prothonotary.

---

[1] A *recognizance* is an obligation to do some particular act (as, to pay a debt, keep the peace, appear in court) recorded in some court or before a magistrate.

in session, he is present in court and keeps a record of the proceedings, calls the jurors, and administers the oath or affirmation to them and to the witnesses.

The returns of the election, required to be filed in his office the next day after the elections of county, State, and national officers (§ 38), are presented by the prothonotary the following day to the judge of the court of common pleas. The judge opens the returns publicly, and the votes are counted and tabulated by such officers of the court and assistants as the judge appoints. A record of the vote is kept in the prothonotary's office, and certificates of election are issued by him to the persons shown to be elected. The prothonotary sends a certified statement of the vote to the secretary of the commonwealth, who lays before the governor the returns of the election of State officers, and sends the returns of the election of federal officers to the proper federal authorities.

Copies of new laws enacted are immediately sent to all the judges, and to the prothonotaries; and they are kept on file in the prothonotary's office for the information of the people.

68. Clerk of the orphans' court. — In counties where the business of the orphans' court is not extensive, one person is elected clerk of the criminal courts and also clerk of the orphans' court. But in counties having separate orphans' courts, and in counties recently made separate judicial districts, the register of wills is clerk of the orphans' court. He has custody of the records and seal of the orphans' court, and enters upon the records the official acts of the court. He preserves the numerous papers in connection with the estates of orphans and of deceased persons. He also issues marriage licenses, after determining that the applicants can legally marry, and reports the marriages to the department of health of the State.

69. District attorney. — In conducting a trial for a District attorney. criminal offense, the commonwealth (§ 41) must of necessity appear in court by a representative. This representative is the district attorney. He is a county officer — an attorney for the commonwealth in criminal matters that come before the courts of the county. To be eligible to the office one must have lived in the county one year, and have been admitted to practice law in the courts of some county within the commonwealth two years. The district attorney prepares and presents to the grand jury bills of indictment in the cases where persons have been held for trial in court (§ 41). He conducts in court the criminal or other prosecutions arising in the county to which the commonwealth is a party.

70. Coroner. — The coroner contributes to the safety of Coroner. the people by investigating the cause of death of any person dying in a violent or sudden manner, or by means unknown. Upon notice of such death, he makes inquiry into the cause, and if there is no reason to believe it a felonious (*i.e.* criminal) destruction of life, no further investigation is made. But if the death may have occurred from any violence done by one person to another, an inquest is held — that is, the coroner summons a jury of Coroner's jury. six persons, over which he presides, to view the body and investigate the cause of death. Witnesses are examined on oath and the facts inquired into, and the jury gives its opinion in writing of the cause and manner of the death.

If the coroner's jury finds the death to have been caused by the felonious act of another, and the person guilty of the act is taken into custody, the coroner may commit him to jail without bail to await trial in the proper court. A full report of the inquest is made to the district attorney, who frames the bill of indictment upon the information contained in the report.[1]

Coroner as sheriff.

If the sheriff is legally removed from office, or dies while in office, the coroner executes the office of sheriff until another sheriff is commissioned. If a writ or process is directed to be served on the sheriff, it is the duty of the coroner to serve it.

Jury commissioners.

71. Jury commissioners. — The two jury commissioners and the county judges constitute a board to select the men who may serve as jurors. For this purpose, they meet at the court-house once a year, at least thirty days before the first term of the court of common pleas in the year.

Selection of jurors.

They must select qualified voters of the county to serve during the year as jurors, and fill the jury wheel with their names. Sober, judicious, and intelligent men must be chosen from the whole county. The judge previously designates the number. In selecting names, the board may be guided by information from others; but if the lists are made up by political or personal favor, the names may be set wholly aside for the reason that the jury wheel was not properly filled. The law aims to exclude partisanship in the selection of jurors. For this reason the jury commissioners are elected from different political parties (§ 63). The names of the persons selected, their occupations, and places of residence are written on slips of paper, which are rolled up or folded and put into the jury wheel. The jury wheel is then locked and sealed by the sheriff and given into the care of the jury commissioners, while the sheriff keeps the

[1] In case a death occurs, or a body is found farther than ten miles from the coroner's office, or the coroner for any reason is unable to act, a justice of the peace may hold the inquest.

key. A list of the jurors selected is filed in the prothonotary's office for public inspection.

At least thirty days before the sitting of each court the prothonotary (if the court of common pleas is about to sit) or the clerk of courts (if a criminal court is to be held) orders the sheriff and the jury commissioners to draw from the jury wheel the names of a certain number of persons to be jurors in the next court. He also bids the sheriff summon these persons to attend the court. Before the names are drawn, the slips are well mixed by turning the jury wheel, and the names must be taken as they are drawn until the panel is complete.

Officers in Charge of Fiscal Affairs

72. County commissioners. — There are three county commissioners in each county. Their chief duty is to cause the taxes to be assessed and levied properly, and the county debts to be paid. The assessment made under their supervision (§ 34) is the basis on which is laid not only the county tax, but all the taxes levied by the local divisions. In arriving at the tax to be levied for county purposes, the county commissioners estimate the expenses of the county for the year, and fix the rate of levy accordingly. They issue warrants of authority to the collectors for the collection of the taxes levied by them, — property tax, occupation tax, and dog tax; and also for the collection of the State tax on mortgages, judgments, and other securities, and on carriages kept for hire (§ 34). *County commissioners. Levying taxes.*

The county commissioners also have charge of the county property, — the court-house, county jail, almshouse, and other county buildings, and the land on which they stand, and the large bridges. They buy whatever is purchased for the county, paying for it out of the county *Care of county property.*

funds. In buying land, and erecting or repairing county buildings, they must have the consent of two successive grand juries and the judge. They furnish the county offices with furniture, books, stationery, fuel, and light, at the expense of the county; and employ janitors and other workmen to care for the county buildings and grounds. They examine all matters in which the county pays out money, borrow money by issuing bonds when necessary, under the close regulation of the law, and conduct all business in which the county is a party. They might well be called the business managers of the county.

Election arrangements. They provide the ballots for the elections, and supply the election officers with ballot-boxes, lists of voters, forms, blanks, and return-sheets. The returns of the primaries (§ 25) are made to the county commissioners, who issue certificates of nomination to the local candidates. They report the vote for State and national candidates to the secretary of the commonwealth, who issues certificates of nomination to the candidates for these offices. Some other duties of a minor character are performed by them for the protection of voters and in the interest of fair and orderly elections.

Clerk to county commissioners. **•73. Clerk to the county commissioners.** — The county commissioners have a clerk, and the office is kept open the year round. The clerk is appointed by the commissioners in some counties, and is elected in others. The duties of the clerk are to keep the books and accounts of the commissioners, record their proceedings, file the papers of the office, and attest the warrants and orders issued by them.

County treasurer. **74. County treasurer.** — The county treasurer takes care of all the county funds and the money belonging to the

State that is received by him. His accounts show where the money comes from, and on what authority it is paid out. The money collected for the State is paid by him to the State treasurer. He furnishes the county commissioners quarterly, or oftener if required, with statements of all public money received and paid out. He is required to give heavy bonds, binding him to an honest handling of the money. Absolute accuracy and a record of all transactions are required of a treasurer. If he fails to perform his duties properly, the county commissioners may enter complaint against him before the court of quarter sessions. If the complaint is found to be true, he will be removed from office, and the men who signed his bond will be held for any loss sustained by the county or the State.

75. Directors of the poor. — In counties having almshouses for the care of the poor there are three directors of the poor. Their term is four years. The entire county is the poor district (§ 21). The directors of the poor manage the almshouse and the farm that is usually connected with it, and furnish relief to the paupers of the county. They admit to the almshouse, or temporarily relieve, those whom they find to be paupers and a burden on the community. Poor persons may be put in the care of the county by the investigation and order of two justices of the peace — in some counties, by the order of only one. Children between the ages of two and sixteen years are not sent to the almshouse; provision is made for their care and education in some home. *Directors of the poor.*

The directors of the poor estimate annually the amount of money needed for the care of the poor, and the county commissioners include the amount in their estimate of the county expenses for the year. In some counties the county commissioners are ex officio[1] directors of the poor.

76. County auditors. — There are three auditors in each county. They meet on the first Monday in January each year, and continue their meetings until they have audited, settled, and adjusted the accounts of the county commissioners, treasurer, directors of the poor, and steward of the almshouse. After examining the accounts they make a full report of their condition, which is presented to the court of common pleas and placed on file in the prothonotary's office, besides being published.

In counties having a population of 150,000 or over, a controller is elected instead of auditors. He has supervision over the fiscal affairs of the county, keeping accounts of the different funds, and directing how the books in the county offices shall be kept. He furnishes the county commissioners with detailed accounts of the different county offices, examines and verifies all bills against the county, and presents the annual report of the receipts and expenditures of the county to the court of common pleas, the same as auditors do.

77. County surveyor. — The duties of the county surveyor are limited to such surveying as remains to be done in connection with public land, and as may be directed by the courts of the county. He is usually selected to do surveying for private persons, because of the reputation his public position gives him and his access to public records. Formerly the State had public land to sell and he surveyed it: the office was then more important. Sev-

---

[1] *Ex-officio* means "by virtue of the office." That is, in this case, any one who holds the office of county commissioner is by reason of that office a director of the poor also.

eral counties do not elect a surveyor, and in some counties the office is combined with that of county engineer.

OFFICERS WHO RECORD WRITTEN INSTRUMENTS

78. Register of wills. — If a person has property, at his death it passes by law to his heirs, unless he has disposed of it otherwise in legal form. He may set forth in a will how his property shall be disposed of. Wills are preserved by being recorded in the office of the register of wills. When a will is presented to the register, the death of the testator (the person who made the will) must be proved; for a will does not go into effect until after the death of the testator. The will must also be proved to be the act of the testator. Two witnesses are required; they usually sign the will as witnesses at the time the document is drawn up. Proving a will is called probating it. If controversy arises over the probate of a will (that is, if the will is contested), the register of wills hears evidence and decides the matter. An appeal from his decision may be taken to the orphans' court. After a will is probated, it is recorded in a book in the register's office. If the testator designated the manner of disposing of his estate and the person by whom it should be done, that person is his executor. He receives from the register papers or "letters," stating his authority as executor, with a copy of the will annexed for his instruction in administering the estate.

If the decedent made no will, and his estate is in such a condition as to require an administrator, — that is, if the estate is insolvent, or if debts owing to the estate must be collected by legal steps, — the law determines to whom letters of administration may be granted. The register of wills grants this authority to the administrator.

Property may be willed by a person of age, or it may

(Marginal notes: Register of wills. Probating a will. Executor. Administrator.)

pass by descent, freely to any of his ancestors (parents or grandparents) and to his descendants (children or grand-children, including the widow of a son). But if it is willed or descends to others than these, the State taxes the estate five per cent, unless its value is very small. The register of wills collects this tax and sends it to the State treasurer, as he does any other money received by him for the use of the commonwealth.

Recorder
of deeds.

79. Recorder of deeds. — A deed is a writing under seal which a person who sells land gives to the purchaser. The owner of land in Pennsylvania must record his deed within ninety days after the deed is made in order to be fully protected in his ownership or title. The object of recording a deed is threefold. It dispenses with the personal delivery of possession of the land to the purchaser, which used to be done by going upon the land and giving him a twig, a tuft of grass, or a clod of earth, as the people gave Penn possession of the province (§ 4). It makes the record and a certified copy of the record evidence of ownership, without further proof. And it protects owners of land against the possible loss of the deed itself, and protects purchasers and others against fraud by enabling them to ascertain from the records the facts as to the ownership of the land.

In the office of the recorder of deeds there are deed books, mortgage books, and other books in which are recorded deeds, mortgages, contracts concerning land, charters, commissions, and the like. None of these instruments can be recorded, however, without full proof of its authority, so that it may be taken as authentic when found on record. Documents executed by private persons must be acknowledged before they can be recorded; that

Acknowl-
edgment
required.

is, the person executing the instrument must go before a notary public, justice of the peace, or other qualified officer, and formally acknowledge the paper as his "act and deed" made for the purposes therein set forth. A fee for recording the instruments is paid the recorder by the persons presenting them, and after they are recorded the papers are returned to the owner.

THE COUNTY SUPERINTENDENT OF SCHOOLS

80. Superintendent of schools. — The public schools of each county are under the supervision of a person of skill and experience in teaching, called county superintendent. In counties having a large number of teachers he appoints assistant superintendents. He is elected every four years by the school directors of the county. The election is held the second Tuesday in April. The city school districts have superintendents of schools; and a township or a borough district with a population of more than 5000 inhabitants may have a superintendent, if the directors of the school district choose to elect one. These districts that have their own superintendent do not share in the election of the county superintendent. A woman may hold the office of superintendent of schools. *[Superintendent of schools.]*

The superintendent of schools has authority to direct the teaching in the schools under his control. He examines publicly persons who wish to teach in the public schools, and gives them certificates setting forth their qualifications. He visits the schools and by suggestions assists the teachers in their work. He has power to annul a teacher's certificate, given by himself or his predecessor, whenever he believes it should be done; but he must give ten days' notice to the teacher and the board of school directors, so that the directors may employ another teacher. A teacher's *[Powers.]*

certificate is annulled only for incompetency, cruelty, negligence, or immorality. A teacher may be dismissed by the board of school directors for the same cause, but only after due notice and a hearing.

Duties.

It is also the duty of the superintendent of schools to see that each board of school directors makes true and proper reports of its schools to him, and to make such reports himself of all the public schools of the county to the State superintendent of public instruction. The law does not permit him in any way to promote the sale of books, apparatus, or supplies used in the public schools; and he is not permitted to receive any pay for teaching in addition to his pay as superintendent. Once a year he invites the teachers of the public schools and other institutions of learning of the county to meet together in a teachers' institute, which is held for the purpose of improving the teaching in the public schools. The institute is held at such time as the superintendent fixes, and continues one week. A teacher who is absent from the institute without sufficient cause forfeits to the school district employing him three dollars for each day absent (§ 46).

Minor county officers.

81. Minor officers. — In counties having a large population, one or more assistant district attorneys may be appointed by the district attorney to aid him in performing the duties of his office, and in some counties the district attorney may appoint special detectives to assist in prosecuting criminals. Some counties have prison inspectors, jail physicians, prison wardens, court interpreters, and assistant coroners. The county commissioners and the directors of the poor usually appoint some lawyer to be their solicitor; he acts as legal adviser for them, and conducts any matter which they must present to the court.

The county commissioners appoint also a mercantile appraiser. He assesses the mercantile tax, which is a charge on each dealer of merchandise in the county for a small license fee and a tax proportional to the business done. The appraiser furnishes the county treasurer with a list of the venders of merchandise in the county, classified according to law, and gives each vender notice of his classification and of the time and place of hearing appeals from the classification. The tax is for the use of the commonwealth, and is paid to the county treasurer, who pays it over to the State treasurer. *Mercantile appraiser.*

82. Salaries of county officers. — Until comparatively recent time the county officials received the fees of their offices in payment for their services, except that in offices where the duties did not require a continuous service, the pay has always been by the day. In all the counties having over 150,000 inhabitants, fixed salaries are now paid county officials. The fees of the office are paid to the county treasurer monthly, except such as are collected for the use of the commonwealth, which are paid to the State treasurer. These counties are graded, and the officials in the more populous ones receive the higher salaries. *County salaries.*

Prothonotaries, clerks of courts, registers of wills, and recorders of deeds, who still receive the fees of their offices, pay over to the county one half of the amount they receive annually above $2000, after deducting clerk hire and office expenses. The highest annual salaries arising from fees do not much exceed $5000, and in many counties they are not much above $1000. Some of the minor officers who are paid by the day receive less than $200 a year. In counties where salaries are paid, they range from $3000 to $10,000. The sheriff in Philadelphia County receives

$15,000 a year, and the prothonotary, treasurer, and register of wills in that county have their salaries increased (but not above $5000) by a percentage on money they receive for the commonwealth. Out of these higher salaries the county officials must pay their deputies and clerks.

83. **Summary.** — The officers of the county fall naturally into four divisions : —

The officers in connection with the courts.

The officers in charge of the business affairs of the county.

The officers who conduct the enrollment of written instruments for preservation and public inspection.

The officer who supervises the teaching in the public schools.

The first division consists of the sheriff, clerk of criminal courts, prothonotary, clerk of orphans' court, district attorney, coroner, and jury commissioners.

The second division is composed of the county commissioners, clerks to the county commissioners, county treasurer, directors of the poor, county auditors or controller, and surveyor.

The third division embraces the recorder of deeds and the register of wills.

The fourth division consists of the superintendent of schools.

QUESTIONS

For how long a term are county officers elected? What limitation is put on the election of sheriff? Treasurer? County commissioners and jury commissioners? How are vacancies in the different offices filled?

What are the duties of the sheriff as a peace officer? As a ministerial officer of the court? In drawing panels of jurors? What are the duties of the clerk of the court of quarter sessions in his office? In the court room? State all the duties of the prothonotary with regard to election returns. Who issues marriage licenses?

Tell the course of a criminal action from the time the copy of the record of a justice's court reaches the district attorney to a finding by the grand jury. If A causes B's death feloniously, give all the steps of the coroner's inquest. What does the coroner do with A, if he arrests him? Tell how the jury wheel is filled. Who keeps the jury wheel? The key? How are jurors summoned to attend court?

What are the duties of county commissioners as to raising money to pay the expenses of the county? As to care of county property? As to elections? Who cares for the county's money? Who removes a county treasurer for any wrong act in office? How is it done? What are the duties of directors of the poor? How are pauper children cared for? What are the duties of county auditors? Of the county surveyor?

How is a will probated? How is the probate contested? Tell each step in the course of administering an estate after the will is probated; if no will was made. Give a case where collateral inheritance tax must be paid. One where it is not paid.

Why should a deed of land be recorded? What are the three purposes of recording a deed? What is required to admit a deed, mortgage, or other instrument to record? Tell the steps taken in recording a deed from the time it is left at the recorder's office till it is received from the recorder.

Who elects the county superintendent of schools? When? What are his duties? For what may he annul a teacher's certificate?

Give the duties of the mercantile appraiser. What does the county treasurer do with the tax?

Make a list of the county officers in your county, and state the salary each receives.

CHAPTER VI

BOROUGHS AND BOROUGH OFFICERS

Reason for incorpora- ting bor- oughs.

84. Incorporation of boroughs. — Whenever the population of a small part of a township increases until several hundred people are living close together, various arrangements for their welfare must be made, such as are not needed by a scattered population. Streets and sidewalks must be provided and some artificial means, perhaps, of supplying the people with pure water and with good drainage. These provisions require powers much more extensive than the townships have. The new community must get its additional powers by a grant from the State. The township does not require a grant from the State to conduct its government; it has the governing power inherent in people living apart in rural sections. Townships have governed themselves thus from time immemorial, but boroughs have always been incorporated, — that is, made by law a corporation with power to transact certain business as one person might.

Origin of borough charters.

Both boroughs and cities are ancient institutions. Boroughs had their origin when kings ruled the people; and the special privileges enjoyed by people living in boroughs were obtained from the sovereign for a price. The price was a tax. This money came later to be used in the borough to defray the expenses of the borough government. The written agreement between the crown and the people, by which they were assured these privileges, came to be the borough charter. Now, borough charters are granted by the State through general borough laws, which give the people of the State the right to have borough government whenever they are in need of it.

85. How a borough is incorporated. — If the majority of the landowners of a town, women as well as men being counted, want borough government for their place, they make application to the court of quarter sessions for the incorporation of the town as a borough. The petition presented to the court sets forth that the majority of the freeholders want the place incorporated, and gives the boundaries of the proposed borough with a map of the territory. Notice of the application to the court is published, and those who favor the application, and any who oppose it, are heard by the court. If the judge of the court finds that the applicants have complied with the law, and he believes, after examining all the facts, that the place should be incorporated, he prepares a decree to that effect. The application and the decree are recorded in the office of the recorder of deeds. The place is thenceforth a borough, and has the right to conduct its government according to the borough laws of the State.

Process of incorporating.

86. Election and term of borough officers. — Nearly all the borough officers are elected, but a few are appointed. The elective officers are chosen at the municipal election (§ 25) by the voters of the borough; they are elected in their respective wards, if the borough is divided into wards. The first borough charter granted in the province of Pennsylvania to Germantown in 1689 limited the members of the borough corporation to eleven men, and these eleven men voted for the officers. In every case since then all citizens of the borough who voted for members of the Assembly had the right to vote for borough officers. Voting for members of the Assembly

Election of officers.

was made the test, for the reason that Penn made that right the broadest of any right of suffrage given the freemen.

The term of office in boroughs is four years and begins on the first Monday in March. Councilmen are elected from wards, if the borough is divided into wards. One half the councilmen is elected every two years. If the number of councilmen is odd, as many as can be, less than one half are elected at the first election and the remainder of them at the next. All the borough officers, except the chief burgess, may be continued in office as long as the voters choose to elect them; but the chief burgess, who is the most important officer, cannot succeed himself.

87. Council. — The council is the legislative body of the borough. It passes the ordinances and resolutions which regulate the government. Ordinances and resolutions must have the signature of the chief burgess, or if he refuses to sign, must be passed by a two-thirds vote of the council; if the council has less than nine members, one more than a majority is required to pass an ordinance. But the council is more than a legislative body; it appoints all the officers of the borough that are not elected, such as the members of the board of health, water commissioners, and policemen. A borough not divided into wards has a council of seven members. Each ward elects one or more councilmen. The council organizes biennially. The presiding officer is chosen from among the members; and some person, not a member, is chosen clerk.

In some of the early borough charters provision was made for town meetings, or assemblies at which all the voters gathered; but the citizens met only when an extra tax was to be discussed, or some other important matter considered. Now, the citizens sometimes attend the council meetings, as is their right, and urge upon the council-men some important action. But the councilmen have the right to do as they believe is for the best interests of the borough, whatever may be the feeling of the citizens at the time. This is true representative government.

88. Chief burgess. — At the head of the borough officers is the chief burgess, so called for the reason that when the office was created there was an assistant burgess, whose office is now abolished. The burgess, as this officer is commonly called, is the chief executive officer of the borough; his duty is to see that the laws are enforced. The part he takes in legislation is small, serving only as a check on the council; ordinances and resolutions must be presented to him for his approval. If he approves them, he signs them; but if not, he returns them with a statement of his objections to the council at their next regular meeting. The council may then accept his objections and dismiss the measure, or pass it over his veto. In enforcing ordinances and collecting fines and penalties, the burgess has the power of a justice of the peace. If a breach of the peace is committed in his view, he may arrest the offender, or issue a warrant and have an officer arrest him.

Chief burgess.

89. Other borough officers. — Many of the borough officers correspond to township officers, — justice of the peace (§ 39), constable (§ 42), assessors (§ 34), collector (§ 35), treasurer (§ 36), and auditors (§ 37). They have the same powers and perform their duties in the same manner as these officers in townships do. In boroughs that are not divided, there is one constable for the entire borough. In boroughs divided into wards, a constable is elected in each ward, and a high constable is chosen in the borough

Other borough officers

at large (§ 42). A policeman of a borough may also be constable.

Filling va-
cancies.

90. Vacancies in office. — A vacancy in the office of chief burgess is filled by appointment of the court of quarter sessions for the rest of the term, upon petition of the council or of any resident citizen. The president of the council acts for the burgess in his absence, or during any incapacity of the burgess. A vacancy in the office of councilman may be filled by the council, or by the court of quarter sessions upon petition of the council, until the next municipal election. Other vacancies in the elective offices are filled in the same way that vacancies in the same offices in townships are filled.

Salaries.

91. Salaries of borough officers. — The borough council fixes the salary of the chief burgess by ordinance. The amount is limited to one hundred dollars a year for each thousand inhabitants, with provision that in boroughs having a population of more than five thousand the salary may be increased fifty dollars a year for each additional thousand. The fees of the office go into the borough treasury. The council fixes the pay of the other borough officers, except such as receive a remuneration fixed by act of the General Assembly. The office of councilman has no salary.

92. Summary. — The State provides by law for the incorporation of boroughs. Application for incorporation is made to the court of quarter sessions. The application and the decree of the court extending to the place the provisions for borough government are recorded in the office of the recorder of deeds.

The officers of a borough are : —

The chief burgess, who enforces the ordinances and the laws of the State applying to the borough, sitting as a magistrate to try offenders of such laws and ordinances ; and who examines the ordinances and resolutions of the council before they go into force and approves' or disapproves them.

The councilmen, who represent the people of the borough in ordinance-making and regulate the affairs of government by ordinances and resolutions.

The officers who have to do with the borough funds, — one or more assessors, a collector, a treasurer, and three auditors.

The officers who are connected with the courts in the borough, — two or more justices of the peace, one or more constables, and a high constable, if the borough is divided into wards.

And such other officers as are provided for in the borough charter or by law, as street commissioner, water commissioner, policemen, and health officers.

QUESTIONS

What are some of the needs which move the people of a place to have it incorporated a borough? How is it done ? What records show whether a town is incorporated a borough or not?

Who elects the borough officers? At which election? For how long a term? Why is it better to elect part of the council each year? How many councilmen has a borough? Name all the officers in any borough you choose.

By whom is a street commissioner in a borough appointed? The members of the board of health? How far may the chief burgess control the passing of an ordinance? How far may the people of the borough control such action? Which is better, for the councilmen to do as they think right, or to do as the people at a council meeting want them to do?

What are the duties of the chief burgess? Can he try to punish a resident of the borough for breach of a borough ordinance? For breaking into the post-office and stealing stamps? If a man is intoxicated and disturbing the peace, in the presence of the burgess, should the burgess arrest him; or should he go to his office and issue a warrant and have the constable arrest him, and take him before the burgess for trial?

What are the duties of the borough assessor? The borough collector? The borough treasurer? The borough auditors? Is there any difference between the duties of a justice of the peace in a borough and a justice of the peace in a township?

How is a vacancy in the office of chief burgess filled? For how long? What is his salary? Does the office of councilman pay a salary?

CHAPTER VII

CITIES AND CITY OFFICERS

Cities incorporated by the State.

93. The incorporation of cities. — A city obtains the authority to conduct its government from the State. The ordinary powers of local government from long-continued practice are recognized as belonging to the people, but the powers exercised by cities are not. They are extraordinary powers, which are granted or withheld by the State as the needs of local government demand. The State never refuses to give to the people the right to maintain municipal government, but it always reserves the control in such matters. Sometimes the people of a city do not govern their city well, and it is then questioned whether it would not be better if the State maintained a closer control of municipal affairs. But to this question it may be answered that municipal government, like all other government, cannot be improved by taking the authority to govern away from the people most interested in the government. Local pride and local interest must be relied on to maintain good government, and neither of these motives grows stronger from inaction in public affairs, but rather from taking part in the affairs of government.

Process of incorporating a city.

94. How a city is incorporated. — A community must have a population of at least 10,000 people in order that it may be made a city. Some cities in the State do not have so large a population, but they were made cities before this requirement was in force. If a borough wishes to become a city, a resolution to submit the matter to a vote of the people must first be passed by the borough council. An election is held at the time of the next general election. The ballots are marked, " For city charter " and " Against city charter." If the vote favors the organization of city government, the returns of the election are sent to the secretary of the commonwealth, who is also furnished with information as to the boundaries of the proposed city. The matter is laid before the governor. If the law has been complied with, the governor issues a charter reciting the facts and defining the boundaries. This charter constitutes the place a "body corporate and politic," with a long list of powers.

In becoming a city, a borough carries into its new organization all its laws, rights, property, and obligations. The borough officers continue to serve until the time for taking office after the next municipal election, when they vacate their positions to the newly elected officials.

If a city wishes to be divided into wards, either the citizens or the council present a petition to the court of quarter sessions. The court appoints a commission of five men, residents of the city. They examine the matter and report their opinion to the court. If the report is favorable, an election in the part of the city affected is held at the time of the municipal election, and on a favorable vote the court orders the new wards erected. *(Division into wards.)*

95. Classification of cities. — For the regulation of municipal affairs the cities of Pennsylvania are divided into three classes : —

Those having a population of 1,000,000 or over are cities of the first class. *(Cities of first class.)*

Those with a population of 100,000 and under 1,000,000 are cities of the second class. *(Second class.)*

Third class.
Those with a population less than 100,000 are cities of the third class.

Legislation by classes.
Laws may be made for cities of the first class, and different laws for cities of the second class, and still different laws for cities of the third class. The number of cities in a class has no effect on the laws, for the reason that laws that are good for a class of cities of more than 1,000,000 depend for their fitness upon the population crowded together in each city, and not upon the number of cities concerned. The same is true of the other classes. If laws were made for each city, as they were before the present Constitution and the present classification came into force (1874), two cities of the same population and presenting the same problems of municipal government might have different laws. This is no longer permitted.

Powers of government in a city.
96. Government of cities. — The government of a city is State government adapted to meet the needs of the people living in that locality. The municipal powers of a city are named in its charter. It is given authority to acquire real estate on which to erect a city building, police stations, hospitals, and other municipal works; to pass ordinances for the regulation of its public affairs; to grant franchises for the development of its resources; to engage in certain public works for its own welfare, such as supplying gas, water, and electric light; to levy taxes for the support of its government; and to do certain other things for the protection and welfare of its citizens.

Absence of municipal courts.
One thing notable in the government of cities is the absence of municipal courts. The judicial authority of the State is adequate for municipal purposes; no additional courts have to be established. The judicial part of the city government is conducted almost wholly by the local

courts of the State, which in no way depend on the municipal government for their existence. It is true the mayor — in some cities assisted by officers belonging to the municipal government — exercises a limited judicial function in the punishment of such offenses as vagrancy, drunkenness, disorderly conduct, and the like. Like the burgess of a borough, he has authority to judge and sentence offenders against the city ordinances and in breaches of the peace, and to settle disputes connected with the collection of penalties imposed by city ordinances. But beyond this the courts of the State administer justice in cities.

The mayor's judicial powers.

97. The legislative department. — In addition to the law of the State, cities require local laws. These local regulations are known as ordinances. They are entirely the work of the city government; the State never enacts them for cities. In each city this legislative power is exercised by a council, consisting of two branches, the common council and the select council. This law-making body constitutes the legislative department of the city. The councilmen are elected by wards. In the smaller cities two common councilmen are usually chosen in each ward, and one select councilman; but in the larger cities only one member of each branch of the council is chosen in each ward. The common councilmen are elected for two years, and the select councilmen for four years. Only part of each branch is elected at a time, so that they never consist wholly of new members. Members of the common council must be at least twenty-one years old, and members of the select council at least twenty-five. Councilmen must reside in the ward they represent. They are not permitted to hold any other public office, except notary public and commis-

Legislative department

Common council; select council.

sioner of deeds. They may not be given employment outside their official duties by the council, nor become financially interested in furnishing supplies for the city. If a matter comes before the council in which a councilman has a private interest, it is not legal for him to vote on it.

Council meetings.

98. Council meetings. — The meetings of the council are held in the council chambers of the municipal building. The common council meets in one chamber, and the select council in another. The time for the meetings is fixed by ordinance; they are usually held every two weeks. Special meetings are also held. Each branch is presided over by one of its members chosen when the body is organized after the new members take their seats. They each have a clerk and such other officers as are necessary for the transaction of business; and each branch keeps a journal of its proceedings. The meetings of the council are public, and the journal of each branch is open to public inspection.

How ordinances are passed.

99. Ordinances. — Ordinances originate in bills which may be presented by members of either branch of the council. After a bill is introduced, it is referred to a committee, usually composed of members of both branches. When it has been duly considered in committee, it is reported back to the branch of the council by which it was referred. If reported favorably, it is printed for fuller consideration by the members. The bill must then pass three readings before it is sent to the other branch.

In the first two readings only the title of the bill is read; but for the third reading, just before the final vote is taken, the bill must be read at length and all members must vote on it unless excused. Only in case of public emergency can a bill be passed the three readings on the day it is introduced. If the bill is approved by a majority of the votes, it is sent to the other branch of the council for consideration. There it goes through the same course. If it again receives a majority vote, it is sent to the mayor for approval. He may sign the bill or veto (*i.e.* reject) it. If vetoed, the bill does not become an ordinance unless Ordinances passed over the veto by a large majority vote of the and the members of each branch — a two-thirds vote in cities of mayor the third class and a three-fifths vote in other cities. The mayor may permit a bill to become an ordinance by failing to act within a certain period — fifteen days in cities of the third class and ten days in other cities. Within one month after their passage, ordinances are recorded in a book in the clerk's office, and are open to the public. If there is a penalty for its violation, the ordinance is published before it goes into effect.

100. The executive department. — The executive power Executive of a city is exercised by the mayor. Closely associated department with the mayor in the government of large cities are the heads of several executive departments. These officers are in most instances appointed by the mayor, the appointment being confirmed by the select council, and they may be removed from office for improper conduct by the mayor. Some of the heads of these departments are elected. The best results seem, however, to come from appointments. In the most highly developed city government there are departments of public safety, public works, public supplies, public health and charities, city controller, collector of taxes, assessors, city treasurer, law, and sinking-fund commission.

Such matters as police affairs, protection against fire, regulation of electric wiring, care of city property and parks, inspection of buildings and steam engines and boilers, come within the department of public safety. The supervision of water works and gas works, — if they are owned and operated by the city, — the paving, cleaning, and lighting of streets, and the important matter of sewerage and drainage of the city, belong to the department of public works. The other departments have the care and regulation of equally important matters, indicated by their names. In the smaller cities these executive functions are not performed through such an elaborate division into departments; but they are always an important part of the administration of municipal government.

Mayor.

101. Mayor. — The mayor is elected by the voters of the city, and holds the office in each city for a term of four years. He must be at least twenty-five years of age, and a citizen and resident of the State and of the city five years; except that in the smaller cities a residence and citizenship in the State of only four years, and in the city of only one year, is all that is required. He is not eligible to the office for the next succeeding term. And in some cities he is not permitted to hold any other municipal office within two years from the expiration of his term as mayor.

Duties and powers.

The mayor is at the head of the city government. It is his duty to see that the ordinances of the city, and the laws of the State so far as they affect the peace of the city, are enforced. He must protect the citizens against all manner of criminal offenses; and to assist him in the performance of this duty he has the entire police force of the city under his direction. If necessary in order to prevent disorder, he may close all places where liquors are sold. He has the power of a sheriff to prevent and suppress assemblages that might lead to riot. He may also regulate any matters whereby the lives, health, and property of citizens are endangered and the public safety is imperiled. It is also his duty to communicate to the councils at least once a year a statement of the finances and general affairs of the city, and to recommend to them such measures as he thinks will promote the public good. He joins in making contracts for the city after the councils have passed ordinances authorizing them. He appoints several city officials, with confirmation of appointment by the select council. The mayor is held responsible for the successful administration of the city government.

102. City controller. — The city controller is elected every four years by the voters of the city. He watches over the finances of the city. It is his duty to countersign all orders on the city treasurer to pay out money. He must, however, be certain that the expenditure has been legally made, that no appropriation has been overdrawn, and that the total of appropriations, estimates, and lawful obligations has been brought within the available income of the city. He is independent of the mayor on the one hand, and of the councils on the other; and it is his duty to watch over the executive and the legislative affairs wherever they affect the finances of the city. He inspects and revises the accounts of the city officials in every department; keeps a record of the receipts and expenditures of the city revenues; and requires reports from all the departments, in order to see that the financial affairs are kept in proper order. *City controller.*

103. City treasurer. — The city treasurer has the care and safekeeping of the public funds of the city. He is elected for a term of four years, and gives a bond in a large sum with sureties for the honest and faithful discharge of his official duties. He has authority to demand and receive all moneys due the city, and pays out the funds of *City treasurer.*

the city only on warrants signed by the mayor, or the head of the department making the appropriation, and countersigned by the city controller. The purpose for which the money is paid out must be explicitly mentioned in the warrant, so that the city controller and the treasurer may know whether the money has been legally appropriated by the councils for that purpose. The treasurer keeps the city's money in such bank or other depositary as the councils direct.

City solicitor.

104. City solicitor. — All the law matters of the city are under the direction and control of the city solicitor, who is chosen in most cities by the councils in joint session, but is appointed by the mayor in some of the large cities. His term of office is three years. He is the legal adviser for all the officers and departments of the city government; he prepares all the contracts to which the city is a party ; and he is custodian of the legal papers and documents of the city. In the large cities he has several assistants. He and his assistants are required to be lawyers.

Other city officers.

105. Other city officers. — There are several other city officers, such as collector or receiver of taxes, who collects the money due the city for taxes, licenses, and rents; assessors, who make the valuation of property for taxation; city clerk and assistant city clerk, who keep the proceedings of the councils and the records of the city, and publish the ordinances and notices when they are required to be published; health officer, who has charge of matters affecting the health of citizens ; city engineer, who assists in directing the curbing and paving of the streets and the laying of sewers; building inspector, who issues permits to erect buildings under the rules and ordinances of the city and inspects them to see that they are built in accordance therewith; and other officers with such duties as an elaborate city government makes necessary.

106. Vacancies in office. — A vacancy in the office of mayor is filled by the people at the next municipal election, if the election occurs more than thirty days after the vacancy; but if not, the vacancy is filled at the second municipal election thereafter. Until the vacancy is so filled, a mayor pro tempore, elected by the councils, acts as executive officer. Vacancies in the offices of controller and treasurer are filled in the same way as a vacancy in the office of mayor, except that in the city of Philadelphia these officers are county officials (the city and the county having the same limits), and a vacancy in either office is filled by the governor (§ 64). Vacancies in the other city offices are filled by the councils or the mayor. *Filling vacancies.*

107. Salaries. — The salaries of the city officials are fixed by ordinance, except that the treasurer and controller of Philadelphia, being classed as county officials, receive salaries fixed by State law. The office of councilman pays no salary. The officers who receive fees pay them into the city treasury. *Salaries.*

108. **Summary.** — Cities receive authority from the State to conduct their government. The State regulates municipal government by laws which apply to all the cities in a class. There are three classes of cities.

The officers of cities are: —

The mayor, who enforces the city ordinances and the laws of the State applying to the city. He is chief magistrate, and in some cities sits as a municipal court and tries the offenses against the ordinances and laws; he appoints most of the city officials, and examines the ordinances and resolutions before they go into force, approving or disapproving them.

The councilmen, who in the select and the common council represent the people of the city in ordinance-making, with power to pass ordinances over the mayor's veto.

The city controller, who watches over the finances of the city.

The city treasurer, who has the care and safe-keeping of the city's money, and pays it out when properly authorized.

The city solicitor, who is the legal adviser for all the officers and departments of the city, and who conducts all legal business in which the city is a party.

The collector of taxes, assessors, city clerk and assistant city clerk, health officer, city engineer, building inspector, and numerous other officers, especially in large cities.

QUESTIONS

From what source do cities get the authority they exercise in municipal government? Could it be withheld? Should it be withheld when the people use it dishonestly? How large a population is now required to obtain city government for a community? How is a borough incorporated a city? What become of the debts of the borough, if it has any, when it is made a city? How is a new ward created in a city?

How are cities classified? Why? Why is it right to make laws for a class of cities, even if only one city is in the class, and not for individual cities?

Does the State have governing power within the limits of a city? Do cities have municipal courts? What judicial power has a mayor? What are ordinances? How do they compare with state laws? How are they enacted? What has the mayor to do with ordinances?

Why should a councilman not vote on an ordinance to buy a piece of land and erect a fire-engine house, if he owns the land? Can a councilman supply his city with gas to light the streets? If he moves out of the ward, can he still keep his seat as councilman?

Name some of the executive departments that assist the mayor in governing a city. In what executive department do police matters come? Paving, cleaning, and lighting the streets?

What assistance has a mayor in protecting the people of a city against thieves? When has a mayor the right to close places where liquors are sold? What are some of the conditions dangerous to life or health which the mayor has power to regulate?

What are the duties of a city controller? Of a city treasurer? Of a city solicitor? Of the city engineer?

How is a vacancy in the office of mayor filled? In the office of city treasurer? In the office of city solicitor?

How are the salaries of city officials fixed?

CHAPTER VIII

THE STATE

109. How the province became the State. — When the Continental Congress in session at Philadelphia recommended, May 15, 1776, that independent governments should be formed by the provinces that had not done so, a resolution to that effect was immediately offered in the Provincial Assembly of Pennsylvania, also in session. It was referred to a committee, which meant delay; and the members of the Assembly who favored immediate action withdrew, and took the matter directly to the people. A convention of the county committees was called to meet June 18. The county committees unanimously resolved that the government of the province was not competent to meet the requirements of public affairs. They called a general convention to form a new government founded on the authority of the people.

The freemen of the province responded promptly to the call, and an election of delegates was held, July 8, at the State House in Philadelphia. The Continental Congress had just adopted the Declaration of Independence, and it was read to the freemen when they assembled in State House Square. The delegates elected at this meeting met one week later to form a State government. Benjamin Franklin was president of this body. They first considered the Declaration of Independence, and gave it their approval. This action severed all relation between the people and the provincial government. A committee of

Government of the State organized, 1776.

87

safety was appointed to direct the government, and the convention proceeded rapidly to the adoption of a constitution, which was completed and went into effect, September 28, 1776, without waiting for a vote of ratification by the people. Provision was made for the election of a new Assembly. The government of the State was organized, March 4, 1777.

Laws of the province and of England adopted, 1776.

110. Former laws reënacted. — The new Assembly at once reënacted the former laws, but it omitted everything in the laws that in any way referred to the authority of Great Britain. Not only were the provincial statutes passed prior to May 15, 1776, adopted, but the common law and the statutes of England in force in the colony were also made a part of the law of the new State. This is how Pennsylvania came to have the great body of common law (§56) which has always distinguished the law of the State and the practice in the State courts.

Government by General Assembly and Executive Council.

111. The new government. — The new State was governed by a General Assembly and an Executive Council, both elected by the freemen. They met annually at Philadelphia. The laws were made by the General Assembly. The Executive Council took no part in making laws, but transacted all the executive business of the government. The president of the Executive Council, who acted as governor, with the advice and consent of the other members of the Council, was chosen by the Executive Council and the General Assembly. All the courts were continued as they were under the provincial government, and the officers of the courts exercised the same powers as before. The officers who were elected by the people remained in office, but those who had been appointed to office were removed. The Executive Council filled the vacancies by appointment. The president of the Council, in addition to acting as governor, was commander-in-chief of the military forces of the State. But he was not permitted to command in person, except with the consent of the Council, and then only so long as they approved, so cautious were the people not to permit power to center in one person. Still greater was their caution not to create a government that could get beyond their control; every seven years they elected a Council of Censors whose duty it was to see that the government was conducted properly.

112. The power of government limited. — Under the new government the people were the source of power. With no limitation of that power, the government was sure to be as inconstant as the minds of the people. Moreover, the people could not themselves conduct the government. They must intrust it to officers selected by them, who must in turn be guided by principles and rules of government agreed upon by the people. These rules and principles of government were set forth in the Constitution adopted by the people, which limited the powers to be exercised by the government. Changes occurred, and the powers of government increased. This body of fundamental rules, as settled upon by the sovereign people, is the guide of the government. The laws made by the State must conform to it, and all things done by authority of the State must be within the scope of powers granted by the Constitution. Questions arising as to the meaning of the Constitution are settled by the State courts, the decision of the supreme court being final.

Power of government limited by the Constitution.

113. The Constitution of the State. — In its history as a State, Pennsylvania has had four Constitutions. The first one was hastily made because war was upon the peo-

First and second Constitutions.

ple, but it carefully safeguarded the rights of the people. The second Constitution, adopted in 1790, was made to fit the relation of the State to the federal government. The rights of the people were more clearly stated, and the legislative, executive, and judicial departments of government were better defined. The executive authority was put in the care of one person elected by the people; the judicial power was embodied in a more complete set of courts; and the law-making branch of the government was made to consist of a Senate and a House of Representatives.

Constitution of 1838.

The third Constitution, adopted in 1838, made still more changes in the details of government. The powers of the General Assembly were enlarged; and offices formerly filled by appointment were made elective. In 1857 representation in the General Assembly was put on the basis of the number of taxable inhabitants, and, in 1864, an amendment gave voters absent from their homes on· military service the right to vote· and have their votes returned to their home districts and counted.

Present Constitution adopted, 1873.

The fourth Constitution was adopted November 3, 1873, and went into force January 1, 1874. It changed the term of office of members of the House óf Representatives from one year to two years, and of senators from two years to four years, and made the sessions of the General Assembly biennial instead of annual. The number of senators was increased from thirty-three to fifty, and the number of representatives from one hundred to two hundred, approximately. Suffrage was extended to every male citizen, instead of being limited to white freemen. The time for holding the general election was changed from the second Tuesday in October to the Tuesday next after the first Monday in November, and the time for holding the municipal election was made uniform throughout the State.

Special legislation, such as granting special favors to persons and places, and such as resulted in a number of different laws for practically the same subject, was prohibited. Numerous other changes were made. Amendments were made in 1901, which permit laws to be passed requiring personal registration of voters in cities (§ 26), and providing other means of voting than by ballot (that is, the use of a voting machine), on condition that secrecy in voting is preserved.

114. How the Constitution is amended. — A general revision of the Constitution requires a convention of delegates elected for that purpose. The General Assembly authorizes the convention and fixes the time it is to meet. The people elect the delegates; and after the work of the convention is completed, they ratify the action of the convention. Amendments do not require the action of a convention. They are proposed in either house of the General Assembly; and if agreed to by a majority of both houses, they are published in two newspapers in each county for three months before the next general election. This gives the people opportunity to elect members to the next General Assembly, who favor or oppose the amendments, as they think best. If the amendments pass the General Assembly at its next session, they are again published in the same way as before, and then submitted to a vote of the people. If approved by the majority of those who vote thereon, they become a part of the Constitution. An amendment that fails in adoption may not again be offered for five years.

How the Constitution is revised.

How amended.

115. The powers of government classified. — The powers of government in the State are divided according to their nature. Three departments are created: the legislative

Depart-
ments of
govern-
ment:
legislative,
executive,
judicial.

department which makes the laws; the executive department, which applies the laws to particular events of government; and the judicial department, which gives to the laws their proper legal construction and application when controversies arise. In practice the powers of government do not admit of so distinct a division. The legislative department does some things which are not legislative in character, such as the election of a United States senator (§ 181), or governor in case of a tie vote; the removal of officers by impeachment (§ 123), and the division of the State into congressional (§ 186), senatorial (§ 119), and other districts (§ 59). The executive department also does things which are not executive, as recommending to the General Assembly measures which the governor thinks should be acted on by that body, and the exercise of the veto power (§ 140). And although the rule is that the courts shall be confined to the decision of matters brought before them, yet in several instances it has been necessary to intrust to the courts of common pleas (§ 55) and the courts of quarter sessions the exercise of functions which are not judicial, but administrative, in their nature (§ 50).

116. **Summary.**— Upon recommendation of the Continental Congress the province of Pennsylvania formed an independent State government. A constitution was adopted September 28, 1776, and a new General Assembly met and the government was organized March 4, 1777. Such provincial laws and such parts of the provincial government as were suited to the new government were adopted by the General Assembly. In 1790, after the Union was formed, a new constitution was adopted to conform to the division of power between the State and the nation. The advancement of the State led to improvements in the Constitution in 1838, and to a thorough revision and enlargement of the Constitution in 1873.

QUESTIONS

What moved the leading men of the province to organize an independent State government ? What steps were taken to bring it about? Who was at the head of the convention that made the first State constitution? When did the new State government begin its course?

What became of the provincial laws and institutions of government? Describe the new State government. When the people became the sole source of power, what prevented everybody from doing as he pleased? What prevented the people as a whole from doing as they pleased? How does a government by all the people without a constitution and a government by a king without a constitution compare?

Give the year in which each of the four Constitutions of the State was adopted. When did the present Constitution go into force? How is a new constitution made? How is an amendment to the Constitution made?

Into how many departments is the government of the State divided? What does each department do? Name some things done by each department that are not strictly of the same nature as the principal work of the department.

OBVERSE   REVERSE

THE GREAT SEAL OF THE STATE OF PENNSYLVANIA.

CHAPTER IX

THE LEGISLATIVE DEPARTMENT

General Assembly.

117. The General Assembly. — The legislative power of the State of Pennsylvania is exercised by the legislature, which is called the General Assembly. This branch of the government consists of the Senate and the House of Representatives. They are called the two houses of the General Assembly. Each house is a check upon the other. The Senate is the more conservative body, while the House of Representatives, being elected every two years, is a better index of the will of the people.

Advantages of representation.

118. The advantages of representation. — A knowledge of the conditions and needs of the people in all parts of the State is necessary in order to make good laws. But if all the people met together to make the laws, it would be impossible to reconcile the local wants, sentiments, and opinions, and get from the multitude the information upon which to enact laws. Under the system of representation, the men who are elected to legislate for the people bring to the General Assembly this knowledge of the conditions in all sections of the State; and by association, mutual information, and comparison of views they acquire a fuller and better knowledge than the people are able to obtain, for the reason that the people do not have the opportunity of the wide view.

119. Senatorial districts and appointment of representatives. — For the purpose of distributing the members

94

THE HOUSE OF REPRESENTATIVES IN THE STATE CAPITOL

of both the Senate and the House of Representatives over the State, so that all the people shall be represented, the State is divided into senatorial districts, and to each county is apportioned one or more representatives according to the population of the county. There are fifty senatorial districts, each of "compact and contiguous" territory and as nearly equal in population as the division of territory will permit. The districts are numbered from one to fifty, Senatorial and each district elects a senator. The people are entitled districts. to two hundred representatives. The population of the State is divided by two hundred, and the number obtained is the population that has the right, given in the Constitution, to have one representative; but it is not an easy Apportion- thing to apportion the representation on this basis, and ment of rep have the number of representatives just two hundred. resenta- tives. By the apportionment made in 1906, the House of Representatives has two hundred and seven members. The General Assembly divides the State into senatorial districts and apportions the representatives after each national census. Sometimes the reapportionment is delayed by politics; and sometimes the dominant political party makes the apportionment in its own favor. Neither of these things is right.

120. Election of senators and representatives.— The elec- Election of tion of senators and representatives occurs biennially, in the senators and representa- even years. The representatives are elected for a term of tives. two years, and the senators for a term of four years. One half the number of senators is chosen every two years, the even-numbered districts alternating with the odd-numbered. Members of both houses of the legislature must have been citizens and inhabitants of the State four years, and residents of the district one year, unless they have been absent on public business; and they must reside in the districts they represent. A man must be at least twenty-five years of age to be eligible to a seat in the Senate, and twenty-one years of age to sit in the House of Representatives.

121. How senators and representatives take their offices. — At noon of the day the General Assembly meets (§ 122) the newly elected senators go to the senate chamber. Assembled there are the senators who continue in office, and the officers of the Senate: the chief clerk, transcribing clerks, sergeant-at-arms, chaplain, messengers, and other officers. The lieutenant governor calls the Senate to order, and the proceedings are opened with prayer by the chaplain. The sergeant-at-arms then introduces the secretary of the commonwealth, who presents to the Senate the election returns from the several senatorial districts electing members. The clerk opens and reads the returns. They show the election of the twenty-five members (§ 120). The roll is then called, and each newly elected senator presents himself to the clerk's desk and takes the oath of office. It is usually administered by one of the judges of the supreme court, but sometimes a judge of the court of common pleas administers the oath. Then the member signs his name to the oath in a book kept for that purpose. After the roll-call is completed, the Senate proceeds to the election of a president pro tempore and other officers, and then takes up the business of the session.

The House of Representatives organizes anew every two years. On the same day that the newly elected senators take their office, the representatives elected, and the officers of the House who return from the last session, meet at eleven o'clock A.M. in the hall of the representatives. One

How senators take office.

How representatives take office.

of the former members, usually the member longest in office, announces from the speaker's desk that the members will meet at noon for the purpose of organizing the House. When that hour arrives, the clerk calls the meeting to order and presents the secretary of the commonwealth, who delivers to the House the returns of the election. The returns are read, and the roll of members is called. All the members take the oath of office as the senators do. Then the House elects its officers and proceeds with its regular business.

122. Sessions of the General Assembly. — The General Assembly meets on the first Tuesday in January in the odd-numbered years. Its sessions are open to the public, unless the business is of such nature that it ought to be kept secret while in progress. A majority of the members of each house is a quorum, but a smaller number may adjourn the house from day to day so that the organization will not be lost, and may compel the attendance of absent members. Each house keeps a journal of its proceedings, which it publishes. The length of the regular session is usually about four months. A special session may be called by the governor on extraordinary occasion.

Sessions of the General Assembly.

123. The Senate. — The Senate has an independent organization. It is judge of the election of its own members, chooses its own officers, and makes its own rules. The lieutenant governor is president of the Senate; but he takes no part in legislation further than to preside over the Senate, enforcing such rules as the members adopt. He has no vote unless the Senate is equally divided on a matter; then he gives the deciding vote. One of the members is always chosen president pro tempore, and he presides when the lieutenant governor is absent or under any dis-

Organization of the Senate.

The lieutenant governor.

President pro tem. of the Senate.

ability. The president pro tempore acts as lieutenant governor, if for any reason the office is vacant; and he may even become governor, if the office of governor cannot be filled by either of the higher officers. He votes on all questions, and may leave the chair and address the Senate on any matter. He performs the important duty of appointing the permanent committees who consider the bills introduced in the Senate, and is ex officio a member of these committees. The Senate approves or rejects appointments made by the governor, and sits as a court for the trial of any impeachments preferred by the House of Rep-

Officers of the senate.

resentatives. The officers of the Senate include : a chief clerk, with assistants, who keeps the records ; a sergeant-at-arms, with assistants, who preserves order on the floor; a chaplain whose duties are of a devotional nature ; a postmaster in charge of the mails ; a doorkeeper, with assistants, who has charge of the senate chamber and its entrances ; and a number of subordinate officers, such as messengers, pages, and janitors.

Organiza-
tion of the
House.

124. The House of Representatives. — The House of Representatives has also an independent organization; it is judge of the election of its members, chooses its own officers, and makes its own rules. The presiding officer, called the speaker, is chosen from among the members.

The speaker.

He appoints the committees, and exercises great power in directing legislation in the House. A member cannot speak until recognized by the speaker. If more than one member arises to speak at the same time, the speaker decides which shall proceed; and it is not an unusual thing for him to ask what a member wishes to call up before recognizing him. If members were permitted to call up anything at any time, the business of the House would be greatly disturbed. In the House of Representatives there are also a number of clerks who keep the records, a chaplain, a sergeant-at-arms with assistants, a postmaster with assistants, a messenger with assistants, a doorkeeper with assistants, a number of pasters and folders, janitors, and pages.

125. Committees. — The committees of the Senate and of the House of Representatives are an important part of their organization. To each committee is intrusted the preparation of some part of the business of legislation. The committee looks into the history and particulars of matters before it, and reports to the house in which the matter is pending what it thinks ought to be done. This enables each house to give to matters before it a fuller investigation, and to secure the advantage of submitting the subjects to members particularly fitted by study and service to decide upon them. Persons who are not members of the legislative body may also be heard. There are a large number of standing committees in both houses, thirty-two in the Senate, and thirty-nine in the House of Representatives, among which are divided the entire business of the General Assembly. New committees are added whenever either house finds it necessary.

Committees of Senate and House.

126. Duties of presiding officers. — Both the Senate and the House of Representatives are governed by rules; but the presiding officers of both houses have certain duties which are obviously right and proper and require no rules. It is the duty of each to call the house to order at the time fixed for meeting and ascertain the presence of a quorum; to cause the journal of the preceding session to be read and passed upon by the house; and to announce the business and lay it before the house in its proper order. He receives

Duties of presiding officers.

propositions from members, puts them to the house, and announces the determination of the body; decides all questions of order, subject to an appeal to the house; preserves order and decorum at all times; receives and announces to the house messages from other branches of the government; and signs in the presence of the house all acts, orders, addresses, and joint resolutions. He acts as the head of the body when judicial proceedings are in progress, and when any matters of state or ceremony are being conducted.

How laws are made.

127. How laws are made. — The chief function of the General Assembly is to enact such laws as will protect and promote the interests of the commonwealth. In all matters of legislation, except for the raising of revenue, the two houses have equal power. Laws are introduced in the form of bills. Bills for raising revenue must originate in the House of Representatives (§11), but the Senate may propose amendments for such bills the same as in considering other bills. Every bill, to become a law, must pass both houses by a majority of all the members elected thereto and must receive the signature of the governor; or if vetoed by the governor, must be passed over his veto by the affirmative vote of two thirds of all the members in each house. A bill can be considered by either house only after it has been referred to a committee, returned therefrom, and printed for the use of the members. It must then be read at length on three different days in each house, and if it is amended the amendments must be printed for the use of the members before the final vote is taken on the bill. The vote on the final passage is taken by yeas and nays, and entered in the journal. The vote on amendments is taken in the same way. Joint resolutions are passed by a majority vote of the two houses without being referred to committees, as they are merely the expression of the will of the two houses.

128. Introduction of a bill. — The progress of a bill through the two houses may be noted by supposing that the representative from Center County introduces a bill for the protection of brook trout in the State. The bill is prepared in duplicate and properly folded; on the back is indorsed the title of the bill, the name of the member, the name of the county he represents, and the date of its presentation. In the order of business a time is set apart for the introduction of bills; when this point is reached, the speaker calls over the counties alphabetically. If any member desires to present a bill, when his county is called he rises in his place and presents it. When the speaker reaches Center County, the representative from that county arises and says, " Mr. Speaker, I read in my place and present to the chair a bill, entitled ——," and hands it to a page, who runs with it to the speaker's desk and gives it to the chief clerk. The speaker says, " The gentleman from Center County reads in his place and presents to the chair a bill, entitled ——; referred to the committee on fish and game." After the bill is numbered by the chief clerk, it is handed to the journal clerk, who enters it in the journal, and later hands it to the chairman of the committee on fish and game, who receipts for it; and the clerk makes another entry in the journal, showing that the bill has been delivered to the committee to whom it was referred.

Introduction of a bill.

129. A bill in committee. — The bill may be held by the committee for several days. Some of the representatives may wish to be heard against the bill before the committee; if so, a time is fixed for a hearing, and members who favor

Committee action on a bill.

the bill, and those who oppose it, are heard. Persons who are not members of the House may also be heard. When the committee has fully considered the bill, its members decide by a vote what report shall be made. If the passage of the bill is recommended, the bill is indorsed, "As committed"; but if it is amended by the committee, it is indorsed, "With amendments." If the committee reports against the bill, or makes a "negative recommend," the bill is indorsed, "Neg. rec."

Committee report of a bill.

130. Reporting a bill. — The report of the bill to the House is made by a member of the committee. He rises in his place, when the order of business of reports of standing committees is reached, and addresses the chair; and a page carries the bill, as indorsed, to the clerk. If a minority report is made by members of the committee who opposed the bill, it also is carried up. Both reports are announced to the House, and a record of them is made in the journal. If the passage of the bill is recommended, it is ordered printed, and is placed on the calendar of bills on first reading.

First reading of a bill.

131. Action on a bill in the House. — In its order the bill is read at length and placed on the calendar of bills on second reading, where it must wait its turn. When the bill is reached under this order of business, the speaker announces its number and title, and the House as a whole

Consideration by committee of the whole.

then becomes a committee to consider the bill. Some member who favors the passage of the bill moves that the House resolve itself into the committee of the whole, and the motion is put by the speaker. The motion carries, and the speaker leaves the chair, calling on some member to preside as chairman of the committee of the whole. The members do not leave their seats. Then the chairman directs the clerk to read the first section of the bill, after which the members vote on the section, and so on through the bill. As each section comes up, it is subject to debate and amendment. When the last section has been acted on, the chairman announces the fact, and says, "The bill has been gone through with." This ends the meeting of the committee of the whole, and the chairman reports the bill back to the House.

Then the speaker, who took the chair when the com- Second mittee of the whole rose, says, "Will the House agree reading. to the report of the committee of the whole?" If it is agreed to, the speaker announces, "The bill is before the House on second reading." As the bill was read through in committee of the whole, it is now open for debate or motion to amend in any part. After being so considered by the House, the speaker says, "The bill has now been read a second time, considered, and agreed to; the question will be on transcribing the bill for a third reading. Shall the bill be transcribed?"

Sometimes the committee of the whole is dispensed with, and the bill is read section by section and considered by the House, and proceeds to the question of transcribing much the same as if it went through the committee of the whole. The bill being ordered transcribed, it lies over and comes up on the calendar of bills on third reading.

When a bill is reached on third reading, it is read Third read- through by the reading clerk, and the speaker says, "This ing and final bill has been read a third time; the question is on agree- bill. vote on a ing to the bill a third time." Following the vote on this question, the speaker announces, "This bill has been read three times at length on three separate days, considered, and agreed to; the question is on its final passage. Agreeable to the provisions of the Constitution, the yeas and nays will be taken on the final passage of the bill." Then the clerk calls the roll; and as his name is called each member arises in his place and votes "aye" or "no." The vote is recorded, and the record shows who voted for the bill, who voted against it, and the members absent or not voting.

Concurrence on a bill by senate.

132. The bill in the Senate. — The speaker then directs the clerk to present the bill to the Senate for its concurrence. A messenger of the House carries the bill to the Senate chamber with a message from the speaker to the president of the Senate, informing him that House Bill No. — has been duly passed by the House. This message serves to introduce the bill in the Senate, where it is referred to the appropriate Senate committee. To receive concurrence of the Senate, the bill must pass through practically the same course that it did in the House. It often happens that a bill passes one house, and is amended in the other; then, if the house which first passed the bill will not concur in the amendments, or if the other house will not recede from them, the member can take but one course to save his bill. He may move the house in

Committee of conference on disagreement.

which the bill originated to appoint a committee of conference, the other house agreeing; and this committee may bring about a compromise by which both bodies agree on the bill. This difference in the action taken by the two houses is sometimes very difficult to harmonize. But it happens only occasionally that the two bodies are unable to come together on bills that have passed the critical stages in both houses, — getting through the committee, passing the committee of the whole, and surviving the final passage.

133. The governor's signature. — After a bill, introduced in the House, is concurred in by the Senate, it is sent to the enrolling clerk of the Senate to be enrolled; that is, it is carefully written out exactly as it was originally passed. When enrolled, the bill is carefully verified, and is then presented to the House for the signature of the speaker, and to the Senate for the signature of the president of the Senate. The bill is then ready to be presented to the governor for his examination. If the governor approves the bill, he signs it, and it becomes a law; but if he does not approve the bill, he returns it to the House, in which it originated, with a message giving his objections to the bill. These objections are entered at large upon the journal, and the House proceeds to reconsider the bill. If two thirds of all the members elected to the House agree to pass the bill, it is sent, with the objections, to the Senate, where it is reconsidered in the same way. If the Senate agrees to the bill by a two-thirds vote of all the members elected to that house, it becomes a law.

134. Limitation of legislative power. — The welfare of the commonwealth is promoted quite as much by not enacting certain laws as it is by enacting others. For this reason the Constitution prohibits the General Assembly from passing laws of a certain nature, on certain subjects, and without certain preliminary steps. For example, a law cannot be revived, amended, or its provisions extended by reference to the title only; but the part that is revived, amended, or extended must be reënacted and published at length. No bill, except a general appropriation bill, can be passed containing more than one subject, and the subject must be clearly expressed in the title. The General Assembly is not permitted to pass any measures having local or special application to the local divisions of the State. It cannot pass measures changing the names of persons or places;

Governor's examination of a bill.

His veto.

Limitation of the legislative power of the General Assembly.

granting divorces; changing the laws of descent or succession; exempting property from taxation; and bearing on numerous other subjects. No law shall extend the term of any public officer, or increase or diminish his salary, after his election or appointment. No money shall be paid out of the Treasury except upon appropriation made by law, and on warrant of the proper officer. There are numerous other restrictions of like character.

Filling vacancies.

135. Vacancy in the general assembly. — If a vacancy occurs in either house, the presiding officer issues a writ of election, directed to the sheriff of the proper county, and fixing the date of election to fill the vacancy for the remainder of the term. The election is held at the general election, unless a special session of the General Assembly is to be held before that time; if so, the election is held before the special session.

Salaries.

136. Compensation of members. — The compensation of members of the General Assembly is $1500 for the regular session, and mileage to and from the homes of the members at twenty cents a mile, and $500 and mileage for a special session.

137. **Summary.** — The people elect representatives to make the laws. They are chosen in small districts, giving the people of every part of the State a fair representation. The representatives meet biennially in the General Assembly; and in considering the subjects of legislation they have the advantage of association, mutual information, and comparison of views. The General Assembly consists of two bodies, — the Senate and the House of Representatives. Laws must be introduced by bills. Each bill to become a law must pass both houses by a majority vote of all the members of each house, and receive the signature of the governor. If the governor does not sign the bill, it requires a two-thirds vote of all the members of each house to make the bill a law.

QUESTIONS

What is the law-making body of the State? Name its two houses. Why has it two houses? What relation do its members bear to the people? What are the advantages of representation in legislation? Why is the State divided into senatorial districts? How are these divisions made? How are representatives apportioned to the counties? How often?

How often are senators and representatives elected? How do they assume the duties of their offices? When does the General Assembly meet? How long are its sessions? Name the officers of the Senate. Of the House. What duties do committees in the two houses perform? What are the ordinary duties of the presiding officers in each house?

How are laws made? Give the ordinary steps in the course of a bill introduced in the House until it goes to the Senate. How is it sent to the Senate? Give its course in the Senate. What is done, if the Senate amends a House bill? Tell all the things that may happen to a bill from the time it goes to the governor till it becomes a law.

Name some of the limitations placed on legislation.

How are vacancies in the General Assembly filled? What compensation do members of the General Assembly receive?

COAT OF ARMS OF THE STATE OF PENNSYLVANIA.

CHAPTER X

THE EXECUTIVE DEPARTMENT

Officers of
the State
executive
department.

138. The chief executive authority. — The highest executive authority (§ 115) of the State is exercised at the capital. The governor is the principal executive officer. He is assisted by a large number of officers connected with this department. Chief among them are the secretary of the commonwealth, attorney general, auditor general, state treasurer, secretary of internal affairs, and superintendent of public instruction. The lieutenant governor performs no executive duties unless he becomes governor (§ 123). There is a large amount of administrative detail in this department, and the work is continually increasing. Insurance, banking, agriculture, manufacturing, and mining, the preservation of forests and of fish and game, and the improvement and maintenance of public roads, have become so important that they are organized as separate divisions in the department. There are also a number of boards and commissions.

Local executive officers.

139. Local officers have executive power. — The executive officers at the capital have charge of the executive business concentrated there; but the laws are also put into force in the local districts by the officers elected in the local divisions. The sheriffs in the counties perform executive duties; so do mayors, burgesses, constables, tax collectors, and other local officers, in their divisions. The local officers are responsible to the people (§ 20), instead of to the governor, for their official conduct. The officers appointed by the governor (§ 151) are responsible in part to the governor and in part to the people, as fixed by law. Every person who keeps the law executes the law so far as he is personally concerned; and it is also his duty to see that others keep the law. He may even arrest any one actually committing a breach of the peace or other criminal offense (§ 41), and may be required to assist an officer in executing the law (§ 42). Always to be law-abiding is a high mark of good citizenship.

140. The governor. — The governor is commander-in-chief of the military forces of the State. In case of war or invasion, or to prevent invasion, suppress riots, or aid civil officers in the execution of the laws, he may order out for service as many of the state militia (§ 148) as are needed. It is his duty to see that the laws are properly executed, and the entire force of the State is behind him for this purpose. This duty does not stop with the governor alone; it extends to every other officer of the State, •and to the citizens as well. The governor is the highest official whose duty it is to make use of the power of the State to execute the laws. *Governor: powers and duties.*

The governor has never been given any control over the legislative department. It is his duty to recommend to the General Assembly such legislation as he believes to be for the welfare of the State, and to examine bills passed by the body, and approve or reject them (§ 133); but this . is as far as his authority goes. The governor issues to all the State officers, except the lieutenant governor and the members of the General Assembly, their commissions, *i.e.* the authority from the commonwealth to perform the duties of their office. He also commissions the district judges, magistrates, aldermen, justices of the peace, notaries public, and the principal county officers.

The governor also has power to remit fines and forfeitures, and to grant reprieves, commutation of sentences, and pardons, except in cases of impeachment; but the commutation of a sentence or the granting of a pardon must be recommended by the board of pardons. Persons accused of serious criminal offenses, who flee from one State to another, are sent back for trial upon request of the governor of the State where the offense was committed, the proper legal steps being taken. Records and contracts, deeds and similar instruments, intended for use in other States, are authenticated by the governor under seal of the State. The governor is a member of State boards and commissions, and is a visitor to the State prisons and other State institutions. He signs important State papers, such as patents for lands; and signs death warrants of persons sentenced to be hanged, and fixes the day for the execution of such sentences.

Qualifications of governor.

No one but a citizen of the State can be governor, and he must be at least thirty years of age, and an inhabitant of the State for seven years next preceding the election. In the election of governor, the returns are sent to the president of the Senate and are opened and publicly declared in the presence of the members of both houses of the General Assembly. In case of a tie vote, the members of the two houses in joint session choose which candidate shall be governor. A governor cannot succeed himself.

Lieutenant governor.

141. Lieutenant governor. — The election, term of office, and qualifications of the lieutenant governor are the same as those of the governor. The duties of the governor devolve upon the lieutenant governor if for any reason the governor is unable to act, but only during the remainder of the term or until the disability is removed. In the absence of this event the lieutenant governor occupies the honorary position of president of the Senate.

142. Secretary of the commonwealth. — The official transactions of the State pass through the office of secretary of the commonwealth. The secretary is custodian of the laws and resolutions passed by the General Assembly, and of the records of death warrants and other official action of the governor in the matter of the punishment of criminals. He prepares the laws for publication and distribution (§ 67), and compiles and publishes the returns of State elections. He is keeper of the seals of the State, and affixes them to and countersigns such State papers as the law directs. He has also numerous duties to perform relating to corporations for profit. Secretary of the commonwealth.

143. Attorney general. — The attorney general is the legal adviser of persons officially connected with the State government, furnishing them, upon request, his oral or written opinion upon all matters arising in their official relation to the State. The claims in favor of the State, not paid when due, are referred to him by the auditor general, and he proceeds to collect them and turn the money over to the State treasurer. He also examines proposed charters of incorporation of State banks and insurance companies, approving them, if he finds them correct. He acts generally for the State in all matters of litigation to which the State is a party, but never in criminal prosecutions in behalf of the State (§ 69). Attorney general.

144. Auditor general. — It is the duty of the auditor general to examine and settle the accounts between the State and any person, officer, department, corporation, or Auditor general.

association. His authority in this respect is very extensive. He may compel the production of books and papers, the presence of persons, and the giving of testimony; and he may also examine the books of any person or institution having accounts with the State, or any who refuse to report to the State as the law directs. In the settlement of claims for taxes and with officers who collect State taxes, and in paying out money belonging to the State, the auditor general enters into many details.

Treasurer.

145. State treasurer. — All the money collected for the State is received and receipted for by the State treasurer. He apportions it among the different funds, putting the money in each instance into the fund to which it belongs, and keeping a separate account of it. He disburses the money on warrants drawn by the proper officers in accordance with appropriations made by the General Assembly. Monthly reports as to the condition of the different funds in the treasury are made by him to the auditor general, and are published. At the beginning of each session of the General Assembly the treasurer makes also a detailed report to that body; and annually he reports to the same body the receipts and expenditures of the previous year. The money belonging to the State is not kept idle in the treasury, but is deposited in banks approved by the banking commissioner and board of revenue commissioners, at two per cent per annum. A State treasurer cannot succeed himself.

Secretary of internal affairs.

146. Secretary of internal affairs. — In the office of the secretary of internal affairs are preserved the records of the original titles of the land and the original surveys. Here are recorded the land titles of the proprietor of the province and of the commonwealth to all the lands within the State, and the grants and conveyances from these owners to purchasers of the land. Here are found also the papers relating to State and county lines, State boundary monuments, and the organization of the counties ; also all the charters, maps, and papers pertaining to the colonial history of the State. It is one of the duties of this office to inquire into the relation of capital and labor in their bearing upon the social, industrial, and educational welfare of the people. The secretary keeps also a close watch upon the railroad, manufacturing, and other business corporations of the State to see that they confine their activities strictly within their limits. Statistics on taxation in the State, on corporations operating railroad, canal, telegraph, and telephone lines, and on the conditions of labor, are furnished the people in the annual report of this office.

Duties regarding records, capital and labor, statistics, etc.

147. Superintendent of public instruction. — The public schools are under the supervision of the superintendent of public instruction and the State board of education. The superintendent of public instruction is at the head of the school system, and commissions the local superintendents of schools, and some of the trustees of the normal schools. There are thirteen normal schools for the professional training of young men and women to be teachers in the public schools. They are, in their strict legal relation to the State, private schools, but they receive liberal aid from the State, and are engaged in a work of public interest. Each school is managed by eighteen trustees residing in the normal school district. Nine of the trustees are chosen by direct election by the stockholders or contributors to the school, and nine are appointed by the superintendent of public instruction from eighteen names submitted to him by vote of the stockholders.

Superintendent of public instruction. State board of education.

Normal schools.

The superintendent or his deputy, with the aid of a board of examiners appointed by him, always conducts the annual examinations for graduation of students of normal schools; and he appoints committees to hold examinations for permanent certificates, and grants these certificates to teachers. He also grants a State certificate to teachers. It is his duty to give to local superintendents, school directors, and citizens, advice and explanations relative to the school law, and the duties of officers of public schools. He may remove county superintendents of schools for neglect of duty, incompetency, or immorality, or for engaging in teaching for compensation while a superintendent. He issues an annual report of the condition of the common schools of the State.

148. Adjutant general. — At the head of the governor's staff in command of the National Guard is the adjutant general. He issues the orders to the National Guard, and sees that his orders are executed, and also inspects the National Guard at the annual encampment. He has charge of the State arsenal, and is custodian of the muster and other rolls of the regiments that served in the Civil War and the Spanish-American War, and of the battle flags belonging to the State. Every able-bodied male citizen resident within the State, of the age of twenty-one and under forty-five, not exempted by law, is liable to military service. The enrollment of the names of these citizens is kept by the adjutant general, and this force in reserve is known as the State militia, only a small part of which is active. The active militia is called the National Guard of Pennsylvania.

149. Other executive officers. — The insurance commissioner sees that the insurance laws of the State are kept. Insurance companies organized in the State are carefully controlled, and those from other States, before they can do any business in Pennsylvania, must file with the commissioner copies of their charters and statements showing their financial condition. If the commissioner believes one of the home companies or any foreign company is insolvent, or is conducting its business fraudulently, he can apply to the courts for an order making such company show why its business should not be closed. Fraternal beneficial societies have also to show that they are responsible, and are legally conducted. *Insurance commissioner.*

The commissioner of banking takes care that the laws relating to banks, trust companies, and saving institutions are properly observed, and that the greatest safety is afforded to their depositors and others interested. He also assists in selecting depositaries for money belonging to the State (§145). *Commissioner of banking.*

The secretary of agriculture looks after the agricultural interests of the farmers of the State by pursuing investigations which they could not well make individually. This work extends to horticulture, forestry, and kindred industries. It embraces information concerning plant diseases, parasites, insect pests, and destructive birds and animals. This department, through the dairy and food commissioner, has charge of enforcing the laws to protect the people against imitation and adulteration of food products, and enforces also the laws to prevent diseases of domestic animals which affect food products. *Secretary of agriculture.*

The commissioner of forestry and four other citizens of the State constitute the State forestry reserve commission, the object of which is to preserve lands for timber culture. The State provides a liberal annual appropriation ($300,000) for the purchase of lands for reservation purposes. Provi- *Forestry reserve commission.*

sion is made also for practical instruction in forestry at the Mont Alto reservation, in Franklin County, and for the maintenance of a sanatorium there for indigent consumptives, now under care of the commissioner of health.

Factory inspector. The factory inspector and deputies whom he appoints, some of them women, enforce the laws for the protection of women and children employed in industrial establishments, the laws to compel the use of proper safeguards about dangerous places of labor, and the laws to prevent overcrowding and foul air in workrooms.

Chief of department of mines. The chief of the department of mines enforces the mining laws to promote the safety of employees in the mines. In the anthracite region the people elect the mine inspectors, for a term of three years. The candidates must first pass an examination to be eligible. In the bituminous region the inspectors are appointed by the governor for a term of four years, from those highest in the list recommended by an examining board.

Highway commissioner. The State highway commissioner is in charge of the work of the State in coöperating with counties and townships in the construction and maintenance of important public roads. The State pays three fourths of the cost of macadamizing such roads as the public desires to have improved, if the improvement meets the approval of the commissioner. The county and township share the other fourth of the expense equally between them. The ancient custom of working out the road tax is giving way to the better regulated work of the State. The commissioner is required to be a competent civil engineer.

Commissioner of health. The commissioner of health is a physician of high professional standing, and associated with him is an advisory board of six members who serve without pay. It is the business of the commissioner to protect the health of the people of the State, and to employ the best means for the prevention of disease. He may regulate any matters harmful to health, enforce quarantine regulations, and take steps to preserve the purity of the waters of the State. Provision is made by law for one or more sanatoria upon large tracts of land for the treatment of indigent persons affected with tuberculosis, the land to be a part of the State forestry reservation. The commissioner has also supervision of the State registration of births, marriages, deaths, and diseases; and of the practice of physicians, surgeons, nurses, and undertakers, in those things which affect the public health.

The State librarian has charge of the State library. He Librarian. receives copies enough of the several documents published by the State, and of the Supreme Court and the Superior Court Reports, to exchange with the other States and Territories, and with foreign countries. Other libraries also exchange publications with him. In the State library there are about 125,000 volumes, and the library is open to the general public as a reference library. All the State officials, judges, and lawyers, while at the capital, are permitted to take books from the library for use, under the regulations.

The superintendent of public grounds and buildings car- Superintend ries out the directions of the board of public grounds and ent of buildings. buildings, and prepares schedules of supplies, repairs, alterations, and improvements needed for the various departments and boards of the government. He receives the articles mentioned in the schedules and delivers them to the proper officials, and sees that all the repairs and improvements ordered by the board are properly done.

The superintendent of public printing and binding takes charge of the reports made to the governor by the heads of

Superintendent of printing.

departments, and also any matter ordered printed by the General Assembly, arranges the material, and turns it over to the person having the contract for the public printing. The State does not do its own printing; every four years the work is let by contract. The superintendent sees that all the work is properly presented to the printer, and that the work is well done.

Commissioner of fisheries.

The commissioner of fisheries has full charge of the enforcement of the laws relating to the protection, propagation, and distribution of fish.

Superintendent of police.

The superintendent of State police under careful regulation appoints the State police force, which consists of four companies, each consisting of a captain, lieutenant, five sergeants, and fifty men. Appointments are made only from citizens of the United States between the ages of twenty-one and forty years, who are able to read and write and are of good moral character. Applicants must pass a physical and mental examination. A member of the police force has the power of a constable as a peace officer (§ 42). Their services are most employed in the mining regions.

Various boards and commissions.

150. Various boards and commissions. — There are also a number of executive boards, councils, and commissions in charge of matters belonging to the executive department. The most important among them are the commission of soldiers' orphan schools, which looks after the education of the orphans of soldiers, sailors, and marines; the board of pardons, to which must be presented applications for pardon and commutation of sentence of criminal offenders before the governor may act; the board of revenue commissioners, which adjusts and equalizes State taxes and approves depositaries of State funds; the board of public charities, which examines all charitable, reformatory, and correctional institutions of the State; and a number of boards of examiners in charge of the granting of licenses to practice medicine, dentistry, burial of the dead, veterinary medicine and surgery. The governor and the heads of the executive departments are ex officio members of most of these boards and commissions.

151. Appointments, vacancies, terms of office, and salaries. — The governor appoints all of the State officers who are not elected. His appointments must be confirmed by the Senate, if it is in session. Appointments made during a recess of the Senate are on the authority of the governor alone, until the Senate convenes; then they must be presented to that body for confirmation. Vacancies in appointive offices are filled by the appointing power; vacancies in the elective offices are filled by the governor by appointment until new officers are elected. If a vacancy in an elective office occurs three months or longer before the time of election, it is filled at the next election; but if it occurs less than three months prior to the time of election, the office is filled at the second ensuing election. The salaries of State officers are generally paid quarterly. by warrant drawn by the auditor general on the State treasurer. Traveling expenses are also paid. The salaries do not remain the same over a long period of time. The General Assembly may change them, but not during the terms of the officers.

Appointments to office.

Filling vacancies.

Salaries.

OFFICERS	HOW CHOSEN	TERM	SALARY
Governor	Elected .	4 years	$10,000 and use of Executive Mansion.
Lieutenant Governor . .	Elected .	4 years	$5000 and $500 (for service on Board of Pardons).

Officers	How Chosen	Term	Salary
Secretary of the Commonwealth.	Appointed	" During pleasure"	$8000 and $500 (Board of Pardons), $300 (Board of Sinking Fund Commissioners), $300 (Board of Revenue Commissioners).
Attorney General. . . .	Appointed	" During pleasure"	$12,000 and $500 (Board of Pardons).
Auditor General	Elected .	4 years	$8000 and $600 (Military Board), $300 (Board of Sinking Fund Commissioners), $300 (Board of Revenue Commissioners).
State Treasurer	Elected .	4 years	$8000 and $600 (Military Board), $300 (Board of Revenue Commissioners).
Secretary of Internal Affairs.	Elected .	4 years	$8000 and $500 (Board of Pardons).
Superintendent of Public Instruction.	Appointed	4 years	$5000.
Adjutant General . . .	Appointed	4 years	$6000 and $600 (Military Board).
Insurance Commissioner .	Appointed	3 years	$6000.
Commissioner of Banking .	Appointed	4 years	$6000.
Secretary of Agriculture .	Appointed	4 years	$3500.
Commissioner of Forestry .	Appointed	4 years	$3000.
Factory Inspector . . .	Appointed	4 years	$5000.
Chief of Dept. of Mines .	Appointed	4 years	$4000.
Highway Commissioner .	Appointed	4 years	$8000.
Commissioner of Health .	Appointed	4 years	$10,000.
Superintendent of Public Grounds and Buildings.	Appointed	4 years	$5000.
Superintendent of Printing and Binding.	Appointed	4 years	$3000.
Commissioner of Fisheries	Appointed	4 years	$3000.
Supt. of State Police . .	Appointed	4 years.	$3000.
State Librarian	Appointed	4 years	$4500.

152. Summary. — The executive department enforces the laws and conducts the work in connection with their enforcement. The governor is the chief officer of the department. The work is divided among a number of subordinate departments, boards, councils, and commissions, each of which has a chief officer, either elected by the people or appointed by the governor with approval of the Senate; and the chief officer is assisted by a number of subordinate officers and clerks.

QUESTIONS

What did Penn mean when he said, " Any government is free to the people under it, whatever be the form, where the laws rule, and the people are a party to those laws "? Do all the people keep the laws? What department of government enforces them? What officer is at the head of this department? What power has he to enforce laws?

Name the chief officers of the executive department·who assist the governor. Do any other officers help execute the laws? What are a mere citizen's duties in this respect? Who may be elected governor? Who takes the office, if the governor dies?

Name the principal duties of the office of secretary of the commonwealth. Of the attorney general. Of the auditor general. Of the State treasurer. Of the secretary of internal affairs. Of the superintendent of public instruction.

What is the national guard? The State militia? When can a Massachusetts fire insurance company do business in Pennsylvania? How can any insolvent or fraudulent company be ousted from the State? Who is at the head of prosecutions for selling impure milk? What is the State doing to preserve forests? If children under fourteen years work in a factory, who hunts up the case and stops it? Who watches to prevent dangerous places for workmen about mines?

What arrangements are made for macadamizing the principal country roads? What is done to preserve the health of the people? How do members of the General Assembly know what laws other States are making? Who attends to the State printing? How are the fish in the waters of the State protected? What State body can be called upon to prevent strikers from tearing up railroad tracks or destroying the works of a mine?

Who appoints State officers not elected? How are vacancies in elective offices filled? Name the salaries of the principal State officers. What are their terms of office?

CHAPTER XI

THE JUDICIAL DEPARTMENT

The State judicial system.

153. The judicial authority. — All the courts of the State belong to the judicial department. They all construe and apply the same law. The courts consist of the supreme court, the superior court, the county courts (§ 51), and the local courts (§ 39). The judicial system is not concentrated at the capital; it is a principle of law that the business of the courts must be done where the causes of action arise. This is specially true of the trial of cases in the local and the county courts. The people then do not have a long way to go for justice, and the lawsuits may be tried before jurors selected from the vicinity in which the litigants live and from which the witnesses come. In the decision of mere questions of law, it does not matter so much, as the law is the same over the whole State. For this reason the higher courts, engaged chiefly in deciding questions of law, meet in cities conveniently accessible from all parts of the State.

Jurisdiction of State and federal courts.

154. Jurisdiction of the courts. — The courts of the State do not in any way depend upon the courts of the nation; they are in themselves a complete system. They administer the law of the State, and they touch federal questions only as far as such questions belong to the State by reason of the federal law being a part of the law of the State (§ 56). In such matters, both the federal courts and the State courts have jurisdiction, running side by side, neither being superior to the other so long as it keeps within its limits. In a matter coming within the jurisdiction of each of the two systems, if the decision of the State court is *against* the title, right, privilege, or immunity claimed under federal authority, it is only fair that the federal courts should be free to pass upon the case. An appeal lies, in such cases, from the State court to the federal court. No appeal is taken, however, if the State court upholds federal authority. With few exceptions, persons are at liberty to bring their suits in the State courts, even though they involve federal questions; but purely federal matters are tried in the federal courts.

155. Influence of the decisions of the courts. — The administration of justice is very uniform. It is confined to the law and the established practice of the courts. Former decisions are followed, and the decisions of the higher courts are freely cited as the proper course of justice in the lower courts. For this reason the decisions are published and become an important part of the libraries of judges and lawyers. Not only are the decisions of the supreme court and of the superior court published, but there are at present thirteen different publications giving important decisions of the county courts, and even one book giving important cases tried before justices of the peace. These reports, and the reports of decisions in other States, are indispensable in the administration of justice.

Influence of decisions of courts.

156. The supreme court. — The supreme court is the highest court of the State. Its jurisdiction extends over the entire State. The greater part of its business is that of reviewing cases, tried in some lower court, in which some error is alleged to have been made. This is known

Supreme court.

as its appellate jurisdiction. It has original jurisdiction — power to try the case from the beginning — in only a few matters.[1]

Appellate jurisdiction. The appellate jurisdiction of the court extends to cases brought to it from any other court of the State, to examine and correct any errors there may be, either in civil or in criminal proceedings. In criminal cases, only defendants are permitted to take appeals; and in cases less grave than homicide, appeals can be taken only when allowed by the higher court. In some instances it is necessary for the court to examine the pleadings and evidence, as in equity cases, to see if the decision presented in the lower court is just and reasonable. Some cases are reviewed with reference to alleged errors, which were pointed out in the court below at the time of the trial. There are also cases in which complaint is made that in the court below the proceedings were not according to law.

Location. For convenience in holding the supreme court, the State is divided into three districts — the eastern, the middle, and the western district. The judges of the court have power to arrange the counties of the State in these districts as best suits the disposal of the business. The court sits in Philadelphia for the eastern district, in Harrisburg for the middle district, and in Pittsburg for the western district. The decisions of the court are prepared for publica-

[1] In cases of injunction against corporations to restrain them from doing, or permitting their servants or others under their control to do, some act which is unjust; in cases of habeas corpus, to bring before the court the matter of an arrest, so that the person arrested may be set at liberty, if his detention is illegal; in cases of mandamus, to force lower courts to do what they have illegally refused to do; and in proceedings of quo warranto affecting officers whose authority extends over the entire State, to prevent them from usurping any franchise or privilege, or to decide whether or not they are entitled to some particular office.

tion by an officer called the State reporter, and published under the title of Pennsylvania State Reports.

There are seven judges of the supreme court, elected by the voters of the State at large for a term of twenty-one years. The number that may be voted for by each voter is limited, so that a political party in minority may elect one judge, whenever two or more are chosen. The judge oldest in commission is the chief justice of the court.

Supreme court judges.

157. The superior court. — The superior court was established in 1895 by an act of the General Assembly, as an intermediate court of appeals, to relieve the supreme court of a part of the increasing amount of work of that court. This court has original jurisdiction only in habeas corpus[1] proceedings (§ 156). The benefit of the writ of habeas corpus is a cardinal right of the liberty of every man; and every court of civil jurisdiction in the State protects him in this right. All the other business of the court is appellate. It is final in all criminal cases, except felonious homicide. Cases of this character go directly to the supreme court, if they are reviewed. In civil cases in which the amount in controversy does not exceed $1500, the jurisdiction of the superior court is final. Civil cases involving more than this sum, when appealed, go directly to the highest court.[2] The decisions are reported by the

Superior court.

[1] *Habeas corpus* is an order issued by a judge or a court requiring that a person kept under restraint be brought to court in order that the lawfulness of the restraint may be determined.

[2] Civil cases brought by the attorney general in his official capacity, and cases involving the right to a public office, may be taken from the superior court to the supreme court, no matter what amount is involved. Also, cases may be appealed to the supreme court, if the jurisdiction of the superior court comes into question; if the case involves the construction or application of federal law, or of the Constitution of the State; or if the appeal is specially allowed by the superior court or by one of the judges of the supreme court.

State reporter, or his assistant, and published under the title of Pennsylvania Superior Court Reports.

The superior court meets once a year in the cities of Philadelphia, Pittsburg, Harrisburg, Scranton, and Williamsport, and the court may fix other places also for its meeting. The court has seven judges, elected in the same manner as judges of the supreme court for a term of ten years, with reëligibility. The judge holding the office longest is the president judge of the court.

Filling vacancies.

158. Vacancies in office. — A vacancy in the office of either a supreme or a superior court judge is filled by appointment of the governor, with approval of the Senate until the next election; then the office is filled for the full term. If it is not three months until the next election, the appointment extends to the second election.

Salaries.

159. Salaries. — The annual salary of the chief justice of the supreme court is $13,500, and of the associate judges, $13,000. The annual salary of the president judge of the superior court is $12,500, and of the associate judges, $12,000.

160. **Summary.** — The judicial power of the State is exercised through a system of State courts which are independent of the federal courts. They are the supreme court, superior court, county courts, and local courts. Justice is administered in them according to State law, which includes federal law whenever it applies to the matter before the court. The supreme court has seven judges, and sits in Philadelphia, Harrisburg, and Pittsburg. It hears and determines not far from one thousand cases a year; its decisions are published as Pennsylvania State Reports. The superior court also has seven judges. It sits in Philadelphia, Pittsburg, Harrisburg, Scranton, and Williamsport. It tries nearly as many cases as the supreme court; its decisions are published as Pennsylvania Superior Court Reports. The greater part of the business of both the supreme court and the superior court is appellate in nature — that of reviewing cases tried in a lower court in which some error is alleged to have been made. Their original jurisdiction — power to try cases from

the beginning — is confined to few matters. All cases of felonious homicide, and civil cases involving over $1500, are appealed directly to the supreme court; other cases are appealed to the superior court. In some instances, cases tried in the superior court may be appealed to the supreme court.

QUESTIONS

What courts belong to the judicial department of the State? Why are the courts that try questions of facts established in the counties and the local divisions? What questions chiefly come before the supreme and the superior court? Who decides them? Are seven judges in each court better than one?

A is sued in the State court on claim of $1000; the next week he goes into bankruptcy under federal law: why do the proceedings in bankruptcy stop the action in the State court?

Why is it best to have the administration of justice uniform? What influence have decisions in the higher courts on the decision of questions in the lower courts? What will result if the lower courts do not observe them?

In what does the supreme court have original jurisdiction? What sort of questions come to the court on appeals? If the supreme court should decide a case wrong, can the error be corrected? Is it likely to decide wrong? Where does the court meet? What is the name of its reports?

When was the superior court established? What for? What civil cases are reviewed by it? What criminal cases? What cases may go from the superior to the supreme court?

For how long are judges in each court elected? Why is a minority party given opportunity to elect some of the judges? How are vacancies filled? What salaries do the judges receive?

GOVERNMENT OF THE NATION

CHAPTER XII

THE COLONIES BECOME A UNION OF STATES

161. Early efforts toward a union. — As early as 1643 the New England colonies formed a league for purposes of defense. This league existed, although not always active, until 1684; but there was no desire on the part of any colony to interfere with the government of any of the other colonies, or to disturb the common relation with the mother country. Again in 1754 there was an effort to unite. Seven of the colonies sent delegates to Albany to plan some method of protection against the French. At this meeting Benjamin Franklin offered a plan of union. He proposed that each of the thirteen colonies should choose, every three years, a number of representatives to attend a federal Grand Council at Philadelphia. The Grand Council was to have power to make treaties with the Indians and regulate Indian trade, and to legislate on all matters affecting the colonies as a whole. The laws passed by the Grand Council were to be subject to the approval of the king. In all matters not of general concern the colonies were to retain intact their individual powers of legislation. Nearly all of the delegates favored Franklin's plan; but when they returned to the colonies, the plan was not adopted. The colonies were unwilling to set up any intercolonial authority for fear they might lose some of their own power.

162. Great Britain taxes the colonies. — The right to tax the people had always been exercised by the assembly in

Great Britain taxes the colonies, 1765.

each colony in which the people of the colony were represented. Parliament, however, undertook to assert absolute British supremacy over the colonists by taxing them without their consent. The colonists regarded this as an act of tyranny, and resisted payment. Delegates from nine of the colonies were chosen to meet at New York to take action against this assault upon their liberties. They met in October, 1765, just before the Stamp Act went into effect. This provincial congress expressed such a strong opposition to the Act that Parliament repealed the law; but in doing so it declared that the British government had the right, nevertheless, to tax the colonists. Soon afterward Parliament laid impost duties on certain merchandise sent to the colonies; the duty on tea became the most famous.

Resistance.

163. The colonies resist. — The next year Massachusetts sent a circular letter to the other colonies inviting them to coöperate with her in measures of resistance. This action made the British government very angry, and it ordered all the assemblies to treat the circular with contempt. As might have been expected, they did just the opposite; every colony responded favorably. Communication between the colonies was slow. Massachusetts had made good use of committees of correspondence between the towns to secure concerted action. Virginia suggested that the plan be extended to the whole country. It was done, and before long a general system of communication was established.

The first blow, 1774.

164. Massachusetts receives the first blow. — Great Britain finally resorted to military force. The troops, on reaching Boston, met a stronger opposition than the British government expected. The people of Massachusetts stood their ground. They were determined to fight in defense of their rights, if necessary. Men from other colonies hastened to Boston to assist them. Not only were British soldiers sent to the colony to punish Massachusetts for daring to resist, but the colonists were made to feel the strong arm of British law. Parliament at once enacted laws closing the port of Boston, annulling the charter of the colony, requiring the trial in England of persons charged with murder, permitting the quartering of British soldiers in any town in the colony, and making such changes in the boundary of Canada that territory claimed by Massachusetts, Connecticut, New York, and Virginia was taken without regard for the rights of these colonies.

165. The colonies unite for defense. — No sooner had Parliament taken away the charter of Massachusetts and closed the port of Boston, than all the other colonies saw that the time for action had arrived, if they were to save their liberties. What the British government had done with Massachusetts, it might do with them. The liberty of every colony was now in jeopardy. The colony of New York suggested that a congress be called to consider the matter. Acting on this suggestion, Virginia invited Massachusetts to appoint a time and place for such a meeting of delegates. By a little strategy Samuel Adams got the assembly of Massachusetts to pass a resolution appointing delegates to this meeting. The resolution was passed, June 17, 1774, and the congress was to meet at Philadelphia in September. During the summer all the other colonies, except Georgia, chose delegates ; Georgia agreed to support whatever action was taken. *The colonies unite.*

166. Meeting of the first Continental Congress. — The delegates met at Philadelphia, September 5, 1774. They remained in session until October 26, and during this time *First Continental Congress, 1774.*

they agreed upon a declaration of rights in which they insisted that the free and exclusive power of legislation belonged to the provincial assemblies, and that the right of legislation on questions of taxation and internal affairs rested with them alone.   Addresses were also prepared to be sent to the king and to the people of Great Britain. The tenth of the following May was fixed as the .time for the meeting of the second Continental Congress.

Colonial
army
organized,
1775.

167. Colonial forces organize. — The British troops were in Boston and war had begun when the Continental Congress met the second time.   The colonial forces which had gathered about Boston were adopted in the name of the United Colonies as the Continental Army, and George Washington was chosen commander-in-chief.   His appointment was made on June 15, 1775, on the motion of John Adams of Massachusetts.   The selection of Washington to lead the Continental Army brought Virginia into close relation with Massachusetts, and did much in forming a union of the colonies to make their efforts successful. Steps were also taken to provide means with which to carry on the war.

Declaration
of Independ-
ence, 1776.

168. The colonies declare their independence. — The Continental Congress met .again in May, 1776.   This session is the most famous.   A recommendation was at once made to the colonies to organize for themselves governments sufficient to conduct their affairs (§ 109).   Still more important was the action taken to prepare the way for a central government.   On the 7th of June, Richard Henry Lee of Virginia offered a resolution that the United Colonies should be free and independent States. This resolution was seconded by John Adams of Massachusetts.   It was discussed for several days, and then postponed till the

INDEPENDENCE HALL AT PHILADELPHIA

first of July for final action.   The resolution passed on the second of July, and its principles were embodied in a formal declaration, which was adopted on the fourth of July, giving to the world the famous Declaration of Independence. This Declaration was read to the people four days later (§ 109) as a proclamation to the world that a new nation had asserted its existence in America.

169. The new States adopt Articles of Confederation. — A committee was also appointed by this Congress to draft a written constitution for the United States.   The Articles of Confederation were framed and presented to the Congress at its next meeting.   They were adopted on September 15, 1777.   Their ratification by all of the States, as required, did not occur until March 1, 1781, at which time the Articles went into effect.   Cornwallis surrendered the same year; and the treaty of peace was signed at Paris, September 3, 1783.   Independence had been declared, fought for, and won.

Articles of Confederation, 1781.

170. The new federal government. — The great work of uniting the several States into a successful federal system was yet to be accomplished.   The interests of war could no longer be relied on to hold the people together; they must now unite in time of peace for the common good. Local interests prevented this union at first.   The Articles of Confederation did not give the general government power to maintain a government.   The people were opposed to creating a central government with power over the States.   A few years, however, convinced them that the safety and welfare of the States demanded a national government with power enough to maintain itself.   Out of this condition came the organization of our federal government.   This central government acts directly upon

The need of a strong central government.

its citizens, as does State government, and has the powers
of a nation in the general affairs of the people and in
foreign relations. Yet it leaves the States in the regulation
of their local affairs as supreme as if they were not parts
of the Union.

Constitu-
tional
convention,
1787.

171. The present Constitution made. — The delegates to
the convention, which met in Philadelphia, May 14, 1787,
were instructed to revise the Articles of Confederation,
and submit to Congress the changes which they thought
it necessary to make. They found, however, that an entirely new constitution must be made; the foundations
were not well laid in the Articles. Of the illustrious men
who composed the convention, one had been superintendent
of finance, two had presided over Congress, one had been
sent to England several times on important missions and
had been minister to France, and Benjamin Franklin, then
almost eighty-two years of age, had taken part in all the
efforts to form a united government, from the time the
Albany plan of union was presented by him thirty-three
years before (§161) to the crowning event now soon to occur.
George Washington was president of the convention. The
delegates followed the spirit of their instructions rather
than the letter, and acting by the supreme authority of the
people whom they represented, they discarded the Articles
and made a new constitution. In drafting the Constitution,
they drew for their material on a long line of English precedent, but incorporated no principle that had not stood the
test of fitness and serviceability under American conditions.
They employed every safeguard to liberty that history
had produced. There were fifty-five delegates in all, and
thirty-nine of them joined in signing the Constitution,
which was completed, September 17, 1787.

172. The Constitution ratified. — As soon as the Con- Constitution ratified, 1788. stitution was completed, it was sent by the convention to Congress. It was passed by Congress without change to the several State assemblies, and by them submitted unaltered to conventions of delegates chosen by the people for the purpose of considering its ratification. Delaware was the first State to ratify it, December 7, 1787, and New Hampshire was the ninth. This was the number required to put it into force. New Hampshire gave the Constitution its ratification, June 21, 1788, at which time the national government under the Constitution became authorized.

Congress fixed the first Wednesday in January for the First President inaugurated, 1789. election of presidential electors, and the first Wednesday in February for the meeting of the electors to choose a President. The date for the inauguration of the President, and the beginning of the new government, was set for the first Wednesday in March. This happened to be the fourth of March, the anniversary of the day on which Penn received his grant from Charles II, and of the day on which the government of Pennsylvania as a State was organized. The inauguration of the President has continued to be on this date. Owing to delay in the assembling of the new Congress, however, Washington was not inaugurated and the government under the Constitution instituted, until April 30, 1789.

173. Amendments made. — A number of the States gave Amendments to the Constitution, 1789. their consent to the Constitution with the understanding that, as soon as the government went into operation, amendments to the Constitution should be adopted which would safeguard the rights of individuals and the States. Congress proposed twelve amendments, September 15,

1789 ; and the States accepted ten of them.   These amendments pertain chiefly to the rights of the people.

Eleventh and twelfth amendments, 1798; 1804.   Five amendments have since been added.   The first of
these grew out of a decision of the Supreme Court of the
United States, in 1793, in which it was held that the court
had power to try a case in which a citizen of South Carolina
sued the State of Georgia for recovery of debt.   Georgia
felt that her dignity as a State had been offended.   As an
outcome of the affair, the eleventh amendment was adopted,
which declares that the judicial power of the United
States does not extend to suits brought against a State
by a citizen of another State or by a citizen of a foreign
country.   A State usually makes provision for the adjustment of such matters in the courts of. the State.   The
twelfth amendment was adopted to provide a better way
of electing the President and the Vice-President, the necessity of which was made plain at the first election of
Jefferson to the presidency.

Thirteenth, fourteenth, and fifteenth amendments, 1865; 1868; 1869.   The last three amendments resulted from the Civil
War.   The thirteenth and fourteenth forbid slavery in
the United States and in any place subject to its control,
and extend equal privileges to all citizens of the United
States.   It is provided that representation in Congress
shall be reduced in any State that denies the right to vote
to any of its male inhabitants twenty-one years of age who
are citizens of the United States.   The fifteenth amendment
eliminates race, color, and previous condition of servitude
from the things that may disqualify a man as a voter.

174. **Summary.** — Great Britain claimed the right to tax her colonies
by act of Parliament.   The colonists insisted that this right belonged
to the people of the colonies, and that the assemblies of the colonies
alone could tax them.   The British government declared that Parliament could legally do so.   The dispute led to war, and the colonies

won. In the contest, the colonies broke away from England, and became separate States. They immediately joined themselves together, first in a league of States, then more effectually in a federal Union. The power of the federal government extends only to those things that affect all the people and to affairs between the Union and other nations. All the other powers of government remain with the people in their State governments.

QUESTIONS

What was the first instance of the American colonies uniting for defense? Give the principal features of Franklin's Albany plan of union. How was the right of taxation exercised in the colonies? What did Parliament attempt to do? With what opposition did the British government meet? What use was made of committees of correspondence?

Where did Great Britain strike the first blow? What did the other colonies do? What legal steps did the British government take to punish Massachusetts? What was the result of this action in America? Tell all you can of the meeting of the first Continental Congress. How far along was the military contest when the Continental Congress met the second time? What was done at the second session?

Describe fully the steps leading to the Declaration of Independence. Who drew up the formal Declaration? What steps were taken to form a government? What can you say of the government under the Articles of Confederation? What did the people soon learn that the general government must be? What steps were taken to make a new Constitution? How was it ratified? When did the national government under the Constitution begin? What amendments were later made to the Constitution?

CHAPTER XIII

THE NATIONAL GOVERNMENT

Steps by
which the
nation
developed. **175. The rise of national power.** — The colonists had the right to have a voice in their own government. The denial and the transgression of this right by the British government (§ 162) aroused the colonists to a knowledge of their power. The first important manifestation of the power was the meeting of the delegates from nine of the colonies in New York in 1765. Separate government was not attempted, only a protest against English tyranny being made; but this meeting was the first step toward an independent government. The meetings of the Continental Congress in Philadelphia followed, and these meetings rapidly developed a government able to carry on the war with England. The success of this war gave to the world a new nation, and this new nation advanced a step farther by organizing a government under the Articles of Confederation. Still another step had to be taken before the nation formed a government able to maintain itself and to answer the requirements of national life. This advancement was made when the people of the States accepted the Constitution of the United States.

Nature of
the govern-
ment of
State and
nation. **176. The nature of the national government.** — The people retained their States, and kept for them the control of the great body of local and domestic affairs. To the nation they gave control over national and international mat-

140

ters. The State and the nation, each acting within its own sphere, administer the entire government of the people. There is but one whole government; part is State and part is national. The relation of the people to each part is the same. The citizen of any State may reach out one hand and touch the State, and reach out the other and touch the nation. He does not have to reach through the State to touch the national government. He may go directly to the State, or to the nation, to protect his civil rights, — to the courts of his State, if the matter complained of comes within the part of the government conducted by the State, or to the courts of the general government, if it is subject to federal control. No person is so high in position, and no interest so great in power, that the citizen may not be sure of protection of his rights.

All the people constitute the nation; the people living in a State compose the State. Each State regulates the social and the legal relations of its people, and is less than national in its character. The nation has authority over the general affairs of all the people, and is distinctively national in its relation to the other countries of the world.

177. Its extent. — The national government extends, on the one hand, to all matters within the States that have to do with the collective interests of the people; and, on the other hand, to all matters of government between nations. Its regulations within the State touch the people of the State as closely as do the laws of the State itself. Federal officers who enforce federal laws reside within the State, and the territory over which they have authority is the same as that of the officers of the State. A marshal is in federal law very nearly what a sheriff is in State law. He may arrest a person for any offense against federal law, and take him before a commissioner (a federal officer with about the same powers as a justice of the peace), who may hear the evidence and hold the accused for trial in a higher federal court; in the same way a charge is investigated before sending a case to the State court. The State and the nation work together in such perfect accord that, if no commissioner is near, a justice of the peace may act, and the accused be held for trial. Not only in cases where federal law is broken, but in the execution of all other civil and military affairs of the nation, federal officers have jurisdiction in all parts of the State. Postmasters, post carriers, revenue collectors, custom officers, pension agents, weather forecasters, and other federal officers reside and perform their duties among the people of the State. No line is drawn dividing the territory of the two jurisdictions; they extend over the same land and affect the same people.

Special powers given to the national government. **178. The distinguishing features.** — There are certain powers given by the people to the national government which clearly distinguish it from State government. Chief among them are the powers to control the monetary system of the country, to maintain post-offices and post-roads, to grant patents and copyrights, to punish crimes committed on the high seas or against the law of nations, to shape the foreign relations of the country, to declare war and control the military forces of the nation, and to regulate commerce both with foreign countries and among the States. These powers may be exercised only by the nation. Other powers are shared by State and nation. The nation has the important power to lay and collect taxes, duties, imposts, and excises for the support of the national government, and also to borrow money on the credit of the United States. But the States also have the right to borrow money, and to raise money by taxation. The nation has the power to establish uniform rules of naturalization, and uniform laws concerning bankruptcy; but if Congress does not make laws governing these matters, the States may enact laws for themselves concerning them.

179. How the powers are vested. — All of the powers of the nation are vested, by the Constitution of the United States, in Congress, the President, and the Supreme Court and such other courts as Congress may establish. This separation of the powers creates the three departments,— the legislative, the executive, and the judicial. Each department is both independent and coördinate. It does not have to rely upon any other department for its authority to act; it is free to administer the affairs of government, within its scope, without interference; and it is responsible to the people for the part it takes in the government. By giving to each department a part of the government to perform, and requiring it to limit its action to that work, the people are protected from the government; no part of it can usurp authority not belonging to it. Thus we have a government of laws, and not of men. The laws are so completely within control of the people that they may be invoked by any citizen, no matter how humble he may be.

The powers are vested in three departments.

180. Summary. — The people have all the authority of government and they created the national government and control it. It is only one part of their whole government; State government is the other part. The national government pertains to national and international affairs; the State directs all the home affairs and ordinary legal relations. All the people are in touch with their whole government, — directly with the State government which is everywhere about them, and also directly with the national government which comes freely into the State, either through its own officers or by use of the State officers. Both the national government and the State government extend over the same land and affect the same people, and taken together constitute the whole government of the people.

QUESTIONS

What power did the Continental Congresses develop? How was it employed? What did it accomplish? Compare the power of government expressed in the Articles of Confederation with that expressed in the Constitution of the United States.

What part of the government is conducted by the State; what part by the nation? If the people are sovereign, and they give part of the power of government to the State, and part to the nation, how far is each sovereign? What is the relation of the people to their whole government, direct or indirect? What is the benefit of this relation? Do the people rule? Give some reasons why the people sometimes rule badly. Can the people correct such evils?

Name as many as you can of the affairs of government conducted by the nation. Name as many as you can that are conducted by the State. What are some of the powers that belong solely to the general government? In the naturalization of foreigners, what law (§ 56) does the State court follow?

What great body of organic laws shows what powers of government are given the nation? In whom are they vested? What are some of the advantages of separating the powers of government? Can any citizen call upon the law to protect him in his rights?

CHAPTER XIV

THE LEGISLATIVE DEPARTMENT

181. Congress. — The Congress of the United States Congress: is the law-making branch of the federal government. It is its composition and composed of two houses, the Senate and the House of term. Representatives. The senators are chosen by the legislatures of the States, two from each State ; and the representatives are elected by the people, the number being fixed by federal law. The term of each Congress is two years. The fourth of March, every second year, is the day on which the old Congress expires and the new Congress begins. This date was fixed for the meeting of the first Congress (§ 172), and the time has never been changed. Congress meets at Washington, the seat of the national government.

Each Congress has two sessions. They both begin on The sessions the first Monday in December. One is the long session, of Congress. and the other the short session. The long session occurs in the odd year, and is the first annual session of each Congress. It is called the long session for the reason that it continues until Congress is adjourned by vote of the members. The short session is scheduled to close on the third of March, but in fact it is usually noon on the fourth, after an all-night session, before the business is completed. The daily sessions of both houses begin at noon, and generally continue four or five hours ; but toward the end of the annual session the work often extends late into the night.

Open and
closed
sessions.

182. Open sessions. — The sessions are now generally open, and the public have access to the galleries. The sessions of the House have always been open, but for a time the Senate held its sessions behind closed doors. Near the end of the Third Congress the Senate passed a resolution that after that annual session the galleries should be open during legislative sittings of the Senate, unless otherwise ordered. Business in either house is transacted in secret session when public interests require it. The doors of the Senate are closed when executive nominations and treaties are under consideration; and of the House, whenever confidential communications are received from the President or the speaker, or when any member offers a communication which ought for a time to be kept secret.

Members
are exempt
from inter-
ference.

183. Privilege of members. — To prevent interference with legislation and enable Congress to perform its work with the aid of all its members, the members of both houses are privileged from arrest during their attendance and in going to and from the sessions, except in cases of treason, felony, and breach of the peace. The members may not be questioned for any speech or debate in either house in any other place than in the house where the speech is made. Thus are the members exempt from the will of others in the performance of their duties as representatives of the people.

Rules of the
Senate and
the House.

184. Rules applying to both houses. — Each house is judge of the election and qualifications of its members; chooses its own officers; makes its own rules; and keeps a journal of its proceedings, which it publishes, except such parts as for reasons of public policy require secrecy. The rules of the House are adopted for each Congress;

but the rules of the Senate remain in force from one Congress to another, subject, however, to such changes as the Senate may make. A majority of each house constitutes a quorum for the transaction of general business. In the Senate, only the members who vote on the question are counted to make a quorum. This was the rule in the House until the Fifty-first Congress, when members present but not voting were counted by Speaker Reed to make a quorum; since then all the members present in the House have been counted. Representatives draw their seats by lot. The seats in the Senate are assigned to members who express a preference for them; a vacant seat, or one about to become vacant, goes to the senator who first chooses it, and he may retain it as long as he is a member of the Senate.

185. Compensation of members. — The salaries of senators and representatives are $7500 a year, with $125 for stationery, and twenty cents a mile for travel to and from each session. The presiding officers get $12,000 a year.

Salaries.

THE HOUSE OF REPRESENTATIVES

186. The membership of the House. — The several members of the federal House of Representatives are elected in each State by the voters who are qualified (§ 26) to choose members of the State legislature. The States divide their territory into congressional districts. The districts are formed so that they will include as many people as the federal law says shall be entitled to one representative in Congress. This ratio of representation is based on the population shown by each census. Under the census of 1910 the ratio is one representative to every 212,407 inhabitants. After March 3, 1913, the House of Representatives will

Representatives: election, qualifications, term.

consist of 435 members. No State, however few its inhabitants, is without one member in the House; and if a State fails to establish a sufficient number of districts to make its full number of representatives, the additional representatives are elected by vote of the State as a whole.

Qualifications and term.

A representative must have been a citizen of the United States seven years, at least twenty-five years of age, and an inhabitant of the State from which he is elected. It is not required that he reside in the district he represents, the English rule being followed in this respect; any qualified citizen may be chosen to represent any district in the State. The House of Representatives is elected anew every two years. Some members are reëlected several times, but all must submit to a vote of the people every two years.

Filling vacancies.

187. A vacancy in the House. — When there is a vacancy in the House, the governor of the State deprived of its full representation issues a writ of election to fill the vacancy. The election is held at the time of the next general election, unless Congress convenes before that date. In that case, a special election is held.

Organization of the House.

188. Organization of the House. — The clerk of the last preceding House makes up a roll of the representatives from the lists sent by the governors of the States after the election. On the fourth of March the members-elect assemble in the hall of the House of Representatives, and the clerk calls the roll. If a quorum is present, he announces the fact, and states that the first business in order is the election of a speaker. Nominations for speaker are made, and the clerk appoints tellers from the members, under whose supervision the vote is taken and the result announced. The member elected speaker immediately takes the oath of office, which is usually administered by the " Father of the House," the member who has had the longest continuous service in the House. The speaker then administers the oath of office to the members. The other principal officers are elected, committees appointed, and rules adopted. Besides the speaker, the House has a clerk, sergeant-at-arms, doorkeeper, postmaster and chaplain. These officers are elected by the members, but are not chosen from the members.

189. The speaker. — The speaker is the presiding officer in the House. His office is one of dignity and importance. In a body as large as the House of Representatives most of the business must be transacted through committees ; the whole House does little more than register by its votes the conclusions which the committees submit. Only a few subjects, such as taxation and appropriations, receive full discussion by the House at large. The speaker appoints the committees, and therefore has great influence in shaping legislation. He always represents the majority, and he must act in a way to keep the majority with him, for he is chosen by the House and may be deposed. The speaker.

A member of the House is not permitted to speak until he has been recognized by the presiding officer, and when two or more rise at the same time, the speaker names the member who is to proceed. It is not thought impertinent for the speaker to inquire what a member desires to call up before recognizing him. This ancient and necessary rule prevents the confusion that would result if any member could call up anything when he desired. The restraint is self-imposed, as the members adopt the rules. Being a member of the House, the speaker may vote on all questions ; but he is not required to vote, except when the vote is by ballot and all members must vote, and when his vote is necessary to decide the question. He may also address the House.

Legislative duties of the House.

190. Duties of the House. — The legislative duties of the House are performed in coöperation with the Senate. When a bill is passed by one house, it must also be passed by the other before it is sent to the President for his approval. The Constitution provides that bills for raising revenue must originate in the House, it being nearest to the people; but the Senate may propose or concur in amendments, as in other bills. Bills for the disbursement of public money also always originate in the House, although there is nothing in law requiring this.

Impeachment.

The sole power of impeachment of federal officers is given the House. The persons liable to impeachment are the President, Vice-President, and all other civil officers of the United States. When a majority of the representatives believe that an officer of the government has been guilty of serious offense and should be removed from office, a statement of the charges is drawn up. A committee is appointed to impeach the person before the Senate and ask the Senate that he be required to appear and answer the impeachment. The House then prepares the articles of impeachment, and appoints a committee to prosecute the impeachment (§ 195) before the Senate. It remains for the Senate to conduct the trial and decide as to the impeached officer's guilt or innocence.

THE SENATE

Senators: term, election, qualifications.

191. Membership and organization. — The members of the Senate of the United States are elected for a term of six years. There are, as we have already noted, two from each State, chosen by the legislatures. In Pennsylvania

THE NATIONAL CAPITOL AT WASHINGTON

the election occurs on the second Tuesday after the legislature organizes. At least two days before the election each house nominates a person for senator, and informs the other house of the nomination. The houses then vote separately, and if they choose the same person by a majority of the votes cast in each house, he is elected; but if not, the two houses meet daily thereafter in joint assembly and vote for a senator until some person is elected. To be eligible to the office of senator a qualified voter must have been a citizen of the United States nine years, and must be at least thirty years of age, and an inhabitant of the State he represents.

The organization of the Senate is continuous. When a new Congress assembles, the presiding officer calls the Senate to order, and the officers and clerks assume their duties. The new members (whose certificates of election from the governors of their respective States have been presented to the Senate by their colleagues) are escorted to the desk, and the oath of office is administered by the president of the Senate. If the Vice-President is not present (§ 204) when the Senate assembles, the secretary, or in his absence the chief clerk, presides till one of the members is elected president pro tempore. The secretary, sergeant-at-arms, chaplain, postmaster, librarian, and doorkeeper are chosen officers of the Senate by the members, but they are not elected from the members. *Organization of the Senate.*

192. A vacancy in the Senate. — A vacancy in the Senate is filled for the unexpired term. If the vacancy occurs during a recess in the State legislature, the position is filled by appointment of the governor until the legislature meets, at which time the vacancy must be filled by action of the legislature. If the legislature refuses or fails *Filling vacancies.*

to fill the vacancy, the appointee of the governor is not entitled to a seat, for the authority of the governor in filling such vacancy is limited to the time during which the legislature is not able to act.

Committees of the Senate.

193. Committees of the Senate. — The standing committees of the Senate are chosen by action of the body. The party in majority arranges an assignment of the senators of that party on the committees, taking, of course a majority of each committee and the chairmanship. The party in minority assigns the senators of that party to their committee places. After the senators are thus assigned, a resolution of the Senate appoints the committees.

Presiding officer.

194. President of the Senate. — There is a wide difference between the powers and influence of the president of the Senate (who is the Vice-President) and the speaker of the House. The president of the Senate has no control in directing the order of business in the Senate, and has no vote unless the votes of the senators are equally divided. He may not speak upon a question, for the reason that he is not a senator. The Constitution makes him the presiding officer; he is not chosen by the members, and may not represent the majority of the body. Out of respect to him, the powers of the president pro tempore as presiding officer, although he is a member of the Senate, cannot be made greater than the powers of the permanent president. In presiding over the business conducted on the floor of the Senate, he has no right to inquire what a senator desires to call up before recognizing him. This leadership of the body remains with the senators themselves; they have not delegated it to the presiding officer. The House may limit debate; but the Senate has never adopted the rule by which debate may be limited and a question brought to a vote. It has always conducted its business without this rule, although at times there seems to be need of such regulation.

195. Duties of the Senate. — The duties of the Senate are Duties of legislative, judicial, and executive in their nature. Its the Senate executive duties consist in approving or disapproving the President's nominations of federal officers, including federal judges, ambassadors, ministers, and consuls; and also in approving or disapproving of treaties. This action can be taken only when two thirds of the senators present agree.

The Senate acts judicially when it sits as a court for Impeach- the trial of impeachments [1] (§ 190). If the President of the ments. United States is on trial, the chief justice of the Supreme Court must preside in place of the Vice-President. A conviction requires a two-thirds vote, and it removes the person from the office he is holding. The Senate cannot change the penalty, and the convict cannot be pardoned. The impeached officer is still liable to be indicted and tried in the courts.

The greater part of the duties of the Senate are of a legislative nature. All the federal laws must pass the Senate. The body is not so large but that each Senator can take part in the consideration of bills, and all important measures brought before the Senate are duly considered in the general debate by the members.

HOW THE LAWS ARE MADE

196. Legislative measures in Congress. — The usual way Procedure in which a bill becomes a law is by passing both houses of of a bill in Congress.

[1] There have been only eight cases of impeachment in the history of the United States, and only twice have the impeached officials been convicted. The most famous impeachment was that of President Johnson in 1868.

How the laws are made.

Congress and receiving the President's signature. When a bill is offered in the Senate, it is carried by a page to the clerk's desk; the title is read, and the clerk refers it to the appropriate committee. In the House, bills of a private nature, to save time, are delivered to the clerk indorsed with the name of the member and the committee to which reference is desired. Other bills are delivered to the speaker and by him referred to the appropriate committees. The committees in charge of bills meet in committee rooms, debate, investigate, and very often hear outside persons on the subject-matter of the bills, and in due time report on them. The bills are numbered and printed, and copies are laid on the desks of the members. Each bill is considered separately and is voted on, in turn, by each house.

Disagreement on a bill.

If the two houses are unable to agree on the passage of a bill, a committee of conference may be requested. Such committees consist usually of three members from each house. After considering the matters referred to them, they report their agreement or disagreement to their respective houses, and take the orders of those bodies until an agreement is reached or a final failure to agree is disclosed. A bill may continue in its course from one annual session of a Congress to another; but if it is not passed by both houses during the two sessions, it fails at the end of the Congress. It must be introduced anew if its further consideration is desired.

The President's signature or veto.

The President has ten days, not counting Sundays, in which to examine a bill before signing it. He usually sends the bill to the department to which the subject-matter belongs for examination by the secretary, who reports to the President any objections to the bill that may occur to him. As to the frame of the bill and any constitutional questions that may be involved, the attorney general is consulted. If the President returns the bill to the house which first passed it with a statement of his reasons for not signing it, the bill is vetoed. In order to become a law it must then pass both houses by a two-thirds vote. If the President keeps the bill longer than the time allowed him to examine it, it becomes a law without his signature, unless its return was prevented by the adjournment of Congress.

Bills and resolutions after they pass Congress and receive the President's signature, or otherwise become laws, are immediately delivered to the secretary of state. He deposits them among the archives of the department after he has copies of them printed by the public printer.

197. **Summary.** — Congress makes the laws of the federal government. It consists of two houses, — the Senate and the House of Representatives. The representatives are elected biennially by the citizens of the States who are qualified to choose members of their State legislatures; the senators are elected by the State legislatures. They are chosen for a term of six years, one third of the number being elected every two years. All bills must pass both houses of Congress and receive the President's approval, or be passed over his veto by a two-thirds vote of both houses, to become laws.

QUESTIONS

Name the two houses of Congress. Which is the larger? How many members has the Senate? The House of Representatives? How are senators elected? Who elects representatives? How are they apportioned to the States? How distributed in each State?

When does the term of a Congress begin? How was the date fixed? How many annual sessions has a Congress? When do they begin? When do they end? How are the sessions distinguished? When are the daily sessions opened? When closed? To what extent are the members privileged from arrest? Why? From being questioned for any speech or debate? Why?

In what respects are the rules of both houses alike? In what do they differ? What compensation do members receive? How does eligibility to membership in the two houses compare? How is a vacancy in the House filled? How often is the House organized? How is it organized? Discuss the powers and duties of the speaker. What are the duties of the House?

How are new senators sworn into office? How is a vacancy in the Senate filled? How are the standing committees of the Senate chosen? What are the duties of the president of the Senate? How do the duties of the Senate compare with those of the House? Tell the steps in the impeachment of a federal judge.

How does the action on a bill by the members in the two houses compare? What laws must be introduced into the House? Why? Trace the passage of a bill through Congress.

CHAPTER XV

THE EXECUTIVE DEPARTMENT

THE PRESIDENT AND THE VICE-PRESIDENT

198. The President. — The executive power of the federal government is vested in the President of the United States. He is the head of the executive branch of the government. Congress has created a number of executive departments and commissions to assist him. The President appoints the heads of these departments, subject to the confirmation of the Senate, and they consult the President on all important matters pertaining to their departments, as he is responsible to the people for all executive action.

199. Election of President and Vice-President. — The President and the Vice-President are elected every four years. They may be reëlected for a second term, but no President has ever been a candidate for a third term. There is no law on this point, but the rule has been established by precedent. Early in the year in which the election occurs each political party fixes on a time and place for holding its national convention. The convention comprises twice as many delegates from all the States and Territories as Congress has members in both houses. These delegates adopt a platform of principles, and nominate as candidates one person for President and one for Vice-President. The candidates must be natural-born citizens of the United States, not less than thirty-five years of age, and fourteen years resident within the United States. On general election day (§ 25), instead of voting directly for the candidates, the voters in each State choose as many electors as their State has senators and representatives in Congress. The electors later choose the President and Vice-President. It was intended by the Constitution that the electors should be a body of well-informed, patriotic men who should act with freedom in the choice of men best fitted for the high offices of President and Vice-President. But, although the election is still conducted in the same manner, no change having been made in the Constitution, the people vote for the electors with the understanding that they will elect the regular party candidates, and the electors always observe this understanding. Thus the result of the election is known as soon as the electors are chosen.

Voting by electors.

200. Voting by the electors. — The electors meet in their respective States on the second Monday in January, and vote by ballot for President and Vice-President. Three lists of the persons voted for, and the number of votes received by each, are certified to and signed by all of the electors, and sealed. One list is deposited with the federal judge of the district in which the electors meet, and the other two are sent by the secretary of state to the president of the Senate, one copy by mail and the other by special messenger. On the second Wednesday in February the lists from the several States are opened by the president of the Senate in the presence of the members of both houses of Congress, and the votes are counted. The candidates having the highest number of votes are declared elected. In case no candidate for President has a majority, the House of Representatives chooses by ballot a President from the three candidates highest in the list ; for the Vice-President in such a case the Senate makes a choice from the two highest.

201. Inauguration of the President. — Formerly the Inauguration. President-elect received official notice of his election, but now he simply takes notice himself, and goes to Washington a few days before the fourth of March, at which time his inauguration takes place. On his arrival he calls upon the President, who returns the call. When it is time for the inaugural escort to start, he goes to the executive mansion and joins the President, and under the escort they are driven in a carriage to the Capitol. The oath of office required by the Constitution is administered, usually by the chief justice of the United States. The President then delivers the inaugural address, which is taken as a forecast of the administrative policies. These ceremonies take place on a platform erected just outside the Capitol, in the presence of a multitude of people. The President then returns to the executive mansion, accompanied by the ex-President, who at once withdraws ; and the President proceeds to review the inaugural procession from a stand in front of the executive mansion. The procession is usually four or five hours in passing.

202. Presidential succession. — If for any reason the Presidential succession. President is not able to serve out his term, the Vice-President succeeds him in the office. In case of removal, death, resignation, or disability of both the President and the Vice-President, the office is filled during the remainder of the term by the members of the Cabinet in the following order : secretary of state, secretary of the treasury, secretary of war, attorney general, postmaster general, secretary of the navy, and secretary of the interior. None of these can act, however, unless he has the qualifications of a President. Never yet in our history have both the President and the Vice-President been unable to hold the office. Five Presidents have died in office — Harrison, Taylor, Lincoln, Garfield, and McKinley; but in each case the succeeding Vice-President survived the term.

President's duties.

203. Duties of the President. — The chief duty of the President is to see that the laws of the United States are faithfully executed. In performance of this comprehensive duty he is to act as commander-in-chief of the army and navy of the United States, and of the militia of the several States when in actual service of the United States; to regulate the foreign relations of the country, receiving foreign ministers, and making treaties, with the assent of two thirds of the senators present, and to appoint and commission all officers of the federal government. From time to time he is to give Congress information of the condition of affairs of government, and recommend to its consideration such measures as he thinks necessary and expedient — which it is customary to do by message to each session of Congress. The President may convene Congress in extra session in case of urgent business.

Vice-President's duties.

204. Duties of the Vice-President. — Unless there is a vacancy in the office of President, and the duties of that office devolve upon the Vice-President, his only official business is to preside in the Senate, administering whatever rules the members adopt.

Salaries.

205. Compensation of President and Vice-President. — The annual salary of the President is $75,000, and of the Vice-President, $12,000 a year. The President has also the use of the White House for his official residence, and an allowance is made by Congress for its care.

EXECUTIVE DEPARTMENTS

206. Subordinate executive officers. — To aid the President in the proper execution of all the laws, provision is made for the appointment of a number of subordinate executive officers. The orderly administration of this branch of the government has led to its division into several departments. At the head of each department is a chief officer, the secretary of the department, under whom are a number of officers. In addition to the departments, there are various boards and commissions. These are similar in their organization to the departments, but their chief officers do not have a place in the President's Cabinet, which is his advisory council.

Nine executive departments.

The executive departments, with the dates of their creation by Congress, are as follows : —

The State Department . . . . July 27, 1789.
The War Department . . . . August 7, 1789.
The Treasury Department . . . . September 2, 1789.
The Post Office Department . . . . September 22, 1789.
The Navy Department . . . . April 30, 1798.
The Interior Department . . . . March 3, 1849.
The Department of Justice . . . . June 22, 1870.
The Department of Agriculture . . . . February 9, 1889.
The Department of Commerce and Labor . . . . February 14, 1903.

207. Organization of the departments. — The heads of all the departments, except the Post Office Department and the Department of Justice, are called secretaries. The heads of these two departments are called postmaster general and attorney general, respectively. Below the secretaries are a number of assistant secretaries. The departments are divided into bureaus, and the bureaus into divisions, and the divisions into rooms. There is a

Organization of the departments.

chief officer over each room, division, and bureau ; and the responsibility is in the order of clerk to chief of division, chief of division to his commissioner, commissioner to the secretary, and secretary to Congress. The President appoints only the secretaries, assistant secretaries, and commissioners. The remaining officers are either appointed by the heads of the departments or are under control of Civil Service Commission. The power of removal goes with the power of appointment, which is a necessary provision in order that the President may fulfil his duty in the execution of the laws.

The Cabinet.

208. President's Cabinet. — Each department has charge of a part of the executive business, and in all important matters the President is consulted by the heads of the departments. These officials collectively are called the President's Cabinet. Such matters as affect the general policy of the administration are discussed in cabinet meetings, but most questions are settled in a conference between the President and the head of the particular department. The members of the Cabinet are in political accord with the President; and they are responsible to him for their acts. The President appoints to these positions such men as have ability and special fitness for the duties they must perform. Each receives an annual salary of $12,000.

State Department.

209. The State Department. — The secretary of state acts as minister of foreign affairs. It is through his office that all the diplomatic functions of the government are exercised. The secretary has custody of the seal and the laws and other official documents of the United States. In conducting affairs with other governments in the name of the President, he may either communicate through the ambassador or minister of the foreign country at Washington, or he may conduct the correspondence through our representative at the foreign court. The highest rank given by our laws to representatives to foreign countries, prior to 1893, was that of envoy extraordinary and minister plenipotentiary. These representatives at many courts had to take second place in the order of their reception for the transaction of business and on social occasions. In 1893 the rank of our representatives at the courts of France, Germany, Great Britain, Russia, and Italy was raised to that of ambassador. The law provides that whenever a foreign government is represented in the United States by an ambassador or other diplomatic officer, the President may direct that our representatives to that country shall have the same designation. Mexico, Brazil, Austria-Hungary, Turkey, and Japan have been added to the list of countries to which our country sends ambassadors.

The rank of diplomatic representatives.

Ministers are the official representatives of the government in political affairs. There are four grades, — ambassadors, envoys extraordinary and ministers plenipotentiary, ministers resident, and charges d'affaires. The United States has ministers at the courts of all the principal countries. Their annual salaries vary from $10,000 to $17,500. Several countries provide homes for their legations at Washington. Our government has recently provided for embassy, legation, and consular buildings abroad, and now owns the embassy premises at Constantinople and Tokyo, and the legation premises at Peking, Bankok, and Tangier.

Four grades of ministers.

Our consuls abroad represent the commercial interests of the United States. They are located in all the important commercial places in the world, and are of three grades, — consuls general, consuls, and commercial agents. They are assisted by interpreters, marshals, and clerks. Their duties in protecting commerce and promoting trade are

Consuls.

numerous; and they do much to increase commercial prosperity by maintaining our friendly business relations with other countries. Consuls receive annual salaries ranging from $2000 to $12,000, and certain fees in addition to the fixed salary.

Treasury Department.

210. The Treasury Department. — The secretary of the treasury receives the revenues of the government. The money is placed in strong vaults, and is paid out only on appropriations made by Congress. Under the secretary's direction the department coins the metallic money and conducts the printing and engraving of the paper money of the nation, supervises the national banks, and audits the accounts of the executive departments.

National banks secure their issue of money by a deposit of United States bonds with the comptroller of the currency. The bills are printed in the Treasury Department at Washington, and when signed by the proper officers of the bank, become notes of the bank, and may be used by the bank like other money. The amount of notes which a national bank may issue does not exceed ninety per cent of the deposit of bonds required to be made by the bank. If the bank fails, its notes are still good, because the bonds held by the comptroller of the currency are of sufficient value for their redemption.

The government makes different kinds of money. It always pays out the kind preferred by the person receiving it. In collecting the revenues there is no way by which the government can require any one, in the payment of any tax or other debt due the government, to pay any particular kind of money. So, if the government makes one kind of money better than another, or one kind that the people for any reason prefer, the better money will all go out of the vaults, and the less desirable come back into them. Then, the only thing the government can do is to recognize the difference in the money, and do business with the people on the basis of the cheaper money. To avoid this trouble it is only necessary to make all kinds of money equally good.

211. The War Department. — The secretary of war has charge of the military forces of the United States, under the direction of the President. He also keeps the army records and the surveys of the public harbors. All the principal officers of the War Department, except the secretary and assistant secretary, are army officers. They have the rank and pay of brigadier general, and are heads of the various subdivisions of the department. The adjutant general issues the military orders of the President, and has charge of the army correspondence and the preservation of the reports. The inspector general visits and inspects the military posts and prisons and the Military Academy at West Point, and reports upon the equipment and discipline of the troops, and the sanitary condition of the posts and prisons. He also examines the accounts of the officers who pay out the money of the department, and of those who have control of the provisions and supplies. The judge advocate general receives and reviews the records of army courts martial, and gives the secretary opinions on law questions submitted to him. The quartermaster general has charge of providing the army supplies, except arms supplied by the chief of ordnance, rations supplied by the commissary general, and medicines supplied by the surgeon general. The paymaster general supervises the payment of the army and the Military Academy. The chief of engineers is at the head of a corps of officers whose duties embrace the location and construction of fortifications, military bridges, pontoons, and lighthouses, and the exten-

War Department.

sive improvement of rivers and harbors undertaken by the government.

212. The Navy Department. — The secretary of the navy executes such orders as he receives from the President relative to the naval forces of the United States. His department issues nautical charts for navigators and publishes nautical books, and has charge of the Naval Observatory at Washington, the Naval Academy at Annapolis, and the Naval War College at Newport harbor. The subdivisions of the department are in charge of naval officers, with the rank of commodore. The names of the bureaus indicate the division of the work. They are: Yards and Docks, Equipment and Recruiting, Navigation, Ordnance, Construction and Repair, Steam Engineering, Supplies and Accounts, and Medicine and Surgery.

In naming the steamships of the navy, the first-class ships are given names of the States; the second-class, of rivers and principal cities and towns; and the third-class, as the President may direct.

213. The Post Office Department. — The postmaster general is at the head of the Post Office Department. He has general supervision of everything relating to the carrying of mails and the establishment of post offices and postal communications. He awards postal contracts, directs routes for mails, negotiates postal treaties, and appoints for a term of no specified limit the fourth-class postmasters — those whose salaries do not exceed $250 for any quarter. The first-, second-, and third-class postmasters are appointed by the President; they receive fixed salaries. Their appointment is usually upon the recommendation of the congressman of the district in which the post office is located. The position of postmaster is thus made a political office.

There are four assistant postmaster generals, and to each of them is assigned the supervision of specified divisions of the department. These assignments are not permanent; they depend upon the discretion of the post-master general, and are frequently modified. The divisions indicate the scope of the work. They are : the Division of Supplies, Free Delivery, Salaries and Allowances, Correspondence, Money Order System, Dead Letter Office, Contracts, Railway Adjustment, Inspection, Mail Equipment, Railway Mail Service, Foreign Mails, Finance, Postage Stamps, Registered Letters, Files, etc., Mail Classification, Appointment, Bonds and Commissions, and Post Office Inspectors and Mail Depredations.

All of the important countries and many of the minor ones are members of the Universal Postal Union. The purpose of this Union is to maintain a uniform rate of postage that can be prepaid to any destination within the Postal Union.

214. The Interior Department. — To the care of the Interior Department is committed the home affairs of the United States, such as the management of the public lands, the dealing with the Indians, the paying of pensions, the issuing and recording of patents, the educational interests of the nation, the scientific investigations of the government, and the supervision of the Territories, national parks, and public property.

The pension relief of the government is extended to veterans of our wars, and to widows and orphans of deceased soldiers and sailors. It is given them upon the principle that in cases where life, or health and strength, have been dedicated to the defense of the nation, it is no more than just that the nation should extend some relief in time of need.

Interior Department.

Pensions.

However subject the pension laws are to abuse, it is commendable for the country to render some aid in the worthy cases of soldiers and sailors who fought the country's battles.

Patents.

Patents are granted to persons who have invented or discovered any new and useful art, machine, manufacture, or composition of matter. Patents are granted also for useful improvements in any of these things. The discovery or improvement, to be patentable, must not be one that is known or used by others in this country, or that has been patented before, or that has been described in any publication in any country, or that has been in public use or on sale for more than two years. A patent secures to the patentee the exclusive use of the thing patented for a period of seventeen years.

Department of Justice; attorney general.

215. The Department of Justice. — The attorney general is the chief officer of the Department of Justice. His duties are: to give advice and opinion upon questions of law, when asked by the President or by the head of any department; to examine titles to lands about to be purchased as sites for public buildings; and to conduct and argue all cases in the Supreme Court in which the United States is interested. He exercises a supervision over the United States district attorneys and marshals, and examines and reports to the President on all applications for pardon. The general organization of the department includes a solicitor general, who is next to the attorney general, an increasing number of assistant attorneys general and assistant attorneys, and solicitors in the other executive departments.

Many important law questions come up in this department, such as involve large sums of money and affect the industrial and financial welfare of the country. The discovery and collection of evidence for the government, and the presentation of its cases, demand laborious, intelligent, and conscientious services. This work of the department is already very large, and is constantly increasing.

216. The Department of Agriculture. — The chief business of the Department of Agriculture is to acquire and diffuse among the people useful information on subjects connected with agriculture. The department inspects and certifies meats intended for export, when the country to which the meats are sent demands it, or when the exporter requests it. It inspects and quarantines live animals imported, with power to destroy any found diseased; inspects and disinfects, when necessary, vessels engaged in transporting live stock, and makes rules in behalf of the humane treatment of such animals; and prevents the transportation of diseased animals from one State to another. The improvement of agricultural industries is an important part of the work of the department. In the interest of this service are conducted a number of experimental gardens and grounds. The Weather Bureau belongs to this department. Its chief duties are to collect meteorological data, distribute information derived, and publish forecasts of the weather by means of bulletins and the display of flags as signals.

Department of Agriculture.

217. The Department of Commerce and Labor. — Although the Department of Commerce and Labor is one of the recently established departments (§ 206), it has taken a prominent place as a part of the executive branch of the government. Its duties are to foster, promote, and develop foreign and domestic commerce; the mining, manufacturing, shipping, and fishery industries; the labor in-

Department of Commerce and Labor.

terests; and the transportation facilities of the United States. The consular officers gather information in respect to the subjects under the care of the Department of Commerce and Labor, in the countries to which they are accredited, and send it to the secretary of this department. In the transfer of the Bureau of Foreign Commerce to this department at the time of its organization, the Consular Service was left with the State Department.

The Census.   The census office, formerly with the Interior Department, but now with this department, has charge of very important duties.   The taking of the census is more than the enumeration of the people.   It embraces a statistical inquiry into the wealth, occupations, education, and health of the people, the progress of agriculture, manufactures, and commerce; the number, age, sex of employees, and wages paid, and other items of interest.   The census is taken every decennial year.   Formerly, the work was not continuous; but now its investigations have the advantage of a permanent corps of officers and an uninterrupted service.

Interstate Commerce Commission.   **218. The Interstate Commerce Commission.** — Congress has power to regulate commerce among the States, and such regulation is committed to the Interstate Commerce Commission created February 4, 1887.   It has no jurisdiction over transportation wholly within one State.   The commission is composed of five members, not more than three of whom are permitted to be of one political party.   It is the duty of the commission to hear complaints of violations of the law, and to take legal steps in the courts to prevent such violations.   The law forbids unjust discrimination among shippers by special rates, rebates, or any other device, and any preferences of localities.   Schedules of freight and passenger rates are required to be printed and posted in public places, and the railroads are not permitted to make changes in such rates until the new rates have been examined by the commission and found to be just. No fares or rates greater or less than those given in the schedules can be received.

219. The Civil Service Commission. — The purpose in establishing the Civil Service Commission, created January 16, 1883, was to withdraw from the influence of politics and favoritism the appointments to positions in the public service. The commission, as representative of the President, recommends candidates for the lower grade of federal service on a basis of competitive examination. At present about one half of the positions in the executive service are classified as competitive positions. The commission consists of three members, not more than two of whom can be of the same political party. The work of the commission tends to protect the public service against political abuses.

Civil Service Commission.

SPECIAL INSTITUTIONS

220. The Smithsonian Institution. — The Smithsonian Institution had its origin in a bequest of James Smithson, an English scientist, who died in 1829. The amount of the bequest was more than half a million dollars, and was given "to found at Washington, under the name of the Smithsonian Institution, an establishment for the increase and diffusion of knowledge among men." The money was paid into the treasury of the United States in 1838, and in 1846 a law was passed organizing the Institution. The President, Vice-President, chief justice, and heads of the executive departments constitute the body in charge of the Institution. Its direct management rests with a Board of

Smithsonian Institution.

Regents composed of the Vice-President, the chief justice, three members of the Senate, three members of the House of Representatives, and six other persons, two of whom are required to be residents of Washington. The members from each house are selected by the presiding officer, and the six other persons are chosen by joint resolution of Congress.

The Smithsonian Institution ranks as one of the world's great institutions of knowledge. It publishes contributions on a large variety of subjects, maintains an annual course of lectures and a great museum, and conducts original investigations and explorations.

Library of Congress.

221. The Library of Congress. — The Library of Congress was established in 1800. It was destroyed in 1814 by the burning of the Capitol by the British, but was afterward replenished by the purchase by Congress of the library of ex-President Jefferson. It was again injured by fire in 1851, which reduced it to 20,000 volumes; but it has increased rapidly since then. The Library remained at the Capitol until 1897, when it was removed to the building erected for it under acts of Congress. The building cost $6,346,000, besides the land, which cost $585,000. It occupies three and three-fourths acres, upon a site ten acres in extent. It is the most magnificent library building in the world. The librarian is appointed by the President. Appropriations for its care are granted by Congress upon the application of the librarian and the superintendent of the building and grounds. The Library is open from nine o'clock A.M. to ten o'clock P.M. every week day, and from two o'clock till ten o'clock P.M. Sundays and most holidays. Any orderly person may use the Library for reference, but the taking of books out of the Library is closely limited.

Two copies of every book, pamphlet, newspaper, photograph, or other form of publication, copyrighted in the United States, are required to be sent to the Library of Congress. Large and valuable additions thus accrue. Congress makes liberal appropriations to the Library, and many gifts and exchanges are received. The collection is now third in point of size in the libraries of the world, and is rich in history, political and social science, public documents, information pertaining to America, important files of newspapers, and original manuscripts.

222. The government printing office. — The Government Printing Office, under the supervision of the government printer, does the printing and binding for the federal government. Its publications consist of the reports of each department, bureau, and division, and the proceedings of Congress. *Printing Office.*

223. **Summary.** — The President is the chief executive officer of the United States. He is elected by the people, and the term of office is four years, with the eligibility limited by precedent to one reëlection. The executive branch of the government is divided into a number of executive departments, at the head of which are men of ability and special fitness, appointed by the President, with the consent of the Senate, to assist him in the faithful execution of the laws. The President is commander-in-chief of the military forces of the nation, and it is his duty to use this force, if necessary, to enforce the laws and to protect the people against foreign or domestic foes.

QUESTIONS

What officer is at the head of the executive branch of the government? Give each step in the nomination and election of the President and Vice-President. In the inauguration of the President. What provision is made to fill the office of President if both President and Vice-President die? What are the duties of the President? Compensation of the President? The Vice-President?

Name the executive departments. The commissions. How are the departments organized? What is the President's Cabinet? What part of the government is conducted through the State Department? How does the secretary of state communicate with other countries? How did the United States come to have ambassadors? Explain the difference between ministers and consuls, and give the grades of each. What department keeps the money of the nation? How is it paid out? Name all of the kinds of money made by the United States. Why should all kinds of money of a government be equally good?

What have the War Department and the Navy Department to do with the executive branch of the government? Give some of the duties of each. What are the duties of the postmaster general? What postmasters receive fixed salaries? What is the Postal Union? What affairs of government does the Interior Department conduct? Are pensions demandable of right, or granted by grace of the government? When is an invention patentable? What are the duties of the attorney general? How does the Department of Agriculture benefit the country? What does the Department of Commerce and Labor do? The Interstate Commerce Commission? The Civil Service Commission?

Give a brief history of the Smithsonian Institution. How is it governed? What does it do? Tell all you can about the Library of Congress. How does it get books and other publications? How does it rank with the great libraries of the world?

CHAPTER XVI

THE JUDICIAL DEPARTMENT

224. Federal courts. — The judicial power of the United States is exercised through a system of federal courts, consisting of a Supreme Court, nine circuit courts of appeals, seventy-eight district courts, a court of claims, a court of customs appeals, and a commerce court. The courts in the Territories and in the District of Columbia depend on the federal government for their authority, but they are not a part of the judicial department of the general government. *System of federal courts.*

The judges of the federal courts, and of the courts in the Territories and the District of Columbia, are appointed by the President, subject to confirmation by the Senate. The federal judges hold their offices during good behavior, as declared by the Constitution, and Congress has no authority to prescribe any limit to their term of office. They may be removed only by impeachment (§ 190) for improper conduct in office. Provision is made, however, for their retirement, without depriving them of the means of support in old age. Any federal justice or judge who has held that position ten years, and has reached the age of seventy, may voluntarily retire, and receives the full salary of his office during life. *Federal judges: appointment, term.*

225. Judicial power limited. — The federal courts have no jurisdiction in matters not of a federal nature. They are confined to the cases which arise within the law of the nation, that is, the Constitution, the acts of Congress, and *Jurisdiction of federal courts.*

the treaties of the United States. Their jurisdiction includes admiralty cases, and questions arising out of diplomatic relations. It extends to cases in which the United States is a party, to controversies between two or more States, and between citizens of different States. The only jurisdiction the federal courts have is that which is conferred upon them; and a State cannot enlarge the federal jurisdiction.

The federal Union has absolute control over national affairs and foreign relations. The States have a like absolute control over the local affairs within their limits. The Supreme Court has always observed this division of government. It has uniformly upheld the national character of the federal Union. But its rulings have never tended to undermine and destroy the legitimate power of the States. On the contrary, it has always ruled so as to uphold full governmental action on the part of the State unembarrassed by federal power.

Supreme
Court

226. The Supreme Court. — The Supreme Court of the United States is an independent court of the highest dignity, removed as far as possible from the sway of human passions and prejudices, and placed under the highest obligations to exercise justice without fear or favor. It is the only court established by the Constitution. Congress has power to establish any number of inferior courts.

The Supreme Court was organized in 1789 and consisted of a chief justice and five associate justices. Since then the number of associate justices has been increased to eight. The sessions of the court are annual, and are held in the Capitol building at Washington. They begin the second Monday in October and continue usually till May. Six justices are a quorum. The daily sessions begin at twelve o'clock and are held every day except Saturdays and Sundays. On Saturday mornings the justices meet together and render decisions in the cases of the week, which are announced the following Monday. Each case is discussed twice by the whole body : once to ascertain. the opinion of the majority, which is directed to be set forth by one of the justices in a written judgment; then again when the written judgment is submitted for criticism and adopted as the judgment of the Court. The annual salary of the chief justice is $15,000, and of the associate justices, $14,500.

227. Circuit courts of appeals. — In 1891 Congress established an additional court in each of the nine circuits into which the States are grouped. This court is the circuit court of appeals. It was created for the purpose of relieving the Supreme Court from an accumulation of business that rendered the prompt decision of cases impossible. In the early history of the Supreme Court few cases arose. At the first term there was no business. In 1801 there were only ten cases on the docket, and for some years the average number of cases was only twenty-four. In 1850 there were seventy-one cases, while from 1875 to 1880 the average number increased to three hundred and ninety-one a year; and the number of cases continued to increase until the relief of the Supreme Court became a necessity.

The circuit court of appeals is held by three judges, two of whom make a quorum. Before the circuit court of appeals was established, there was one circuit judge in each circuit; he held the circuit court. When the circuit court of appeals was erected, the circuits were each given an additional judge, and others have been added as the work of the courts has required. Any of the federal judges in the circuit may hold the circuit court of appeals, whether it

Nine circuit courts of appeals.

be a circuit judge, a district judge, or one of the justices of the Supreme Court. The justices of the Supreme Court still go circuit and hold the circuit courts. But no judge can sit on a case in the circuit court of appeals if the case was tried before him in a lower federal court.

Appeal to Supreme Court.

Appeals in some cases lie direct to the Supreme Court; in all others they are taken to the circuit court of appeals. The appeals taken to the Supreme Court are in cases involving the jurisdiction of the court; final sentences in cases growing out of captures made on the high seas in time of war; convictions of capital or other infamous crime; cases involving the construction or application of the Constitution of the United States or of a treaty; and all cases in which the Constitution or laws of a State are claimed to be in conflict with the Constitution of the United States.

Questions before the State courts do not go to the federal courts unless they involve federal law. Such matters belong to the federal courts, and their litigation may be begun in the federal courts, or be taken to the proper federal court on appeal at any stage in their progress, if the State court decides adversely to federal right.

The annual salary of circuit judges is $7000.

District courts.

228. District courts. — District courts are the lowest federal courts and are held by one judge. A district is a part or the whole of a State. The court for a district is held in the district, and the records are kept there. There are seventy-eight districts and ninety-six judges. Others are added as the business of the courts require it. The jurisdiction of the district courts embraces chiefly criminal cases, admiralty cases, bankruptcy proceedings, suits for penalties, and the like.

In nearly every district the President appoints a federal

district attorney, whose duty it is to prosecute criminal cases before the federal judges of his district; also a United States marshal, who acts as a federal sheriff of any federal circuit or district court of the United States.

The annual salary of district judges is $6000.

229. Court of claims. — The United States gives its citizens the privilege of suing the federal government if they have a claim against it. The court of claims is held by five judges, one of whom is chief justice of the court. The court meets at Washington. Its jurisdiction extends to claims founded on any act of Congress, or on any regulation of an executive department, or on any contract with the government. The judgments of the court cannot be paid till Congress appropriates money for their payment. Cases involving $3000 or more may be appealed to the Supreme Court.

Court of claims.

The annual salary of the chief justice is $6500, and of the associate judges $6000.

230. Court of Customs Appeals. — This court consists of a presiding judge and four associate judges. It is held whenever business requires and wherever convenient, and decides finally appeals from the Board of General Appraisers as to classification of merchandise and rates of duty imposed thereon. One has sixty days in which to carry a complaint to this court.

Court of customs appeals.

The annual salary of the judges is $7000.

231. Commerce court. — Five circuit judges, assigned by the chief justice of the Supreme Court, hold the commerce court. Its sessions are held at Washington. This court has jurisdiction in certain matters of interstate commerce coming to it from the Interstate Commerce Commission.

Commerce court.

Most questions arising out of commerce with foreign nations go to the higher courts.

Summary. — The judicial power of the United States is exercised through a system of federal courts, — a Supreme Court, circuit courts of appeals, district courts, court of claims, court of customs appeals, and commerce court. Their jurisdiction is limited to federal questions, and it does not include any of the legitimate powers of the States. Cases go from the lower to the higher federal courts on appeal. Questions before the state courts do not go to the federal courts unless they involve federal law. Such matters come within the jurisdiction of the federal courts, and their litigation may be begun in the federal courts, or be taken to the proper federal court on appeal at any stage in their progress, if the state court decides adversely to federal right.

QUESTIONS

Name the federal courts. Who appoints the federal judges? For how long a term? Can Congress shorten the term? When may a federal judge retire from office?

What limitation is there upon the jurisdiction of federal courts? Of what does the federal law consist? If litigation arises over the line between two States, in what court is the case brought? If John Doe of Pittsburg sells iron to Richard Doe of Cleveland, in what court at Pittsburg can he sue Richard Doe to collect payment?

By what authority is the Supreme Court established? If Congress enacted a law and the Supreme Court declared it unconstitutional, could Congress pass a law doing away with the Supreme Court, and in that way make a freer way for its laws? What danger would there be in such a course? Tell how the Supreme Court arrives at decisions.

Why were the circuit courts of appeals established? By what judges may they be held? What appeals go directly to the Supreme Court? What amount must a case involve to be brought originally in the circuit court? In what court is it brought if the amount is less than $2000?

What is the chief duty of federal district attorneys? Of marshals? Tell all you can about the court of claims. Give the salaries of the different federal judges.

CHAPTER XVII

FEDERAL TERRITORY

232. The federal domain. — Certain territory that is Federal domain. not within the limits of the States belongs to the United States as a nation. The District of Columbia and the thinly populated sections of the country that are not organized as States are federal domain, over which the United States has dominion. The Constitution gives Congress authority to make laws to govern this territory, and no other division of the government can do it. Within the borders of the States there are federal building sites, arsenals, and dockyards. Congress controls these properties, and the States have no right to make use of lands that are thus used by the federal government. The government of the State, however, applies to them as it does to every other portion of the State.

233. Territorial Government. — The government of the Government of territories. thinly populated sections, organized as Territories, is much like that of a State. It has the three departments of government, but they are not so highly developed as in State government. The governor and the judges are appointed by the President, with the confirmation of the Senate, for a term of four years. The legislature, which consists of a Council of twelve members and a House of Representatives of twenty-four, is chosen by the people. The scope of legislation is almost as wide as in a State; it extends to all proper subjects not inconsistent with the

Constitution of the United States. The courts are of three grades,— supreme, circuit, and district; and they administer federal laws, and the laws made by the territorial legislature. A Territory has representation in the national government by means of a delegate who is permitted to sit and to speak in the House of Representatives, but not to vote.

Citizens in territories.

The position of a citizen in a Territory differs from that of a citizen in a State. He is entitled to the protection of the United States as respects his private rights in life, liberty, and pursuit of happiness, the same as if he lived in a State; but he does not enjoy the same political privileges, and he does not participate so fully in the national government. In federal domain not yet made a Territory, the part a citizen takes in the local government may be limited; Congress is responsible for the government, and may put it into such hands as it thinks best.

Government of the District of Columbia.

234. District of Columbia. — The District of Columbia was governed directly by Congress until 1871, when it was placed under territorial government. In 1874 the government was put into the care of three commissioners appointed by the President, with the consent of the Senate. This manner of government still continues. The residents of the District have no voice in the appointment of any of the officers; they are appointed by the Commission. The large number of persons holding federal office and in federal employ in the District keep their former residences and go home to vote at all important elections.

Alaska.

235. Alaska. — The government of Alaska is still that of an unorganized Territory, there being no legislative body. The Territory has a governor, who resides at Sitka, a surveyor general, and several judges, attorneys, and commissioners appointed by the territorial courts. These officials act as justices of the peace, recorders, probate judges, and perform other duties of both a civil and a criminal nature. The large towns are permitted to incorporate and elect governing bodies similar to those of towns in organized Territories.

236. Hawaii. — The Hawaiian Islands became a republic July 4, 1894, and were annexed to the United States as unorganized territory by resolution of Congress July 7, 1898. They were made a Territory April 30, 1900, and the territorial government was inaugurated June 14 following. The legislature has two houses, a Senate of fifteen members and a House of Representatives of thirty members. Its sessions are biennial.

Hawaii.

237. Porto Rico. — The island of Porto Rico was ceded to the United States by Spain December 10, 1898. Congress provided a civil government for the island April 12, 1900, but did not raise it to the rank of a Territory, nor extend to the island the Constitution and laws of the United States. The inhabitants are citizens of Porto Rico, and as such they are entitled to the protection of the United States, but they are not citizens of the United States. The legislature consists of a Council and a House of Delegates. The Council has eleven members, five of whom are natives, appointed by the President with consent of the Senate. The House of Delegates is elected biennially by the people of the island. The courts are similar to other territorial courts.

Porto Rico.

238. Philippines. — The Philippine Islands came into the possession of the United States the same time that Porto Rico did. Civil government was established July 1, 1902. All of the inhabitants who were citizens of Spain at the

Philippines.

time the islands were received are citizens of the Philippines and are entitled to the protection of the United States, but they are not citizens of the United States. The legislature is composed of the Philippine Commission, consisting of the governor and eight commissioners, as the upper house; and the Philippine Assembly, consisting of not less than fifty nor more than one hundred members, elected by the people, as the lower house. The sessions of the legislature are held annually. The courts are similar to other territorial courts. Natives are allowed to hold the lower courts. Some of the judges of the higher courts also are natives.

Pacific Islands.

239. Other islands. — Federal domain includes also the island of Guam, ceded by Spain in 1898; the island of Tutuila, obtained by treaty in 1899, and noted for its fine harbor; and Wake Island, and a number of scattered islands in the Pacific Ocean — some of them hardly more than rocks or coral reefs — over which the flag has been raised from time to time. The only government in these islands is the maritime regulations of the coaling stations established in some of them.

Panama Canal Zone.

240. Panama Canal Zone. — The United States received from the Republic of Panama, by treaty which went into effect February 26, 1904, a strip of land five miles wide on each side of the center line of the route of the Panama Canal. The United States has the perpetual right of use, occupation, and control of this land. Other lands and waters outside this zone, which may be necessary for the construction, maintenance, operation, sanitation, and protection of the Canal, may also be used and occupied perpetually. The United States thus has from sea to ocean, across the Isthmus of Panama, all in the way of territorial rights that could be desired. The Canal Zone is governed by a Commission.

241. **Summary.** — The government of federal domain outside the States is given into the care of Congress. All but a small part of the territory of the West is organized into States. The authority of Congress to govern this territory is well established. The government of territory far away from the home country is founded upon the same right: distance does not affect the right, although it may affect the benefit to be derived from the acquisition.

QUESTIONS

What branch of the national government has control over federal domain not yet organized as States? Are there any Territories yet in the State group? How does their government differ from that of the States? In what are the rights of citizens of a State and a Territory alike? In what do they differ? How is the District of Columbia governed? Do residents vote in the District?

Describe the government of Alaska. Of Hawaii. Of Porto Rico. Of the Philippines. What rights have the United States along the Panama Canal? How is this Canal Zone governed? Tell some advantages to the United States derived from possessions far from the home country. Some of the disadvantages.

APPENDIX

ORGANIZATION OF COUNTIES AND COUNTY TOWNS

COUNTIES	TAKEN FROM	FORMED	COUNTY TOWNS LAID OUT	
Chester	Original	1682	West Chester	1786
Bucks	Original	1682	Doylestown	1778
Philadelphia	Original	1682	Philadelphia	1682
Lancaster	Chester	1729	Lancaster	1730
York	Lancaster	1749	York	1741
Cumberland	Lancaster	1750	Carlisle	1751
Berks	Philadelphia, Bucks, Lancaster	1752	Reading	1748
Northampton	Bucks	1752	Easton	1738
Bedford	Cumberland	1771	Bedford	1766
Northumberland	Lancaster, Cumberland, Berks, Bedford, Northampton	1772	Sunbury	1772
Westmoreland	Bedford, and purchase of 1784	1773	Greensburg	1782
Washington	Westmoreland	1781	Washington	1782
Fayette	Westmoreland	1783	Uniontown	1767
Franklin	Cumberland	1784	Chambersburg	1764
Montgomery	Philadelphia	1784	Norristown	1784
Dauphin	Lancaster	1785	Harrisburg	1785
Luzerne	Northumberland	1786	Wilkesbarre	1783
Huntingdon	Bedford	1787	Huntingdon	1767
Allegheny	Westmoreland, Washington	1788	Pittsburg	1765
Delaware	Chester	1789	Media	1849
Mifflin	Cumberland, Northumberland	1789	Lewistown	1790
Somerset	Bedford	1795	Somerset	1795
Lycoming	Northumberland	1795	Williamsport	1796
Greene	Washington	1796	Waynesburg	1796
Wayne	Northumberland	1796	Honesdale	1826
Armstrong	Allegheny, Westmoreland, Lycoming	1800	Kittanning	1804
Adams	York	1800	Gettysburg	1780
Butler	Allegheny	1800	Butler	1803
Beaver	Allegheny, Washington	1800	Beaver	1791
Centre	Mifflin, Northumberland, Lycoming, Huntingdon	1800	Bellefonte	1795
Crawford	Allegheny	1800	Meadville	1795
Erie	Allegheny	1800	Erie	1795

Counties	Taken from	Formed	County Towns	Laid Out
Mercer	Allegheny	1800	Mercer	1803
Venango	Allegheny, Lycoming	1800	Franklin	1795
Warren	Allegheny, Lycoming	1800	Warren	1795
Indiana	Westmoreland, Lycoming	1803	Indiana	1805
Jefferson	Lycoming	1804	Brookville	1830
McKean	Lycoming	1804	Smethport	1807
Potter	Lycoming	1804	Coudersport	1807
Tioga	Lycoming	1804	Wellsboro	1806
Cambria	Huntingdon, Somerset, Bedford	1804	Ebensburg	1805
Clearfield	Lycoming	1804	Clearfield	1805
Bradford	Luzerne, Lycoming	1810	Towanda	1812
Susquehanna	Luzerne	1810	Montrose	1811
Schuylkill	Berks, Northampton	1811	Pottsville	1816
Lehigh	Northampton	1812	Allentown	1751
Lebanon	Dauphin, Lancaster	1813	Lebanon	1750
Columbia	Northumberland	1813	Bloomsburg	1802
Union	Northumberland	1813	Lewisburg	1785
Pike	Wayne	1814	Milford	1800
Perry	Cumberland	1820	New Bloomfield	1822
Juniata	Mifflin	1831	Mifflintown	1791
Monroe	Northampton, Pike	1836	Stroudsburg	1806
Clarion	Venango, Armstrong	1839	Clarion	1840
Clinton	Lycoming, Centre	1839	Lockhaven	1833
Wyoming	Luzerne	1842	Tunkhannock	1790
Carbon	Northampton, Monroe	1843	Mauchchunk	1815
Elk	Jefferson, Clearfield, McKean	1843	Ridgway	1843
Blair	Huntingdon, Bedford	1846	Hollidaysburg	1820
Sullivan	Lycoming	1847	Laporte	1850
Forest	Jefferson, Venango	1848 ?	Tionesta	1852
Fulton	Bedford	1850	McConnellsburg	1786
Lawrence	Beaver, Mercer	1850	New Castle	1802
Montour	Columbia	1850	Danville	1790
Snyder	Union	1855	Middleburg	1800
Cameron	Clinton, Elk, McKean, Potter	1860	Emporium	1861
Lackawanna	Luzerne	1878	Scranton	1840

SUPERINTENDENTS OF COMMON SCHOOLS
OF PENNSYLVANIA

	Commissioned
Henry C. Hickok	1857
Thomas H. Burrows	1860
Charles R. Coburn	1863
James P. Wickersham	1866
James P. Wickersham	1869
James P. Wickersham	1872

SUPERINTENDENTS OF PUBLIC INSTRUCTION
OF PENNSYLVANIA

James P. Wickersham	June 1, 1875
E. E. Higbee (died in office Dec. 13, 1899) . . .	Mar. 17, 1881
D. J. Waller, Jr.	Mar. 1, 1890
Nathan C. Schaeffer	June 1, 1893

NORMAL SCHOOL DISTRICTS

DISTRICT	LOCATION OF SCHOOL	COUNTIES IN THE DISTRICT
1st	West Chester	Delaware, Chester, Bucks, and Montgomery.
2d	Millersville	Lancaster, York, and Lebanon.
3d	Kutztown	Berks, Schuylkill, and Lehigh.
4th	East Stroudsburg . .	Northampton, Carbon, Monroe, Pike, Luzerne, Wayne, and Lackawanna.
5th	Mansfield	Wyoming, Sullivan, Susquehanna, Lycoming, Bradford, and Tioga.
6th	Bloomsburg	Dauphin, Northumberland, Columbia, Montour, Union, Snyder, Perry, Juniata, and Mifflin.
7th	Shippensburg	Cumberland, Adams, Franklin, Fulton, Bedford, Huntingdon, and Blair.
8th	Lock Haven	Centre, Clinton, Clearfield, Elk, Potter, and Cameron.
9th	Indiana	Cambria, Indiana, Armstrong, and Westmoreland.
10th	California	Washington, Fayette, Greene, and Somerset.
11th	Slippery Rock	Allegheny, Butler, and Beaver.
12th	Edinboro	Lawrence, Mercer, Venango, Crawford, and Erie.
13th	Clarion	Jefferson, Clarion, Forest, Warren, and McKean.

GOVERNORS OF PENNSYLVANIA

Under Constitution of 1790

	1790–1793	Thomas Mifflin.
	1793–1796	(Reëlected.)
	1796–1799	(Reëlected.)
	1799–1802	Thomas McKean.
	1802–1805	(Reëlected.)
Democrat	1805–1808	(Reëlected.)

Under Constitution of 1790

	1808–1811	Simon Snyder.
	1811–1814	(Reëlected.)
	1814–1817	(Reëlected.)
	1817–1820	William Findlay.
Federalist	1820–1823	Joseph Heister.
	1823–1826	John Andrew Schulze.
Democrat	1826–1829	(Reëlected.)
	1829–1832	George Wolf.
	1832–1835	(Reëlected.)
Anti-Mason	1835–1839	Joseph Ritner.

Under Constitution of 1838

Democrat	1839–1842	David Rittenhouse Porter.
	1842–1845	(Reëlected.)
	1845–1848	Francis Rawn Shunk.
Whig	1848–1852	William Freame Johnston.
Democrat	1852–1855	William Bigler.
Whig-American	1855–1858	James Pollock
Democrat	1858–1861	William Fisher Packer.
	1861–1864	Andrew Gregg Curtin.
	1864–1867	(Reëlected.)
Republican	1867–1870	John White Geary.
	1870–1873	(Reëlected.)
	1873–1876	John Frederick Hartranft.

Under Constitution of 1873

	1876–1879	(Reëlected.)
	1879–1883	Henry Martyn Hoyt.
Democrat	1883–1887	Robert Emory Pattison.
Republican	1887–1891	James Addams Beaver.
Democrat	1891–1895	Robert Emory Pattison.
	1895–1899	Daniel Hartman Hastings.
	1899–1903	William Alexis Stone.
Republican	1903–1907	Samuel Whitaker Pennypacker.
	1907–1911	Edwin Snyder Stuart.
	1911–	John Kinley Tener.

THINGS FIRST IN PENNSYLVANIA

1685 First book printed in the middle colonies, "The Excellent Privilege of Liberty & Property," by William Bradford, at Philadelphia.

1688 April 18, first antislavery protest in America, by the German Quakers of Germantown.

1690 First paper mill in America erected on the Wissahickon by William Rittenhouse.·

1696 First book in High German printed in America at Philadelphia, by William Bradford, for Heinrich Bernard Köster.

1716 First successful effort in America to establish iron works, on the Schuylkill, near Pottstown.

1719 December 22, First newspaper in the middle colonies, *The American Weekly Mercury*, published at Philadelphia, by Andrew Bradford.

1730 First Masonic lodge opened in America at Philadelphia.

1731 July, "Library Company of Philadelphia," founded by Benjamin Franklin, first subscription library in America.

1732 June 21, First German newspaper in America, *Die Philadelphische Zeitung*, published by Benjamin Franklin.

1736 First volunteer fire company in America organized in Philadelphia.

1738 First German printing press in America set up at Germantown.

1740 First medical book in America, published by Dr. Thomas Cadwalader, at Philadelphia.

1741 January, Benjamin Franklin published at Philadelphia *The American Magazine*, the first magazine in America.

1743 German Bible printed in Germantown by Christopher Saur, the first Bible printed in a European tongue in America.

1745 Ephrata Cloister press set up, the first in America to print in both German and English.

1746 February, Christopher Sauer of Germantown began publication of the first religious magazine in America.

1751 First medical school in the colonies established at Philadelphia.
"Pennsylvania Hospital" chartered, first in America devoted to the relief of the sick.

1752 September, First lightning rod used in the world, set up by Benjamin Franklin at the southeast corner of Second and Race streets, Philadelphia.
The "Philadelphia Contributorship," the first fire insurance company in the colonies, founded.

1753 March 4, First Arctic expedition in America, fitted out by Philadelphia merchants.

1762 First school of anatomy in America, opened by Dr. William Shippen at
     Philadelphia.

1769 Obediah Gore burned, first in America, anthracite coal in his smith
     forge near where Wilkesbarre now stands.

1773 Oliver Evans of Pennsylvania first suggested steam as motor power for
     land carriage.

1774 First daily newspaper in America, *Pennsylvania Packet*, under D. C.
     Claypoole, begun in 1771 by John Dunlap as a weekly.

     First society for promotion of abolition of slavery formed at Phila-
     delphia.

     September 5, First Continental Congress met in Carpenters' Hall in
     Philadelphia.

1776 July 4, Declaration of Independence adopted at State House, Phila-
     dephia.

1777 June 14, Flag made by Betsy Ross of Philadelphia adopted by Congress
     as flag of United States.

1780 First abolition law in America enacted, providing that slavery be abol-
     ished in Pennsylvania.

1782 First edition of the Bible in English printed in America, by Robert
     Aitken at Philadelphia.

1785 September, John Fitch exhibited first models of a steamboat, before the
     American Philosophical Society of Philadelphia.

1786 First American dispensary founded at Philadelphia by Dr. Benjamin
     Rush.

     July 27, John Fitch navigated first steam vessel on the Delaware
     River.

1789 First Greek book, "Lucian's Dialogues," printed in America, by Joseph
     James, at Philadelphia.

1790 Philadelphia became Capital of the United States.
     John Fitch's steamboat made regular trips on Delaware River.

1791 February 25, "First Bank of the United States" established at Phila-
     delphia.

1792 First turnpike company in the United States incorporated, Philadelphia
     to Lancaster.

     April 2, First United States Mint established at Philadelphia.

     April 19, "Schuylkill & Delaware Canal" chartered, the first public
     canal in the United States.

1795 November 4, The schooner *White Fish*, built at Presque Isle, arrived
     at Philadelphia, — the first vessel to demonstrate that transportation
     could be established between Lake Erie and the Hudson River.

1802 Anthracite coal first burned in grates, in Philadelphia.

1804 First bituminous coal sent down the Susquehanna River.

First cotton spun in the United States by carding and spinning jenny, at Pittsburg.

First steam dredging machine in United States, constucted by Oliver Evans, at Philadelphia. Being placed on wheels, it propelled itself one and one half miles to the Schuylkill River, the first propulsion of a carriage on land by steam in the United States.

1805 First agency in the United States for the sale of American manufactures established in Philadelphia by Elijah Waring.

1808 First flint glass manufactured in the United States by Bakewell & Co. of Pittsburg.

1809 September, Experimental railroad constructed at Bull's Head tavern, Third Street, above Callowhill, Philadelphia, — the first railroad laid down in America.

Thomas and George Leiper built railroad at their quarries in Delaware County.

1814 First successful experiment in the use of anthracite coal in an iron furnace, made in Delaware County by Mellon & Bishop.

1816 First steam paper mill in the United States started at Pittsburg.

1822 First cylinders for printing calico engraved in the United States at Philadelphia.

1823 March 31, First railway act in the United States passed by General Assembly of Pennsylvania.

1827 Paper first made from straw at Meadville by Colonel William McGraw.

1829 First locomotive in the United States used on Carbondale and Honesdale Road.

1856 First Republican National Convention met in Philadelphia.

1859 August 29, Colonel E. L. Drake successfully bored for petroleum at Titusville.

1861 April 16, Pennsylvania troops first to reach Washington in defense of the Union.

CONSTITUTION OF THE COMMONWEALTH OF PENN-SYLVANIA

(This Constitution shall take effect on January 1, 1874, for all purposes not otherwise provided for therein. — Sec. 1, Schedule.)

PREAMBLE

WE, the people of the Commonwealth of Pennsylvania, grateful to Almighty God for the blessings of civil and religious liberty, and humbly invoking His guidance, do ordain and establish this Constitution.

ARTICLE I

Declaration of Rights

That the general, great and essential principles of liberty and free government may be recognized and unalterably established, WE DECLARE THAT—

Inherent Rights of Mankind

Sec. 1. All men are born equally free and independent, and have certain inherent and indefeasible rights, among which are those of enjoying and defending life and liberty, of acquiring, possessing and protecting property and reputation, and of pursuing their own happiness.

Political Power

Sec. 2. All power is inherent in the people, and all free governments are founded on their authority and instituted for their peace, safety and happiness. For the advancements of these ends they have at all times an inalienable and indefeasible right to alter, reform or abolish their government in such manner as they may think proper.

Religious Freedom

Sec. 3. All men have a natural and indefeasible right to worship Almighty God according to the dictates of their own consciences; no man can of right be compelled to attend, erect or support any place of worship, or to maintain any ministry against his consent; no human authority can, in any case whatever, control or interfere with the rights of conscience, and no preference shall ever be given by law to any religious establishments or modes of worship.

Religion

Sec. 4. No person who acknowledges the being of a God and a future state of rewards and punishments shall, on account of his religious sentiments, be disqualified to hold any office or place of trust or profit under this Commonwealth.

Elections

Sec. 5. Elections shall be free and equal; and no power, civil or military, shall at any time interfere to prevent the free exercise of the right of suffrage.

Trial by Jury

Sec. 6. Trial by jury shall be as heretofore, and the right thereof remain inviolate.

Freedom of Press and Speech — Libels

Sec. 7. The printing press shall be free to every person who may undertake to examine the proceedings of the legislature or any branch of government, and no law shall ever be made to restrain the right thereof. The free communication of thoughts and opinions is one of the invaluable rights of man, and every citizen may freely speak, write and print on any subject, being responsible for the abuse of that liberty. No conviction shall be had in any prosecution for the publication of papers relating to the official conduct of officers or men in public capacity, or to any other matter proper for public investigation or information, where the fact that such publication was not maliciously or negligently made shall be established to the satisfaction of the jury; and in all indictments for libels the jury shall have the right to determine the law and the facts under the direction of the court, as in other cases.

Security from Searches and Seizures

Sec. 8. The people shall be secure in their persons, houses, papers and possessions from unreasonable searches and seizures, and no warrant to search any place or to seize any person or things shall issue without describing them as nearly as may be, nor without probable cause, supported by oath or affirmation subscribed to by the affiant.

Rights of Accused in Criminal Prosecutions

Sec. 9. In all criminal prosecutions the accused hath a right to be heard by himself and his counsel, to demand the nature and cause of the accusation against him, to meet the witnesses face to face, to have compulsory process for obtaining witnesses in his favor, and, in prosecutions by indictment or information, a speedy public trial by an impartial jury of the vicinage; he cannot be compelled to give evidence against himself, nor can he be deprived of his life, liberty or property, unless by the judgment of his peers or the law of the land.

Criminal Informations — Twice in Jeopardy

Sec. 10. No person shall, for any indictable offence, be proceeded against criminally by information, except in cases arising in the land or naval forces, or in the militia, when in actual service, in time of war or public danger, or by leave of the court for oppression or misdemeanor in office. No person shall, for the same offence, be twice put in jeopardy of life or limb; nor shall private property be taken or applied to public use, without authority of law and without just compensation being first made or secured.

Courts to be Open — Suits Against the State

Sec. 11. All courts shall be open; and every man for an injury done him in his lands, goods, person or reputation shall have remedy by due course of law, and right and justice administered without sale, denial or delay. Suits may be brought against the Commonwealth in such manner, in such courts and in such cases as the legislature may by law direct.

Power of Suspending Laws

Sec. 12. No power of suspending laws shall be exercised unless by the legislature or by its authority.

Bail — Fines and Punishments

Sec. 13. Excessive bail shall not be required, nor excessive fines imposed, nor cruel punishments inflicted.

Prisoners to be Bailable — Habeas Corpus

Sec. 14. All prisoners shall be bailable by sufficient sureties, unless for capital offences when the proof is evident or presumption great; and the privilege of the writ of *habeas corpus* shall not be suspended, unless when in case of rebellion or invasion the public safety may require it.

Oyer and Terminer, &c.

Sec. 15. No commission of Oyer and Terminer or Jail Delivery shall be issued.

Insolvent Debtors

Sec. 16. The person of a debtor, where there is not strong presumption of fraud, shall not be continued in prison after delivering up his estate for the benefit of his creditors in such manner as shall be prescribed by law.

Ex Post Facto Laws — Impairment of Contracts

Sec. 17. No *ex post facto* law, nor any law impairing the obligation of contracts, or making irrevocable any grant of special privileges or immunities, shall be passed.

Attaint

Sec. 18. No person shall be attainted of treason or felony by the legislature.

Effect of Attainder Limited — No Forfeiture for Suicide or in Case of Death by Casualty

Sec. 19. No attainder shall work corruption of blood, nor except during the life of the offender, forfeiture of estate to the Commonwealth. The estate of such persons as shall destroy their own lives shall descend or vest as in cases of natural death, and if any person shall be killed by casualty there shall be no forfeiture by reason thereof.

Right of Petition

Sec. 20. The citizens have a right in a peaceable manner to assemble together for their common good, and to apply to those invested with the powers of government for redress of grievances or other proper purposes, by petition, address or remonstrance.

Right to Bear Arms

Sec. 21. The right of the citizens to bear arms in defence of themselves and the State shall not be questioned.

No Standing Army — Military Subordinate to Civil Power

Sec. 22. No standing army shall, in time of peace, be kept up without the consent of the legislature, and the military shall in all cases and at all times be in strict subordination to the civil power.

Quartering of Troops

Sec. 23. No soldier shall in time of peace be quartered in any house without the consent of the owner, nor in time of war but in a manner to be prescribed by law.

Titles and Offices

Sec. 24. The legislature shall not grant any title of nobility or hereditary distinction, nor create any office the appointment to which shall be for a longer term than during good behavior.

Emigration

Sec. 25. Emigration from the State shall not be prohibited.

Exceptions from the General Powers of Government

Sec. 26. To guard against transgressions of the high powers which we have delegated, we declare that everything in this article is excepted out of the general powers of government and shall forever remain inviolate.

ARTICLE II

The Legislature — Power Vested in — Consists of a Senate and House

Sec. 1. The legislative power of this Commonwealth shall be vested in a General Assembly which shall consist of a Senate and a House of Representatives.

Election of Members — Vacancies

Sec. 2. Members of the General Assembly shall be chosen at the general election every second year. Their term of service shall begin on the first day of December next after their election.   Whenever a vacancy shall occur in either House, the presiding officer thereof shall issue a writ of election to fill such vacancy for the remainder of the term.

Terms of Senators and Representatives

Sec. 3. Senators shall be elected for the term of four years and Representatives for the term of two years.

Meetings of the General Assembly — Filling of Vacancy in Office of United States Senator

Sec. 4. The General Assembly shall meet at twelve o'clock, noon, on the first Tuesday of January every second year, and at other times when convened by the Governor, but shall hold no adjourned annual session after the year one thousand eight hundred and seventy-eight.   In case of a vacancy in the office of United States Senator from this Commonwealth, in a recess between sessions, the Governor shall convene the two Houses, by proclamation on notice not exceeding sixty days, to fill the same.

Qualifications of Senators and Representatives — Residence

Sec. 5. Senators shall be at least twenty-five years of age and Representatives twenty-one years of age.   They shall have been citizens and inhabitants of the State four years, and inhabitants of their respective districts one year next before their election (unless absent on the public business of the United States or of this State,) and shall reside in their respective districts during their terms of service.

Disqualifications

Sec. 6. No Senator or Representative shall, during the time for which he shall have been elected, be appointed to any civil office under this Commonwealth, and no member of Congress or other person holding any office (except of attorney-at-law or in the militia) under the United States or this Commonwealth shall be a member of either House during his continuance in office.

Persons Convicted of Infamous Crimes to be Disqualified

Sec. 7. No person hereafter convicted of embezzlement of public moneys, bribery, perjury or other infamous crime, shall be eligible to the General Assembly, or capable of holding any office of trust or profit in the Commonwealth.

Compensation not to be Increased During Term

Sec. 8. The members of the General Assembly shall receive such salary and mileage for regular and special sessions as shall be fixed by law, and no other compensation whatever, whether for service upon committee or otherwise. No member of either House shall, during the term for which he may have been elected, receive any increase of salary, or mileage, under any law passed during such term.

Election of President pro tempore of the Senate and Speaker of the House — Other Officers — Each House shall Judge as to Election of its Members, &c.

Sec. 9. The Senate shall, at the beginning and close of each regular session and at such other times as may be necessary, elect one of its members President *pro tempore*, who shall perform the duties of the Lieutenant-Governor, in any case of absence or disability of that officer, and whenever the said office of Lieutenant-Governor shall be vacant. The House of Representatives shall elect one of its members as Speaker. Each House shall choose its other officers, and shall judge of the election and qualifications of its members.

Quorum

Sec. 10. A majority of each House shall constitute a quorum, but a smaller number may adjourn from day to day and compel the attendance of absent members.

Powers of Each House — Expulsion

Sec. 11. Each House shall have power to determine the rules of its proceedings and punish its members or other persons for contempt or disorderly behavior in its presence, to enforce obedience to its process, to protect its members against violence or offers of bribes or private solicitation, and, with the concurrence of two-thirds, to expel a member, but not a second time for the same cause, and shall have all other powers necessary for the legislature of a free State. A member expelled for corruption shall not thereafter be eligible to either House, and punishment for contempt or disorderly behavior shall not bar an indictment for the same offence.

Journals — Yeas and Nays

Sec. 12. Each House shall keep a journal of its proceedings and from time to time publish the same, except such parts as require secrecy, and the yeas and nays of the members on any question shall, at the desire of any two of them, be entered on the journal.

Sessions Shall be Open

Sec. 13. The sessions of each House and of Committees of the Whole shall be open, unless when the business is such as ought to be kept secret.

Adjournments

Sec. 14. Neither House shall, without the consent of the other, adjourn for more than three days, nor to any other place than that in which the two Houses shall be sitting.

Privileges of Members

Sec. 15. The members of the General Assembly shall in all cases, except treason, felony, violation of their oath of office, and breach or surety of the peace, be privileged from arrest during their attendance at the sessions of their respective Houses and in going to and returning from the same; and for any speech or debate in either House they shall not be questioned in any other place.

Senatorial Districts — Ratio

Sec. 16. The State shall be divided into fifty senatorial districts of compact. and contiguous territory as nearly equal in population as may be, and each district shall be entitled to elect one Senator. Each county containing one or more ratios of population shall be entitled to one Senator for each ratio, and to an additional Senator for a surplus of population exceeding three-fifths of a ratio, but no county shall form a separate district unless it shall contain four-fifths of a ratio, except where the adjoining counties are each entitled to one or more Senators, when such county may be assigned a Senator on less than four-fifths and exceeding one-half a ratio, and no county shall be divided unless entitled to two or more Senators. No city or county shall be entitled to separate representation exceeding one-sixth of the whole number of Senators. No ward, borough or township shall be divided in the formation of a district. The senatorial ratio shall be ascertained by dividing the whole population of the State by the number fifty.

Representative Districts — Ratio

Sec. 17. The members of the House of Representatives shall be apportioned among the several counties, on a ratio obtained by dividing the population of the State as ascertained by the most recent United States census by two hundred. Every county containing less than five ratios shall have one representative for every full ratio, and an additional representative when the surplus exceeds half a ratio; but each county shall have at least one representative. Every county containing five ratios or more shall have one representative for every full ratio. Every city containing a population equal to a ratio shall elect separately its proportion of the representatives allotted to the county in which it is located. Every city entitled to more than four representatives, and every county having over one hundred thousand inhabitants shall be divided into districts of compact and contiguous territory, each district to elect its proportion of representatives according to its population, but no district shall elect more than four representatives.

Apportionment of the State

Sec. 18. The General Assembly at its first session after the adoption of this Constitution, and immediately after each United States decennial census, shall apportion the State into senatorial and representative districts agreeably to the provisions of the two next preceding sections.

ARTICLE III

Legislation — Passage of Bills

Sec. 1. No law shall be passed except by bill, and no bill shall be so altered or amended, on its passage through either House, as to change its original purpose.

Reference and Printing

Sec. 2. No bill shall be considered, unless referred to a committee, returned therefrom, and printed for the use of the members.

Form of Bills

Sec. 3. No bill, except general appropriation bills, shall be passed containing more than one subject, which shall be clearly expressed in its title.

Three Readings — Amendments — Yeas and Nays

Sec. 4. Every bill shall be read at length on three different days in each House; all amendments made thereto shall be printed for the use of the members before the final vote is taken on the bill, and no bill shall become a law, unless on its final passage the vote be taken by yeas and nays, the names of the persons voting for and against the same be entered on the journal, and a majority of the members elected to each House be recorded thereon as voting in its favor.

Votes on Concurring in Amendments — Reports of Committees of Conference

Sec. 5. No amendment to bills by one House, shall be concurred in by the other, except by the vote of a majority of the members elected thereto, taken by yeas and nays, and the names of those voting for and against recorded upon the journal thereof; and reports of committees of conference shall be adopted in either House only by the vote of a majority of the members elected thereto, taken by yeas and nays, and the names of those voting recorded upon the journals.

Revival and Amendment of Laws

Sec. 6. No law shall be revived, amended, or the provisions thereof extended or conferred, by reference to its title only, but so much thereof as is revived, amended, extended or conferred shall be re-enacted and published at length.

Special and Local Legislation Limited

Sec. 7. The General Assembly shall not pass any local or special law authorizing the creation, extension or impairing of liens:

Regulating the affairs of counties, cities, townships, wards, boroughs or school districts:

Changing the names of persons or places:

Changing the venue in civil or criminal cases:

Authorizing the laying out, opening, altering or maintaining, roads, highways, streets or alleys:

Relating to ferries or bridges, or incorporating ferry or bridge companies, except for the erection of bridges crossing streams which form boundaries between this and any other State:

Vacating roads, town plats, streets or alleys:

Relating to cemeteries, grave-yards, or public grounds not of the State:

Authorizing the adoption or legitimation of children:

Locating or changing county seats, erecting new counties or changing county lines:

Incorporating cities, towns or villages, or changing their charters:

For the opening and conducting of elections, or fixing or changing the place of voting:

Granting divorces:

Erecting new townships or boroughs, changing township lines, borough limits or school districts:

Creating offices, or prescribing the powers and duties of officers in counties, cities, boroughs, townships, election or school districts:

Changing the law of descent or succession:

Regulating the practice or jurisdiction of, or changing the rules of evidence in, any judicial proceeding or inquiry before courts, aldermen, justices of the peace, sheriffs, commissioners, arbitrators, auditors, masters in chancery or other tribunals, or providing or changing methods for the collection of debts, or the enforcing of judgments, or prescribing the effect of judicial sales of real estate:

Regulating the fees, or extending the powers and duties of aldermen, justices of the peace, magistrates or constables:

Regulating the management of public schools, the building or repairing of school-houses and the raising of money for such purposes:

Fixing the rate of interest:

Affecting the estates of minors or persons under disability, except after due notice to all parties in interest, to be recited in the special enactment:

Remitting fines, penalties and forfeitures, or refunding moneys legally paid into the treasury:

Exempting property from taxation:

Regulating labor, trade, mining or manufacturing:

Creating corporations, or amending, renewing or extending the charters thereof:

Granting to any corporation, association or individual any special or exclusive privilege or immunity, or to any corporation, association or individual the right to lay down a railroad track:

Nor shall the General Assembly indirectly enact such special or local law by the partial repeal of a general law; but laws repealing local or special acts may be passed:

Nor shall any law be passed granting powers or privileges in any case where the granting of such powers and privileges shall have been provided for by general law, nor where the courts have jurisdiction to grant the same or give the relief asked for.

Notice of Local and Special Bills

Sec. 8. No local or special bill shall be passed unless notice of the intention to apply therefor shall have been published in the locality where the matter or the thing to be effected may be situated, which notice shall be at least thirty days prior to the introduction into the General Assembly of such bill and in the manner to be provided by law; the evidence of such notice having been published, shall be exhibited in the General Assembly before such act shall be passed.

Signing of Bills

Sec. 9. The presiding officer of each House shall, in the presence of the House over which he presides, sign all bills and joint resolutions passed by the General Assembly, after their titles have been publicly read immediately before signing, and the fact of signing shall be entered on the journal.

Officers of the General Assembly

Sec. 10. The General Assembly shall prescribe by law the number, duties and compensation of the officers and employes of each House, and no payment shall be made from the State treasury, or be in any way authorized, to any person, except to an acting officer or employe elected or appointed in pursuance of law.

Extra Compensation Prohibited — Payment of Claims Against the Commonwealth

Sec. 11. No bill shall be passed giving any extra compensation to any public officer, servant, employe, agent or contractor, after services shall have been rendered or contract made, nor providing for the payment of any claim against the Commonwealth without previous authority of law.

Public Contract for Supplies

Sec. 12. All stationery, printing, paper and fuel used in the legislative and other departments of government shall be furnished, and the printing, binding and distribution of the laws, journals, department reports, and all other printing and binding, and the repairing and furnishing the halls and rooms used for the meetings of the General Assembly and its committees, shall be performed under contract to be given to the lowest responsible bidder below such maximum price and under such regulations as shall be prescribed by law; no member or officer of any department of the government shall be in any way interested in such contracts, and all such contracts shall be subject to the approval of the Governor, Auditor General and State Treasurer.

Extension of Official Terms and Increase of Salaries Prohibited

Sec. 13. No law shall extend the term of any public officer, or increase or diminish his salary or emoluments, after his election or appointment.

Revenue Bills

Sec. 14. All bills for raising revenue shall originate in the House of Representatives, but the Senate may propose amendments as in other bills.

Appropriation Bills

Sec. 15. The general appropriation bill shall embrace nothing but appropriations for the ordinary expenses of the executive, legislative and judicial departments of the Commonwealth, interest on the public debt and for public schools; all other appropriations shall be made by separate bills, each embracing but one subject.

Public Moneys — How Paid Out

Sec. 16. No money shall be paid out of the treasury, except upon appropriations made by law, and on warrant drawn by the proper officer in pursuance thereof.

Appropriations to Charitable and Educational Institutions

Sec. 17. No appropriations shall be made to any charitable or educational institution not under the absolute control of the Commonwealth, other than normal schools established by law for the professional training of teachers for the public schools of the State, except by a vote of two-thirds of all the members elected to each House.

Appropriations — How Limited

Sec. 18. No appropriations, except for pensions or gratuities for military services, shall be made for charitable, educational or benevolent purposes, to any person or community, nor to any denominational or sectarian institution, corporation or association.

Appropriations to Institutions for Soldiers' Widows and Orphans

Sec. 19. The General Assembly may make appropriations of money to institutions wherein the widows of soldiers are supported or assisted, or the orphans of soldiers are maintained and educated; but such appropriations shall be applied exclusively to the support of such widows and orphans.

Municipal Powers not to be Delegated to Special Commissions, &c.

Sec. 20. The General Assembly shall not delegate to any special commis-sion, private corporation or association, any power to make, supervise or in-terfere with any municipal improvement, money, property or effects, whether held in trust or otherwise, or to levy taxes or perform any municipal function whatever.

Suits for Damages in Case of Injuries Resulting in Death, or for Injuries to Persons or Property — How not to be Limited

Sec. 21. No act of the General Assembly shall limit the amount to be re-covered for injuries resulting in death, or for injuries to persons or property, and, in case of death from such injuries, the right of action shall survive, and the General Assembly shall prescribe for whose benefit such actions shall be prosecuted. No act shall prescribe any limitations of time within which suits may be brought against corporations for injuries to persons or property, or for other causes different from those fixed by general laws regulating actions against natural persons, and such acts now existing are avoided.

Investment of Trust Funds by Executors, &c.

Sec. 22. No act of the General Assembly shall authorize the investment of trust funds by executors, administrators, guardians or other trustees, in the bonds or stock of any private corporation, and such acts now existing are avoided saving investments heretofore made.

Change of Venue

Sec. 23. The power to change the venue in civil and criminal cases shall be vested in the courts, to be exercised in such manner as shall be provided by law.

Corporate Obligations Owned by the Commonwealth

Sec. 24. No obligation or liability of any railroad or other corporation, held or owned by the Commonwealth, shall ever be exchanged, transferred, re-mitted, postponed or in any way diminished by the General Assembly, nor shall such liability or obligation be released, except by payment thereof into the State treasury.

Legislation at Special Sessions

Sec. 25. When the General Assembly shall be convened in special session, there shall be no legislation upon subjects other than those designated in the proclamation of the Governor calling such sessions.

Actions on Concurrent Resolutions, &c.

Sec, 26. Every order, resolution or vote, to which the concurrence of both Houses may be necessary, except on the question of adjournment, shall be presented to the Governor and before it shall take effect be approved by him, or being disapproved, shall be re-passed by two-thirds of both Houses according to the rules and limitations prescribed in case of a bill.

Inspectors of Merchandise

Sec. 27. No State office shall be continued or created for the inspection or measuring of any merchandise, manufacture or commodity, but any county or municipality may appoint such officers when authorized by law.

Changing Location of State Capital

Sec. 28. No law changing the location of the Capital of the State shall be valid until the same shall have been submitted to the qualified electors of the Commonwealth at a general election and ratified and approved by them.

Members of the General Assembly — When Guilty of Bribery — Punishment

Sec. 29. A member of the General Assembly who shall solicit, demand or receive, or consent to receive, directly or indirectly, for himself or for another, from any company, corporation or person, any money, office, appointment, employment, testimonial, reward, thing of value or enjoyment, or of personal advantage, or promise thereof, for his vote, or official influence, or for withholding the same, or with an understanding, expressed or implied, that his vote or official action shall be in any way influenced thereby, or who shall solicit or demand any such money or other advantage, matter or thing aforesaid for another, as the consideration of his vote or official influence, or for withholding the same, or shall give or withhold his vote or influence in consideration of the payment or promise of such money, advantage, matter or thing to another, shall be held guilty of bribery within the meaning of this Constitution, and shall incur the disabilities provided thereby for said offence, and such additional punishment as is or shall be provided by law.

Bribery of State Officers Defined

Sec. 30. Any person who shall, directly or indirectly, offer, give or promise, any money, or thing of value, testimonial, privilege or personal advantage, to any executive or judicial officer, or member of the General Assembly, to influence him in the performance of any of his public or official duties, shall be guilty of bribery and be punished in such manner as shall be provided by law.

Corrupt Solicitation of Officials to be Defined by Law — Punishment

Sec. 31. The offence of corrupt solicitation of members of the General Assembly or of public officers of the State or of any municipal division thereof, and any occupation or practice of solicitation of such members or officers to influence their official action, shall be defined by law and shall be punished by fine and imprisonment.

Bribery or Corrupt Solicitation — Testimony Against Persons Accused of — Disqualification on Conviction

Sec. 32. Any person may be compelled to testify in any lawful investigation or judicial proceeding against any person who may be charged with having committed the offence of bribery or corrupt solicitation, or practices of solicitation, and shall not be permitted to withhold his testimony upon the ground that it may incriminate himself or subject him to public infamy; but such testimony shall not afterwards be used against him in any judicial proceeding, except for perjury in giving such testimony, and any person convicted of either of the offences aforesaid shall, as part of the punishment therefor, be disqualified from holding any office or position of honor, trust or profit in this Commonwealth.

Members Interested not to Vote

Sec. 33. A member who has a personal or private interest in any measure or bill proposed or pending before the General Assembly shall disclose the fact to the House of which he is a member, and shall not vote thereon.

ARTICLE IV

THE EXECUTIVE

Executive Department — of What Consisting

Sec. 1. The executive department of this Commonwealth shall consist of a Governor, Lieutenant Governor, Secretary of the Commonwealth, Attorney General, Auditor General, State Treasurer, Secretary of Internal Affairs and a Superintendent of Public Instruction.

Governor — Election — Returns — Tie Vote — Contested Elections

Sec. 2. The supreme executive power shall be vested in the Governor, who shall take care that the laws be faithfully executed; he shall be chosen on the day of the general election, by the qualified electors of the Commonwealth, at the places where they shall vote for Representatives. The returns of every election for Governor shall be sealed up and transmitted to the seat of government, directed to the President of the Senate, who shall open and publish them in the presence of the members of both Houses of the General Assembly. The person having the highest number of votes shall be Governor, but if two or more be equal and highest in votes, one of them shall be chosen Governor by the joint vote of the members of both Houses. Contested elections shall be determined by a committee, to be selected from both Houses of the General Assembly, and formed and regulated in such manner as shall be directed by law.

Term of Office

Sec. 3. The Governor shall hold his office during four years from the third Tuesday of January next ensuing his election, and shall not be eligible to the office for the next succeeding term.

Lieutenant Governor — To be President of the Senate

Sec. 4. A Lieutenant Governor shall be chosen at the same time, in the same manner, for the same term, and subject to the same provisions as the Governor; he shall be president of the Senate, but shall have no vote unless they be equally divided.

Qualifications of Governor and Lieutenant Governor

Sec. 5. No person shall be eligible to the office of Governor or Lieutenant Governor except a citizen of the United States, who shall have attained the age of thirty years, and have been seven years next preceding his election an inhabitant of the State, unless he shall have been absent on the public business of the United States or of this State.

Disqualifications for Offices of Governor and Lieutenant Governor

Sec. 6. No member of Congress or person holding any office under the United States or this State shall exercise the office of Governor or Lieutenant Governor.

Military Power

Sec. 7. The Governor shall be commander-in-chief of the army and navy of the Commonwealth, and of the militia, except when they shall be called into the actual service of the United States.

Appointing Power — Filling Vacancies — Confirmations

Sec. 8. He shall nominate and, by and with the advice and consent of two-thirds of all the members of the Senate, appoint a Secretary of the Commonwealth and an Attorney General during pleasure, a Superintendent of Public Instruction for four years, and such other officers of the Commonwealth as he is or may be authorized by the Constitution or by law to appoint; he shall have power to fill all vacancies that may happen, in offices to which he may appoint, during the recess of the Senate, by granting commissions which shall expire at the end of their next session; he shall have power to fill any vacancy that may happen, during the recess of the Senate, in the office of Auditor General, State Treasurer, Secretary of Internal Affairs or Superintendent of Public Instruction, in a judicial office, or in any other elective office which he is or may be authorized to fill; if the vacancy shall happen during the session of the Senate, the Governor shall nominate to the Senate, before their final adjournment, a proper person to fill said vacancy; but in any such case of vacancy, in an elective office, a person shall be chosen to said office of the next general election, unless the vacancy shall happen within three calendar months immediately preceding such election, in which case the election for such said office shall be held at the second succeeding general election.   In acting on executive nominations the Senate shall sit with open doors, and, in confirming or rejecting the nominations of the Governor, the vote shall be taken by yeas and nays, and shall be entered on the journal.

Pardoning Power — Board of Pardons

Sec. 9.   He shall have power to remit fines and forfeitures, to grant reprieves, commutations of sentence and pardons, except in cases of impeachment; but no pardon shall be granted, nor sentence commuted, except upon the recommendation in writing of the Lieutenant Governor, Secretary of the Commonwealth, Attorney General and Secretary of Internal Affairs, or any three of them, after full hearing, upon due public notice and in open session, and such recommendation, with the reasons therefor at length, shall be recorded and filed in the office of the Secretary of the Commonwealth.

Information from Officers

Sec. 10.   He may require information in writing from the officers of the executive department, upon any subject relating to the duties of their respective offices.

Information to the Legislature

Sec. 11.   He shall, from time to time, give to the General Assembly information of the state of the Commonwealth, and recommend to their consideration such measures as he may judge expedient.

May Convene, and in Certain Cases, Adjourn the Legislature

Sec. 12.   He may, on extraordinary occasions, convene the General Assembly, and in case of disagreement between the two Houses, with respect to the time of adjournment, adjourn them to such time as he shall think proper, not exceeding four months.   He shall have power to convene the Senate in extraordinary session by proclamation for the transaction of executive business.

When Lieutenant Governor to Act as Governor

Sec. 13.   In case of death, conviction on impeachment, failure to qualify, resignation, or other disability of the Governor, the powers, duties and emoluments of the office for the remainder of the term, or until the disability be removed, shall devolve upon the Lieutenant Governor.

President pro tempore of Senate — May Become Lieutenant Governor and Governor

Sec. 14.   In case of a vacancy in the office of Lieutenant Governor, or when the Lieutenant Governor shalt be impeached by the House of Representatives, or shall be unable to exercise the duties of his office, the powers, duties and emoluments thereof for the remainder of the term, or until the disability be removed, shall devolve upon the President *pro tempore* of the Senate; and the President *pro tempore* of the Senate shall in like manner become Governor if a vacancy or disability shall occur in the office of Governor; his seat as Senator shall become vacant whenever he shall become Governor, and shall be filled by election as any other vacancy in the Senate.

Bills — Approval of — How Vetoed — Passing over Veto — Not Signed or Vetoed Become Laws

Sec. 15. Every bill which shall have passed both Houses shall be presented to the Governor; if he approve he shall sign it, but if he shall not approve he shall return it with his objections to the House in which it shall have originated, which House shall enter the objections at large upon their journal, and proceed to reconsider it. If, after such reconsideration, two-thirds of all the members elected to that House shall agree to pass the bill, it shall be sent with the objections to the other House by which likewise it shall be reconsidered, and if approved by two-thirds of all the members elected to that House it shall be a law; but in such cases the votes of both Houses shall be determined by yeas and nays, and the names of the members voting for and against the bill shall be entered on the journals of each House, respectively. If any bill shall not be returned by the Governor within ten days after it shall have been presented to him, the same shall be a law in like manner as if he had signed it, unless the General Assembly, by their adjournment, prevent its return, in which case it shall be a law, unless he shall file the same, with his objections, in the office of the Secretary of the Commonwealth, and give notice thereof by public proclamation within thirty days after such adjournment.

Partial Disapproval of Appropriation Bills

Sec. 16. The Governor shall have power to disapprove of any item or items of any bill, making appropriations of money, embracing distinct items, and the part or parts of the bill approved shall be the law, and the item or items of appropriation disapproved shall be void, unless repassed according to the rules and limitations prescribed for the passage of other bills over the executive veto.

Governor and Lieutenant Governor — Trial of Contested Elections of — Hold Office until Successors are Qualified

Sec. 17. The Chief Justice of the Supreme Court shall preside upon the trial of any contested election of Governor or Lieutenant Governor and shall decide questions regarding the admissibility of evidence, and shall, upon request of the committee, pronounce his opinion upon other questions of law involved in the trial. The Governor and Lieutenant Governor shall exercise the duties of their respective offices until their successors shall be duly qualified.

Secretary of the Commonwealth — Duties of

Sec. 18. The Secretary of the Commonwealth shall keep a record of all official acts and proceedings of the Governor, and when required lay the same, with all papers, minutes and vouchers relating thereto, before either branch of the General Assembly, and perform such other duties as may be enjoined upon him by law.

Secretary of Internal Affairs — Duties of

Sec. 19. The Secretary of Internal Affairs shall exercise all the powers and perform all the duties of the Surveyor General, subject to such changes as shall be made by law. His department shall embrace a bureau of industrial statistics, and he shall discharge such duties relating to corporations, to the charitable institutions, the agricultural, manufacturing, mining, mineral, timber and other material or business interests of the State as may be prescribed by law. He shall annually, and at such other times as may be required by law, make report to the General Assembly.

Superintendent of Public Instruction — Duties of

Sec. 20. The Superintendent of Public Instruction shall exercise all the powers and perform all the duties of the Superintendent of Common Schools, subject to such changes as shall be made by law.

Terms of Office

Sec. 21. The term of the Secretary of Internal Affairs shall be four years; of the Auditor General three years; and of the State Treasurer two years. These officers shall be chosen by the qualified electors of the State at general elections. No person elected to the office of Auditor General or State Treasurer shall be capable of holding the same office for two consecutive terms.

State Seal — Commissions

Sec. 22. The present Great Seal of Pennsylvania shall be the seal of the State. All commissions shall be in the name and by the authority of the Commonwealth of Pennsylvania, and be sealed with the State seal and signed by the Governor.

ARTICLE V

THE JUDICIARY

Judicial Power — How Vested

Sec. 1. The judicial power of this Commonwealth shall be vested in a Supreme Court, in courts of Common Pleas, courts of Oyer and Terminer and General Jail Delivery, courts of Quarter Sessions of the Peace, Orphans'

Courts, Magistrates' Courts, and in such other courts as the General Assembly may from time to time establish.

Supreme Court — Terms of Judges — Chief Justice

Sec. 2. The Supreme Court shall consist of seven judges, who shall be elected by the qualified electors of the State at large. They shall hold their office for the term of twenty-one years, if they so long behave themselves well but shall not be again eligible. The judge whose commission shall first expire shall be chief justice, and thereafter each judge whose commission shall first expire shall in turn be chief justice.

Supreme Court — Jurisdiction and Powers of

Sec. 3. The jurisdiction of the Supreme Court shall extend over the State, and the judges thereof shall, by virtue of their offices, be justices of Oyer and Terminer and General Jail Delivery in the several counties; they shall have original jurisdiction in cases of injunction where a corporation is a party defendant, of *habeas corpus* of *mandamus* to courts of inferior jurisdiction, and of *quo warranto* as to all officers of the Commonwealth whose jurisdiction extends over the State, but shall not exercise any other original jurisdiction; they shall have appellate jurisdiction by appeal, *certiorari* or writ of error in all cases, as is now or may hereafter be provided by law.

Common Pleas Courts

Sec. 4. Until otherwise directed by law, the courts of Common Pleas shall continue as at present established, except as herein changed; not more than four counties shall, at any time, be included in one judicial district organized for said courts.

Judicial Districts — Associate Judges

Sec. 5. Whenever a county shall contain forty thousand inhabitants it shall constitute a separate judicial district, and shall elect one judge learned in the law; and the General Assembly shall provide for additional judges, as the business of the said districts may require. Counties containing a population less than is sufficient to constitute separate districts shall be formed into convenient single districts, or, if necessary, may be attached to contiguous districts as the General Assembly may provide. The office of associate judge, not learned in the law, is abolished in counties forming separate districts; but the several associate judges in office when this Constitution shall be adopted shall serve for their unexpired terms.

Common Pleas Courts of Philadelphia and Allegheny Counties — a Number of Judges in any County may be Increased

Sec. 6. In the counties of Philadelphia and Allegheny all the jurisdiction and powers not vested in the District courts and courts of Common Pleas, subject to such changes as may be made by this Constitution or by law, shall be in Philadelphia vested in four, and in Allegheny in two, distinct and separate courts of equal and co-ordinate jurisdiction, composed of three judges each; the said courts in Philadelphia shall be designated respectively as the court of Common Pleas number one, number two, number three and number four, and in Allegheny as the court of Common Pleas number one and two, but the number of said courts may be by law increased, from time to time, and shall be in like manner designated by successive numbers; the number of judges in any of said courts, or in any county where the establishment of an additional court may be authorized by law, may be increased from time to time, and whenever such increase shall amount in the whole to three, such three judges shall compose a distinct and separate court as aforesaid, which shall be numbered as aforesaid. In Philadelphia all suits shall be instituted in the said courts of Common Pleas without designating the number of said court, and the several courts shall distribute and apportion the business among them in such manner as shall be provided by rules of court, and each court, to which any suit shall be thus assigned, shall have exclusive jurisdiction thereof, subject to change of venue, as shall be provided by law. In Allegheny each court shall have exclusive jurisdiction of all proceedings at law and in equity, commenced therein, subject to change of venue as may be provided by law.

Prothonotary of Philadelphia — Term — Assistants — Salaries — Fees — Court Dockets

Sec. 7. For Philadelphia there shall be one prothonotary's office, and one prothonotary for all said courts to be appointed by the judges of said courts, and to hold office for three years, subject to removal by a majority of the said judges; the said prothonotary shall appoint such assistants as may be necessary and authorized by said courts; and he and his assistants shall receive fixed salaries, to be determined by law and paid by said county; all fees collected in said office, except such as may be by law due to the Commonwealth, shall be paid by the prothonotary into the county treasury. Each court shall have its separate dockets, except the judgment docket, which shall contain the judgments and liens of all the said courts, as is or may be directed by law.

Criminal Courts in Philadelphia and Allegheny Counties — Assignment of Judges to

Sec. 8. The said courts in the counties of Philadelphia and Allegheny, respectively, shall, from time to time, in turn detail one or more of their judges to hold the courts of Oyer and Terminer and the courts of Quarter Sessions of the peace of said counties, in such manner as may be directed by law.

Duties of Common Pleas Judges

Sec. 9. Judges of the courts of Common Pleas learned in the law shall be judges of the courts of Oyer and Terminer, Quarter Sessions of the Peace and

General Jail Delivery, and of the Orphans' Court and within their respective districts shall be Justices of the Peace as to criminal matters.

Judges of Common Pleas Courts may Issue Writs of Certiorari

Sec. 10. The judges of the courts of Common Pleas, within their respective counties, shall have power to issue writs of *certiorari* to justices of the peace and other inferior courts not of record, and to cause their proceedings to be brought before them, and right and justice to be done.

Justices of the Peace and Aldermen — Election, Term, Number and Qualification

Sec. 11. Except as otherwise provided in this Constitution, justices of the peace or aldermen shall be elected in the several wards, districts, boroughs and townships at the time of the election of constables, by the qualified electors thereof, in such manner as shall be directed by law, and shall be commissioned by the Governor for a term of five years. No township, ward, district or borough shall elect more than two justices of the peace or aldermen without the consent of a majority of the qualified electors within such township, ward or borough; no person shall be elected to such office unless he shall have resided within the township, borough, ward or district for one year next preceding his election. In cities containing over fifty thousand inhabitants, not more than one alderman shall be elected in each ward or district.

Magistrates Courts in Philadelphia — Election — Salaries — Jurisdiction

Sec. 12. In Philadelphia there shall be established, for each thirty thousand inhabitants, one court not of record, of police and civil causes, with jurisdiction not exceeding one hundred dollars; such courts shall be held by magistrates whose term of office shall be five years, and they shall be elected on general ticket by the qualified voters at large; and in the election of the said magistrates no voter shall vote for more than two-thirds of the number of persons to be elected when more than one are to be chosen; they shall be compensated only by fixed salaries, to be paid by said county; and shall exercise such jurisdiction, civil and criminal, except as herein provided, as is now exercised by aldermen, subject to such changes, not involving an increase of civil jurisdiction or conferring political duties, as may be made by law. In Philadelphia the office of alderman is abolished.

Fees, Fines and Penalties

Sec. 13. All fees, fines and penalties in said courts shall be paid into the county treasury.

Right of Appeal from Decisions of Courts not of Record

Sec. 14. In all cases of summary conviction in this Commonwealth, or of judgment in suit for a penalty before a magistrate, or court not of record, either party may appeal to such court of record as may be prescribed by law, upon allowance of the appellate court or judge thereof upon cause shown.

Election of Judges — Term of Office — Removal for Cause

Sec. 15. All judges required to be learned in the law, except the judges of the Supreme Court, shall be elected by the qualified electors of the respective districts over which they are to preside, and shall hold their offices for the period of ten years, if they shall so long behave themselves well; but for any reasonable cause, which shall not be sufficient ground for impeachment, the Governor may remove any of them on the address of two-thirds of each house of the General Assembly.

Voting for Judges of Supreme Court

Sec. 16. Whenever two judges of the Supreme Court are to be chosen for the same term of service each voter shall vote for one only, and when three are to be chosen he shall vote for no more than two; candidates highest in vote shall be declared elected.

Priority of Judges' Commissions

Sec. 17. Should any two or more judges of the Supreme Court, or any two or more judges of the court of Common Pleas for the same district, be elected at the same time, they shall, as soon after the election as convenient, cast lots for priority of commission, and certify the result to the Governor, who shall issue their commissions in accordance therewith.

Compensation of Judges

Sec. 18. The judges of the Supreme Court and the judges of the several courts of Common Pleas, and all other judges required to be learned in the law, shall at stated times receive for their services an adequate compensation, which shall be fixed by law, and paid by the State. They shall receive no other compensation, fees or perquisites of office for their services from any source, nor hold any other office of profit under the United States, this State or any other State.

Residences of Judges

Sec. 19. The judges of the Supreme Court, during their continuance in office, shall reside within this Commonwealth; and the other judges, during their continuance in office, shall reside within the districts for which they shall be respectively elected.

Common Pleas Courts — Chancery Powers of

Sec. 20. The several courts of Common Pleas, besides the powers herein conferred, shall have and exercise within their respective districts, subject to such changes as may be made by law, such chancery powers as are now vested by law in several courts of Common Pleas of this Commonwealth, or as may hereafter be conferred upon them by law.

Supreme Court — Limitations to Duties and Powers of — Court of Nisi Prius Abolished

Sec. 21. No duties shall be imposed by law upon the Supreme Court or any of the judges thereof except such as are judicial, nor shall any of the judges thereof exercise any power of appointment except as herein provided. The court of *Nisi Prius* is hereby abolished, and no court of original juris- diction to be presided over by any one or more of the judges of the Supreme Court shall be established.

Orphans' Courts — Auditing of Accounts — Registers' Courts Abolished

Sec. 22. In every county wherein the population shall exceed one hun- dred and fifty thousand the General Assembly shall, and in any other county may, establish a separate Orphans' Court to consist of one or more judges who shall be learned in the law, which court shall exercise all the jurisdiction and powers now vested in or which may hereafter be conferred upon the Orphans' courts, and thereupon the jurisdiction of the judges of the court of Common Pleas within such county, in Orphans' court proceedings, shall cease and determine. In any county in which a separate Orphans' Court shall be established, the register of wills shall be clerk of such court and subject to its directions in all matters pertaining to his office; he may appoint assistant clerks, but only with the consent and approval of said court. All accounts filed with him as register or as clerk of the said separate Orphans' Court shall be audited by the court without expense to parties, except where all parties in interest in a pending proceeding shall nominate an auditor whom the court may, in its discretion, appoint. In every county Orphans' courts shall possess all the powers and jurisdiction of a Registers' court, and separate Registers' courts are hereby abolished.

Style of Criminal Process — Prosecutions

Sec. 23. The style of all process shall be "The Commonwealth of Penn- sylvania." All prosecutions shall be carried on in the name and by the authority of the Commonwealth of Pennsylvania, and conclude "against the peace and dignity of the same."

Right of Appeal in Criminal Cases

Sec. 24. In all cases of felonious homicide, and in such other criminal cases as may be provided for by law, the accused after conviction and sen- tence may remove the indictment, record and all proceedings to the Supreme Court for review.

Vacancies in Courts of Record — How Filled

Sec. 25. Any vacancy happening by death, resignation or otherwise, in any court of record, shall be filled by appointment by the Governor, to continue till the first Monday of January next succeeding the first general election which shall occur three or more months after the happening of such vacancy.

Laws Relating to Courts to be Uniform — Certain Courts not to be Created

Sec. 26. All laws relating to courts shall be general and of uniform operation, and the organization, jurisdiction and powers of all courts of the same class or grade, so far as regulated by law, and the force and effect of the process and judgments of such courts, shall be uniform; and the General Assembly is hereby prohibited from creating other courts to exercise the powers vested by this Constitution in the judges of the courts of Common Pleas and Orphans' courts.

Jury Trials may be Dispensed with in Civil Cases

Sec. 27. The parties, by agreement filed, may in any civil case dispense with trial by jury, and submit the decision of such case to the court having jurisdiction thereof, and such court shall hear and determine the same; and the judgment thereon shall be subject to writ of error as in other cases.

ARTICLE VI

IMPEACHMENT AND REMOVAL FROM OFFICE

Power of Impeachment

Sec. 1. The House of Representatives shall have the sole power of impeachment.

Trials of Impeachment

Sec. 2. All impeachments shall be tried by the Senate; when sitting for that purpose the Senators shall be upon oath or affirmation; no person shall be convicted without the concurrence of two-thirds of the members present.

Who may be Impeached — Judgment — Civil Trial

Sec. 3. The Governor and all other civil officers shall be liable to impeachment for any misdemeanor in office, but judgment in such cases shall not extend further than to removal from office and disqualification to hold any office of trust or profit under this Commonwealth; the person accused, whether convicted or acquitted, shall nevertheless be liable to indictment, trial, judgment and punishment, according to law.

Public Officers may be Removed for Cause — How Removed

Sec. 4. All officers shall hold their offices on the condition that they behave themselves well while in office, and shall be removed on conviction of misbehavior in office or of any infamous crime. Appointed officers, other than judges of the courts of record and the Superintendent of Public Instruction, may be removed at the pleasure of the power by which they shall have been appointed. All officers elected by the people, except Governor, Lieutenant Governor, members of the General Assembly and judges of the courts of record learned in the law, shall be removed by the Governor for reasonable cause, after due notice and full hearing, on the address of two-thirds of the Senate.

ARTICLE VII

OATH OF OFFICE

Official Oaths — How Administered

Sec. 1. Senators and Representatives and all judicial, State and county officers shall, before entering on the duties of their respective offices, take and subscribe the following oath or affirmation:

" I do solemnly swear (or affirm) that I will support, obey and defend the Constitution of the United States, and the Constitution of this Commonwealth, and that I will discharge the duties of my office with fidelity; that I have not paid or contributed, or promised to pay or contribute, either directly or indirectly, any money or other valuable thing, to procure my nomination or election, (or appointment,) except for necessary and proper expenses expressly authorized by law; that I have not knowingly violated any election law of this Commonwealth, or procured it to be done by others in my behalf; that I will not knowingly receive, directly or indirectly, any money or other valuable thing for the performance or non-performance of any act or duty pertaining to my office, other than the compensation allowed by law."

The foregoing oath shall be administered by some person authorized to administer oaths, and in case of state officers and judges of the Supreme Court, shall be filed in the office of the Secretary of the Commonwealth, and in the case of other judicial and county officers, in the office of the prothonotary of the county in which the same is taken; any person refusing to take said oath or affirmation shall forfeit his office; and any person who shall be convicted of having sworn or affirmed falsely, or of having violated said oath or affirmation, shall be guilty of perjury, and be forever disqualified from holding any office of trust or profit within this Commonwealth. The oath to the members of the Senate and House of Representatives shall be administered by one of the judges of the Supreme Court, or of a court of Common Pleas, learned in the law, in the hall of the House to which the members shall be elected.

ARTICLE VIII

SUFFRAGE AND ELECTIONS

Qualifications of Electors

*Sec. 1. Every male citizen twenty-one years of age, possessing the following qualifications, shall be entitled to vote at all elections, subject however to such laws requiring and regulating the registration of electors as the General Assembly may enact:

1. He shall have been a citizen of the United States at least one month.

2. He shall have resided in the State one year (or, having previously been a qualified elector or native born citizen of the State, he shall have removed therefrom and returned, then six months), immediately preceding the election.

3. He shall have resided in the election district where he shall offer to vote at least two months immediately preceding the election.

4. If twenty-two years of age and upwards, he shall have paid within two years a State or county tax, which shall have been assessed at least two months and paid at least one month before the election.

General Elections — When Held

Sec. 2. The general election shall be held annually on the Tuesday next following the first Monday of November, but the General Assembly may by law fix a different day, two-thirds of all the members of each house consenting thereto.

Municipal Elections — When Held

Sec. 3. All elections for city, ward, borough and township officers, for regular terms of service, shall be held on the third Tuesday of February.

Elections to be by Ballot or Other Method — Secrecy in Voting to be Preserved

† Sec. 4. All elections by the citizens shall be by ballot or by such other

---

* Section 1 of Article 8, as given above, is Amendment No. 1, as adopted by a vote of the people November 5, 1901. The section previously read as follows:

Sec. 1. Every male citizen twenty-one years of age, possessing the following qualifications, shall be entitled to vote at all elections:

First. He shall have been a citizen of the United States at least one month.

Second. He shall have resided in the State one year, (or if, having previously been a qualified elector or native-born citizen of the State, he shall have removed therefrom and returned, then six months,) immediately preceding the election.

Third. He shall have resided in the election district where he shall offer to vote at least two months immediately preceding the election.

Fourth. If twenty-two years of age or upwards, he shall have paid within two years a State or county tax, which shall have been assessed at least two months and paid at least one month before the election.

† Section 4 of Article 8, as given above, is Amendment No. 3 as adopted by a vote of the people November 5, 1901. The section previously read as follows:

method as may be prescribed by law: Provided, That secrecy in voting be preserved.

Electors Privileged from Arrest

Sec. 5. Electors shall in all cases except treason, felony and breach or surety of the peace, be privileged from arrest during their attendance on elections and going to and returning therefrom.

Privileges of Electors in Actual Military Service

Sec. 6. Whenever any of the qualified electors of this Commonwealth shall be in actual military service, under a requisition from the President of the United States, or by the authority of this Commonwealth, such electors may exercise the right of suffrage in all elections by the citizens, under such regulations as are or shall be prescribed by law, as fully as if they were present at their usual places of election.

Election and Registration Laws to be Uniform — Registration Laws for Cities May be Enacted

*Sec. 7. All laws regulating the holding of elections by the citizens or for the registration of electors shall be uniform throughout the State, but laws regulating and requiring the registration of electors may be enacted to apply to cities only: Provided, That such laws be uniform for cities of the same class.

Bribery of Electors — Penalty

Sec. 8. Any person who shall give, or promise or offer to give, to an elector, any money, reward or other valuable consideration for his vote at an election, or for withholding the same, or who shall give or promise to give such consideration to any other person or party for such elector's vote or for the withholding thereof, and any elector who shall receive or agree to receive, for himself or for another, any money, reward or other valuable consideration for his vote at an election, or for withholding the same shall thereby forfeit the right to vote at such election, and any elector whose right to vote shall be challenged for such cause before the election officers shall be required to swear or affirm that the matter of the challenge is untrue before his vote shall be received.

Sec. 4. All elections by the citizens shall be by ballot. Every ballot voted shall be numbered in the order in which it shall be received, and the number recorded by the election officers on the list of voters, opposite the name of the elector who presents the ballot. Any elector may write his name upon his ticket or cause the same to be written thereon and attested by a citizen of the district. The election officers shall be sworn or affirmed not to disclose how any elector shall have voted unless required to do so as witnesses in a judicial proceeding.

*Section 7 of Article 8, as given above, is Amendment No. 2 as adopted by a vote of the people November 5, 1901. The section previously read as follows:

Sec. 7. All laws regulating the holding of elections by the citizens or for the registration of electors shall be uniform throughout the State, but no elector shall be deprived of the privilege of voting by reason of his name not being registered.

Violation of Election Laws — By Candidates and Others — Penalties

Sec. 9. Any person who shall, while a candidate for office, be guilty of bribery, fraud, or wilful violation of any election law, shall be forever disqualified from holding an office of trust or profit in this Commonwealth; and any person convicted of wilful violation of the election laws shall, in addition to any penalties provided by law, be deprived of the right of suffrage absolutely for a term of four years.

Contested Elections — Witnesses Compelled to Testify

Sec. 10. In trials of contested elections and in proceedings for the investigation of elections, no person shall be permitted to withhold his testimony upon the ground that it may criminate himself or subject him to public infamy; but such testimony shall not afterwards be used against him in any judicial proceeding except for perjury in giving such testimony.

Election Districts — Formation of — How Divided

Sec. 11. Townships, and wards of cities or boroughs, shall form or be divided into election districts of compact and contiguous territory, in such manner as the court of Quarter Sessions of the city or county in which the same are located may direct; but districts in cities of over one hundred thousand inhabitants shall be divided by the Courts of Quarter Sessions, having jurisdiction therein, whenever at the next preceding election more than two hundred and fifty votes shall have been polled therein; and other election districts whenever the court of the proper county shall be of opinion that the convenience of the electors and the public interests will be promoted thereby.

Viva Voce Elections — When Used

Sec. 12. All elections by persons in a representative capacity shall be *viva voce.*

Residence and Right to Vote of Government Officials and Certain Other Electors

Sec. 13. For the purpose of voting no person shall be deemed to have gained a residence by reason of his presence, or lost it by reason of his absence, while employed in the service, either civil or military, of this State or of the United States, nor while engaged in the navigation of the waters of the State or of the United States, or on the high seas, nor while a student of any institution of learning, nor while kept in any poorhouse or other asylum at public expense, nor while confined in public prison.

District Election Boards — Of what Consisting — Privileges

Sec. 14. District election boards shall consist of a judge and two inspectors, who shall be chosen annually by the citizens. Each elector shall have the right to vote for the judge and one inspector, and each inspector shall appoint one clerk. The first election board for any new district shall be selected, and vacancies in election boards filled, as shall be provided by law. Election officers shall be privileged from arrest upon days of election, and while engaged in making up and transmitting returns, except upon warrant of a court of record or judge thereof, for an election fraud, for felony, or for wanton breach of the peace. In cities they may claim exemption from jury duty during their terms of service.

Election Officers — Qualifications of — Eligibility to Civil Office

Sec. 15. No person shall be qualified to serve as an election officer who shall hold, or shall within two months have held any office, appointment or employment in or under the government of the United States or of this State, or of any city, or county, or of any municipal board, commission or trust in any city, save only justices of the peace and aldermen, notaries public and persons in the militia service of the State; nor shall any election officer be eligible to any civil office to be filled at an election at which he shall serve, save only to such subordinate municipal or local offices, below the grade of city or county offices, as shall be designated by general law.

Overseers of Election — How Appointed — Number of — Qualifications — Powers of

Sec. 16. The courts of Common Pleas of the several counties of the Commonwealth shall have power, within their respective jurisdictions, to appoint overseers of election to supervise the proceedings of election officers and to make report to the court as may be required; such appointments to be made for any district in a city or county upon petition of five citizens, lawful voters of such election district, setting forth that such appointment is a reasonable precaution to secure the purity and fairness of elections; overseers shall be two in number for an election district, shall be residents therein, and shall be persons qualified to serve upon election boards, and in each case members of different political parties; whenever the members of an election board shall differ in opinion the overseers, if they shall be agreed thereon, shall decide the question of difference; in appointing overseers of election all the law judges of the proper court, able to act at the time, shall concur in the appointments made.

Trial of Contested Elections — To be by Courts of Law — Legislature to Pass Laws Regulating

Sec. 17. The trial and determination of contested elections of electors of President and Vice-President, members of the General Assembly, and of all public officers, whether state, judicial, municipal or local, shall be by the courts of law, or by one or more of the law judges thereof; the General Assembly shall, by general law, designate the courts and judges by whom the several classes of election contests shall be tried, and regulate the manner of trial and all matters incident thereto; but no such law assigning jurisdiction, or regulating its exercise, shall apply to any contest arising out of an election held before its passage.

ARTICLE IX

TAXATION AND FINANCE

Uniformity of Taxation — Exemptions Under General Laws

Sec. 1. All taxes shall be uniform, upon the same class of subjects, within the territorial limits of the authority levying the tax, and shall be levied and collected under general laws; but the General Assembly may, by general laws, exempt from taxation public property used for public purposes, actual places of religious worship, places of burial not used or held for private or corporate profit, and institutions of purely public charity.

Exemption from Taxation Restricted

Sec. 2. All laws exempting property from taxation, other than the property above enumerated, shall be void.

Taxation of Corporations

Sec. 3. The power to tax corporations and corporate property shall not be surrendered or suspended by any contract or grant to which the State shall be a party.

State Debts — Creation of, Restricted

Sec. 4. No debt shall be created by or on behalf of the State except to supply casual deficiencies of revenue, repel invasion, suppress insurrection, defend the State in war, or to pay existing debt; and the debt created to supply deficiencies in revenue shall never exceed, in the aggregate at any one time, one million of dollars.

Laws Authorizing State Indebtedness Shall Specify the Purpose

Sec. 5. All laws authorizing the borrowing of money by and on behalf of the State, shall specify the purpose for which the money is to be used, and the money so borrowed shall be used for the purpose specified and no other.

Pledging of State Credit — Holding of Certain Securities Prohibited

Sec. 6. The credit of the Commonwealth shall not be pledged or loaned to any individual, company, corporation or association, nor shall the Commonwealth become a joint-owner or stockholder in any company, association or corporation.

Municipalities not to become Stockholders in Corporations, &c. •

Sec. 7. The General Assembly shall not authorize any county, city, •
borough, township or incorporated district to become a stockholder in any
company, association or corporation, or to obtain or appropriate money
for, or to loan its credit to, any corporation, association, institution or individual.

Municipal Debt, Amount of, Limited

Sec. 8. The debt of any county, city, borough, township, school district
or other municipality or incorporated district, except as herein provided,
shall never exceed seven per centum upon the assessed value of the taxable property therein, nor shall any such municipality or district incur any
new debt, or increase its indebtedness to an amount exceeding two per
centum upon such assessed valuation of property, without the assent of the
electors thereof at a public election in such manner as shall be provided by
law; but any city, the debt of which now exceeds seven per centum of such
assessed valuation, may be authorized by law to increase the same three per
centum, in the aggregate at any one time, upon such valuation.

State not to Assume Municipal Debts — Exceptions

Sec. 9. The Commonwealth shall not assume the debt, or any part thereof,
of any city, county, borough or township, unless such debt shall have been
contracted to enable the State to repel invasion, suppress domestic insurrection, defend itself in time of war, or to assist the State in the discharge of any
portion of its present indebtedness.

*Municipalities Incurring Indebtedness must Provide for Payment by
Annual Tax*

Sec. 10. Any county, township, school district or other municipality, incurring any indebtedness shall, at or before the time of so doing, provide for
the collection of an annual tax sufficient to pay the interest and also the
principal thereof within thirty years.

*State Sinking Fund — of what Consisting — To be Increased — How
Expended*

Sec. 11. To provide for the payment of the present State debt, and any
additional debt contracted as aforesaid, the General Assembly shall continue
and maintain the sinking fund, sufficient to pay the accruing interest on such
debt, and annually to reduce the principal thereof by a sum not less than
two hundred and fifty thousand dollars; the said sinking fund shall consist
of the proceeds of the sales of the public works or any part thereof, and of
the income or proceeds of the sale of any stocks owned by the Commonwealth, together with other funds and resources that may be designated

by law, and shall be increased from time to time by assigning to it any part of the taxes or other revenues of the State not required for the ordinary and current expenses of government; and unless in case of war, invasion or insurrection, no part of the said sinking fund shall be used or applied otherwise than in the extinguishment of the public debt.

Surplus Funds Applied to State Indebtedness — Sinking Fund Investments

Sec. 12. The moneys of the State, over and above the necessary reserve, shall be used in the payment of the debt of the State, either directly or through the sinking fund, and the moneys of the sinking fund shall never be invested in or loaned upon the security of anything, except the bonds of the United States, or of this State.

Reserve Funds Limited — Monthly Statements to be Published

Sec. 13. The moneys held as necessary reserve shall be limited by law to the amount required for current expenses, and shall be secured and kept as may be provided by law. Monthly statements shall be published showing the amount of such moneys, where the same are deposited, and how secured.

Misuse of Public Moneys — Penalty For

Sec. 14. The making of profit out of the public moneys, or using the same for any purpose not authorized by law by any officer of the State, or member or officer of the General Assembly, shall be a misdemeanor and shall be punished as may be provided by law, but part of such punishment shall be disqualification to hold office for a period of not less than five years.

ARTICLE X

EDUCATION

Public Schools Provided For

Sec. 1. The General Assembly shall provide for the maintenance and support of a thorough and efficient system of public schools, wherein all the children of this Commonwealth above the age of six years may be educated, and shall appropriate at least one million dollars each year for that purpose.

Sectarian Schools not to Receive Public School Money

Sec. 2. No money raised for the support of the public schools of the Commonwealth shall be appropriated to or used for the support of any sectarian school.

Females Eligible as School Officers

Sec. 3. Women twenty-òne years of age and upwards, shall be eligible to any office of control or management under the school laws of this State.

ARTICLE XI

Militia to be Organized — Maintenance — Exemption from Military Service

Sec. 1. The freemen of this Commonwealth shall be armed, organized and disciplined for its defence when and in such manner as may be directed by law. The General Assembly shall provide for maintaining the militia by appropriations from the treasury of the Commonwealth, and may exempt from military service persons having conscientious scruples against bearing arms.

ARTICLE XII

PUBLIC OFFICERS

Selection of Officers not Otherwise Provided for in Constitution

Sec. 1. All officers, whose selection is not provided for in this Constitution, shall be elected or appointed as may be directed by law.

United States Officers Cannot Hold Remunerative State Offices — Incompatible Offices

Sec. 2. No member of Congress from this State, nor any person holding or exercising any office or appointment of-trust or profit under the United States, shall at the same time hold or exercise any office in this State to which a salary, fees or perquisites shall be attached. The General Assembly may by law declare what offices are incompatible.

Dueling Disqualifies from Holding Office — Further Punishment

Sec. 3. Any person who shall fight a duel or send a challenge for that purpose, or be aider or abettor in fighting a duel, shall be deprived of the right of holding any office of honor or profit in this State, and may be otherwise punished as shall be prescribed by law.

ARTICLE XIII

New Counties — Restrictions in Forming

Sec. 1. No new county shall be established which shall reduce any county to less than four hundred square miles, or to less than twenty thousand inhabitants ; nor shall any county be formed of less area, or containing a less population ; nor shall any line thereof pass within ten miles of the county seat of any county proposed to be divided.

ARTICLE XIV

COUNTY OFFICERS

County Officers Enumerated — Sheriff and Treasurer Ineligible to Succeed Themselves

Sec. 1. County officers shall consist of sheriffs, coroners, prothonotaries, registers of wills, recorders of deeds, commissioners, treasurers, surveyors, auditors or controllers, clerks of the courts, district attorneys and such others as may from time to time be established by law; and no sheriff or treasurer shall be eligible for the term next succeeding the one for which he may be elected.

Election of County Officers — Terms — Vacancies

Sec. 2. County officers shall be elected at the general elections and shall hold their offices for the term of three years, beginning on the first Monday of January next after their election, and until their successors shall be duly qualified; all vacancies not otherwise provided for, shall be filled in such manner as may be provided by law.

One Year's Residence Necessary to Qualify for Appointment to a County Office

Sec. 3. No person shall be appointed to any office within any county, who shall not have been a citizen and an inhabitant therein one year next before his appointment, if the county shall have been so long erected, but if it shall not have been so long erected, then within the limits of the county or counties out of which it shall have been taken.

County Seat — Certain Offices to be Located at

Sec. 4. Prothonotaries, clerks of the courts, recorders of deeds, registers of wills, county surveyors and sheriffs, shall keep their offices in the county town or the county in which they respectively shall be officers.

Compensation of County Offices — Those Salaried not to Retain Fees

Sec. 5. The compensation of county officers shall be regulated by law, and all county officers who are or may be salaried shall pay all fees which they may be authorized to receive, into the treasury of the county or State, as may be directed by law. In counties containing over one hundred and fifty thousand inhabitants all county officers shall be paid by salary, and the salary of any such officer and his clerks, heretofore paid by fees, shall not exceed the aggregate amount of fees earned during his term and collected by or for him.

Accountability of County, Township and Borough Officers for Public Moneys

Sec. 6. The General Assembly shall provide by law for the strict accountability of all county, township and borough officers, as well for the fees which may be collected by them, as for all public or municipal moneys which may be paid to them.

Election of County Commissioners and Auditors — Vacancies — How Filled

Sec. 7. Three county commissioners and three county auditors shall be elected in each county where such officers are chosen, in the year one thousand eight hundred and seventy-five and every third year thereafter; and in the election of said officers each qualified elector shall vote for no more than two persons, and the three persons having the highest number of votes shall be elected; any casual vacancy in the office of county commissioner or county auditor shall be filled, by the court of Common Pleas of the county in which such vacancy shall occur, by the appointment of an elector of the proper county who shall have voted for the commissioner or auditor whose place is to be filled.

ARTICLE XV

CITIES AND CITY CHARTERS

When Cities May be Chartered

Sec. 1. Cities may be chartered whenever a majority of the electors of any town or borough having a population of at least ten thousand shall vote at any general election in favor of the same.

Municipal Commissions — Contracting of Debts by

Sec. 2. No debt shall be contracted or liability incurred by any municipal commission, except in pursuance of an appropriation previously made therefor by the municipal government.

City Sinking Funds

Sec. 3. Every city shall create a sinking fund, which shall be inviolably pledged for the payment of its funded debt.

ARTICLE XVI

PRIVATE CORPORATIONS

Certain Charters to be Void

Sec. 1. All existing charters, or grants of special or exclusive privileges, under which a *bona fide* organization shall not have taken place and business been commenced in good faith, at the time of the adoption of this Constitution, shall thereafter have no validity.

Corporate Privileges not to be Increased — Exception

Sec. 2. The General Assembly shall not remit the forfeiture of the charter of any corporation now existing, or alter or amend the same, or pass any other general or special law for the benefit of such corporation, except upon the condition that such corporation shall thereafter hold its charter subject to the provisions of this Constitution.

State's Right of Eminent Domain and Police Power to be Supreme

Sec. 3. The exercise of the right of eminent domain shall never be abridged or so construed as to prevent the General Assembly from taking the property and franchises of incorporated companies, and subjecting them to public use, the same as the property of individuals; and the exercise of the police power of the State shall never be abridged or so construed as to permit corporations to conduct their business in such manner as to infringe the equal rights of individuals or the general well-being of the State.

Cumulative Voting Permitted in Corporation Elections

Sec. 4. In all elections for directors or managers of a corporation each member or shareholder may cast the whole number of his votes for one candidate, or distribute them upon two or more candidates, as he may prefer.

Foreign Corporations — Regulations Concerning

Sec. 5. No foreign corporation shall do any business in this State without having one or more known places of business and an authorized agent or agents in the same upon whom process may be served.

Corporations — Scope of Business Limited — Holding of Real Estate

Sec. 6. No corporation shall engage in any business other than that expressly authorized in its charter, nor shall it take or hold any real estate except such as may be necessary and proper for its legitimate business.

Corporate Stocks and Bonds — Increase of Stock and Indebtedness — Regulated

Sec. 7. No corporation shall issue stocks or bonds except for money, labor done, or money or property actually received; and all fictitious increase of stock or indebtedness shall be void. The stock and indebtedness of corporations shall not be increased except in pursuance of general law, nor without the consent of the persons holding the larger amount in value of the stock, first obtained at a meeting to be held after sixty days' notice given in pursuance of law.

Compensation for Property Taken or Affected Under Right of Eminent Domain — Appeals

Sec. 8. Municipal and other corporations and individuals invested with the privilege of taking private property for public use shall make just compensation for property taken, injured or destroyed by the construction or enlargement of their works, highways or improvements, which compensation shall be paid or secured before such taking, injury or destruction. The General Assembly is hereby prohibited from depriving any person of an appeal from any preliminary assessment of damages against any such corporations or individuals made by viewers or otherwise; and the amount of such damages in all cases of appeal shall on the demand of either party be determined by a jury according to the course of the common law.

State Banking Laws — Requirements

Sec. 9. Every banking law shall provide for the registry and countersigning, by an officer of the State, of all notes or bills designed for circulation, and that ample security to the full amount thereof shall be deposited with the Auditor General for the redemption of such notes or bills.

Alterations and Revocation of Charters — No Law shall Create, Renew or Extend More than One Charter

Sec. 10. The General Assembly shall have the power to alter, revoke or annul any charter or incorporation now existing and revocable at the adoption of this Constitution, or any that may hereafter be created, whenever in their opinion it may be injurious to the citizens of this Commonwealth, in such manner, however, that no injustice shall be done to the corporators. No law hereafter enacted shall create, renew or extend the charter of more than one corporation.

Public Notice Required of Application for Banking Powers — Duration of Charter

Sec. 11. No corporate body to possess banking and discounting privileges shall be created or organized in pursuance of any law without three months' previous public notice, at the place of the intended location, of the intention to apply for such privileges, in such manner as shall be prescribed by law, nor shall a charter for such privilege be granted for a longer period than twenty years.

Right to Construct Telegraph Lines — Consolidation of Competing Lines Prohibited

Sec. 12. Any association or corporation organized for the purpose, or any individual, shall have the right to construct and maintain lines of telegraph within this State, and to connect the same with other lines, and the General Assembly shall, by general law of uniform operation, provide reasonable regulations to give full effect to this section. No telegraph company shall consolidate with, or hold a controlling interest in the stock or bonds of, any other telegraph company owning a competing line, or acquire, by purchase or otherwise, any other competing line of telegraph.

Joint-Stock Companies or Associations Treated as Corporations

Sec. 13. The term " corporations," as used in this article, shall be construed to include all joint-stock companies or associations having any of the powers or privileges of corporations not possessed by individuals or partnerships.

ARTICLE XVII

RAILROADS AND CANALS

To be Public Highways and Common Carriers — Rights and Duties of Railroad Companies

Sec. 1. All railroads and canals shall be public highways, and all railroad and canal companies shall be common carriers.   Any association or corporation oganized for the purpose shall have the right to construct and operate a railroad between any points within this State, and to connect at the State line with railroads of other States.   Every railroad company shall have the right with its road to intersect, connect with or cross any other railroad; and shall receive and transport each the other's passengers, tonnage, and cars loaded or empty, without delay or discrimination.

Companies Organized in this State to Maintain Offices and Stock Books Therein

Sec. 2. Every railroad and canal corporation organized in this State shall maintain an office therein where transfers of its stock shall be made, and where its books shall be kept for inspection by any stockholder or creditor of such corporation, in which shall be recorded the amount of capital stock subscribed or paid in, and by whom, the names of the owners of its stock and the amounts owned by them, respectively, the transfers of said stock, and the names and places of residence of its officers.

Transportation of Persons and Property — Undue Discrimination Prohibited — Special Rate Tickets

Sec. 3. All individuals, associations and corporations shall have equal right to have persons and property transported over railroads and canals, and no undue or unreasonable discrimination shall be made in charges for, or in facilities for, transportation of freight or passengers within the State or coming from or going to any other State.   Persons and property transported over any railroad shall be delivered at any station at charges not exceeding the charges for transportation of persons and property of the same class in the same direction to any more distant station; but excursion and commutation tickets may be issued at special rates.

Parallel or Competing Lines not to be Consolidated— Officers of, Restricted
—Juries to Decide Whether Companies Are

Sec. 4. No railroad, canal or other corporation, or the lessees, purchasers or managers of any railroad or canal corporation, shall consolidate the stock, property or franchises of such corporation with, or lease, or purchase the works or franchises of, or in any way control any other railroad or canal corporation owning or having under its control a parallel or competing line; nor shall any officer of such railroad or canal corporation act as an officer of any other railroad or canal corporation owning or having the control of a parallel or competing line; and the question whether railroads or canals are parallel or competing lines shall, when demanded by the party complainant, be decided by a jury as in other civil issues.

Powers of Incorporated Common Carriers Limited— Privileges of Mining
and Manufacturing Companies

Sec. 5. No incorporated company doing the business of a common carrier shall, directly or indirectly, prosecute or engage in mining or manufacturing articles for transportation over its works; nor shall such company, directly or indirectly, engage in any other business than that of common carriers, or hold or acquire lands, freehold or leasehold, directly or indirectly, except such as shall be necessary for carrying on its business; but any mining or manufacturing company may carry the products of its mines and manufactories on its railroad or canal not exceeding fifty miles in length.

Officers and Employes not to be Interested in Companies' Contracts or
Transportation Business

Sec. 6. No president, director, officer, agent or employe of any railroad or canal company shall be interested, directly or indirectly, in the furnishing of material or supplies to such company, or in the business of transportation as a common carrier of freight or passengers over the works owned, leased, controlled or worked by such company.

Discriminations and Preferences in Charges and Facilities Forbidden

Sec. 7. No discrimination in charges or facilities for transportation shall be made between transportation companies and individuals, or in favor of either, by abatement, drawback or otherwise, and no railroad or canal company or any lessee, manager or employe thereof, shall make any preferences in furnishing cars or motive power.

Granting of Passes Limited

Sec. 8. No railroad, railway or other transportation company shall grant free passes, or passes at a discount, to any person except officers or employes of the company.

Consent of Local Authorities Necessary for Construction of Street Railways

Sec. 9. No street passenger railway shall be constructed within the limits of any city, borough or township, without the consent of its local authorities.

Acceptance of this Article Necessary for Future Legislation

Sec. 10. No railroad, canal or other transportation company, in existence at the time of the adoption of this article, shall have the benefit of any future legislation by general or special laws, except on condition of complete acceptance of all the provisions of this article.

Powers and Duties as Secretary of Internal Affairs in Regard to Transportation Companies

Sec. 11. The existing powers and duties of the Auditor General in regard to railroads, canals and other transportation companies, except as to their accounts, are hereby transferred to the Secretary of Internal Affairs, who shall have a general supervision over them, subject to such regulations and alterations as shall be provided by law; and, in addition to the annual reports now required to be made, said secretary may require special reports at any time upon any subject relating to the business of said companies from any officer or officers thereof.

General Assembly to Enforce Provisions of this Article

Sec. 12. The General Assembly shall enforce by appropriate legislation the provisions of this article.

ARTICLE XVIII

FUTURE AMENDMENTS

Amendments to Constitution — How Made

Sec. 1. Any amendment or amendments to this Constitution may be proposed in the Senate or House of Representatives, and, if the same shall be agreed to by a majority of the members elected to each House, such proposed amendment or amendments shall be entered on their journals with the yeas and nays taken thereon, and the Secretary of the Commonwealth shall cause the same to be published three months before the next general election, in at least two newspapers in every county in which such newspapers shall be published; and if, in the General Assembly next afterwards chosen, such proposed amendment or amendments shall be agreed to by a majority of the members elected to each House, the Secretary of the Commonwealth shall cause the same again to be published in the manner aforesaid; and such proposed amendment or amendments shall be submitted to the qualified electors of the State in such manner, and at such time at least three months after being so agreed to by the two Houses, as the General Assembly shall prescribe; and, if such amendment or amendments shall be approved by a majority of those voting thereon, such amendment or amendments shall become a part of the Constitution; but no amendment or amendments shall be submitted oftener than once in five years. When two or more amendments shall be submitted they shall be voted upon separately.

SCHEDULE

When Constitution Shall Take Effect

That no inconvenience may arise from the changes in the Constitution of the Commonwealth, and in order to carry the same into complete operation, it is hereby declared that: .

Sec. 1. This Constitution shall take effect on the first day of January, in the year one thousand eight hundred and seventy-four, for all purposes not otherwise provided for therein.

What Laws, Rights, &c., to Remain in Force

Sec. 2. All laws in force in this Commonwealth at the time of the adoption of this Constitution and not inconsistent therewith, and all rights, actions, prosecutions and contract shall continue as if this Constitution had not been adopted.

Election of Senators in 1874 and 1875

Sec. 3. At the general election in the years one thousand eight hundred and seventy-four and one thousand eight hundred and seventy-five Senators shall be elected in all districts where there shall be vacancies. Those elected in the year one thousand eight hundred and seventy-four shall serve for two years, and those elected in the year one thousand eight hundred and seventy-five shall serve for one year. Senators now elected and those whose terms are unexpired shall represent the districts in which they reside until the end of the terms for which they were elected.

Election of Senators in 1876

Sec. 4. At the general election in the year one thousand eight hundred and seventy-six, Senators shall be elected from even numbered districts to serve for two years, and from odd numbered districts to serve for four years.

Election of Governor in 1875 and 1878

Sec. 5. The first election of Governor under this Constitution shall be at the general election in the year one thousand eight hundred and seventy-five, when a Governor shall be elected for three years, and the term of the

Governor elected in the year one thousand eight hundred and seventy-eight and of those thereafter elected shall be for four years, according to the provisions of this Constitution.

Election of Lieutenant Governor in 1874

Sec. 6. At the general election in the year one thousand eight hundred and seventy-four a Lieutenant Governor shall be elected according to the provisions of this Constitution.

Election of Secretary of Internal Affairs — Office of Surveyor General Abolished

Sec. 7. The Secretary of Internal Affairs shall be elected at the first general election after the adoption of this Constitution, and, when the said officer shall be duly elected and qualified, the office of Surveyor General shall be abolished. The Surveyor General in office at the time of the adoption of this Constitution shall continue in office until the expiration of the term for which he was elected.

Office of Superintendent of Common Schools Abolished

Sec. 8. When the Superintendent of Public Instruction shall be duly qualified the office of Superintendent of Common Schools shall cease.

Eligibility to Re-election of Present State Officers

Sec. 9. Nothing contained in this Constitution shall be construed to render any person now holding any State office for a first official term ineligible for re-election at the end of such term.

Judges of Supreme Court — Expiration of Terms — Additional Judges to be Elected

Sec 10. The judges of the Supreme Court in office when this Constitution shall take effect shall continue until their commissions severally expire. Two judges in addition to the number now composing the said court, shall be elected at the first general election after the adoption of this Constitution.

Certain Courts Abolished on Dec. 1, 1875 — Court of First Criminal Jurisdiction for Counties of Schuylkill, Lebanon and Dauphin Abolished

Sec. 11. All courts of record and all existing courts which are not specified in this Constitution shall continue in existence until the first day of December, in the year one thousand eight hundred and seventy-five, without abridgement of their present jurisdiction, but no longer. The Court of First Criminal Jurisdiction for the counties of Schuylkill, Lebanon and Dauphin is hereby abolished, and all causes and proceedings pending therein in the county of Schuylkill shall be tried and disposed of in the courts of Oyer and Teminer and Quarter Sessions of the peace of said county.

Register's Courts Abolished

Sec. 12. The Register's courts now in existence shall be abolished on the first day of January next succeeding the adoption of this Constitution.

When Judicial Districts to be Designated— Assignment of Judges to Districts

Sec. 13. The General Assembly shall, at the next session after the adoption of this Constitution, designate the several judicial districts as required by this Constitution. The judges in commission when such designation shall be made shall continue during their unexpired terms judges of the new districts in which they reside ; but, when there shall be two judges residing in the same district, the President Judge shall elect to which district he shall be assigned and the additional law judge shall be assigned to the other district.

How Often Judicial Districts shall be Designated

Sec. 14. The General Assembly shall, at the next succeeding session after each decennial census and not oftener, designate the several judicial districts as required by this Constitution.

Expiration of Terms of Certain Judges —Judge of Common Pleas Court of Schuylkill County

Sec. 15. Judges, learned in the law, of any court of record holding commissions in force at the adoption of this Constitution shall hold their respective offices until the expiration of the terms for which they were commissioned, and until their successors shall be duly qualified. The Governor shall commission the President Judge of the Court of First Criminal Jurisdiction for the counties of Schuylkill, Lebanon and Dauphin as a judge of the Court of Common Pleas of Schuylkill county, for the unexpired term of his office.

Who shall Become President Judges — Terms of Associate Judges

Sec. 16. After the expiration of the term of any President Judge of any court of Common Pleas in commission at the adoption of this Constitution, the judge of such court learned in the law and oldest in commission shall be the President Judge thereof, and when two or more judges are elected at the same time in any judicial district they shall decide by lot which shall be President Judge; but when the President Judge of a court shall be re-elected he shall continue to be President Judge of that court. Associate judges, not learned in the law, elected after the adoption of this Constitution, shall be commissioned to hold their offices for the term of five years from the first day of January next after their election.

Fixing Compensation of Judges

Sec. 17. The General Assembly, at the first session after the adoption of this Constitution, shall fix and determine the compensation of the judges of the Supreme Court and of the judges of the several judicial districts of the

Commonwealth, and the provisions of the fifteenth section of the article on Legislation shall not be deemed inconsistent herewith. Nothing contained in this Constitution shall be held to reduce the compensation now paid to any law judge of this Commonwealth now in commission.

Common Pleas Court in Philadelphia and Allegheny Counties — Organizations of, in Philadelphia

Sec. 18. The courts of Common Pleas in the counties of Philadelphia and Allegheny shall be composed of the present judges of the District Court and court of Common Pleas of said counties until their offices shall severally end, and of such other judges as may from time to time be selected. For the purpose of first organization in Philadelphia the judges of the court number one shall be Judges Allison, Pierce and Paxson; of the court number two Judges Hare, Mitchell and one other judge to be elected; of the court number three Judges Ludlow, Finletter and Lynd; and of the court number four Judges Thayer, Briggs and one other judge to be elected. The judge first named shall be the President Judge of said courts respectively, and thereafter the President Judge shall be the judge oldest in commission; but any President Judge, re-elected in the same court or district, shall continue to be President Judge thereof. The additional judges for courts numbers two and four shall be voted for and elected at the first general election after the adoption of this Constitution, in the same manner as the two additional judges of the Supreme Court, and they shall decide by lot to which court they shall belong. Their term of office shall commence on the first Monday of January, in the year one thousand eight hundred and seventy-five.

Organization of Common Pleas Courts in Allegheny County

Sec. 19. In the county of Allegheny, for the purpose of first organization under this Constitution, the judges of the court of Common Pleas, at the time of the adoption of this Constitution, shall be the judges of the court number one, and the judges of the District Court, at the same date, shall be the judges of the Common Pleas number two. The President Judges of the Common Pleas and District Court shall be President Judge of said courts number one and two, respectively, until their offices shall end; and thereafter the judge oldest in commission shall be President Judge; but any President Judge re-elected in the same court, or district, shall continue to be President Judge thereof.

When Organization of Common Pleas Courts in Philadelphia and Allegheny Counties shall Take Effect

Sec. 20. The organization of the courts of Common Pleas under this Constitution for the counties of Philadelphia and Allegheny shall take effect on the first Monday of January, one thousand eight hundred and seventy-five, and existing courts in said counties shall continue with their present powers and jurisdiction until that date, but no new suits shall be instituted in the courts of Nisi Prius after the adoption of this Constitution.

Trial and Disposition of Causes and Transfer of Records in Philadelphia County

Sec. 21. The causes and proceedings pending in the court of *Nisi Prius* court of Common Pleas, and District Court in Philadelphia shall be tried and disposed of in the court of Common Pleas. The records and dockets of said courts shall be transferred to the prothonotary's office of said county.

Trial and Disposition of Causes in Allegheny County

Sec. 22. The causes and proceedings pending in the court of Common Pleas in the county of Allegheny shall be tried and disposed of in the court number one; and the causes and proceedings pending in the District Court shall be tried and disposed of in the court number two.

Appointment of Prothonotary in Philadelphia — Clerk of Quarter Sessions

Sec. 23. The Prothonotary of the court of Common Pleas of Philadelphia shall be first appointed by the judges of said court on the first Monday of December, in the year one thousand eight hundred and seventy-five, and the present Prothonotary of the District Court in said county shall be the Prothonotary of the said court of Common Pleas until said date when his commission shall expire, and the present Clerk of the court of Oyer and Terminer and Quarter Sessions of the Peace in Philadelphia shall be the Clerk of such court until the expiration of his present commission on the first Monday of December, in the year one thousand eight hundred and seventy-five.

Aldermen in Cities, other than Philadelphia, Containing over Fifty Thousand Inhabitants

Sec. 24. In cities containing over fifty thousand inhabitants, except Philadelphia, all aldermen in office at the time of the adoption of this Constitution shall continue in office until the expiration of their commissions, and at the election for city and ward officers in the year one thousand eight hundred and seventy-five one alderman shall be elected in each ward as provided in this Constitution.

Magistrates to Succeed Aldermen in Philadelphia

Sec. 25. In Philadelphia magistrates in lieu of aldermen shall be chosen, as required in this Constitution, at the election in said city for city and ward officers in the year one thousand eight hundred and seventy-five ; their term of office shall commence on the first Monday of April succeeding their election. The terms of office of aldermen in said city holding or entitled to commissions at the time of the adoption of this Constitution shall not be affected thereby.

Expiration of Term of Present Officers

Sec. 26. All persons in office in this Commonwealth at the time of the adoption of this Constitution, and at the first election under it, shall hold their respective offices until the term for which they have been elected or appointed shall expire, and until their successors shall be duly qualified, unless otherwise provided in this Constitution.

Administration of Oath of Office

Sec. 27. The seventh article of this Constitution prescribing an oath of office shall take effect on and after the first day of January, one thousand eight hundred and seventy-five.

Expiration of Terms of Present County Commissioners and Auditors

Sec. 28. The terms of office of County Commissioners and County Auditors, chosen prior to the year one thousand eight hundred and seventy-five, which shall not have expired before the first Monday of January in the year one thousand eight hundred and seventy-six, shall expire on that day.

Compensation of Present Officers may Include Fees

Sec. 29. All state, county, city, ward, borough and township officers in office at the time of the adoption of this Constitution, whose compensation is not provided for by salaries alone, shall continue to receive the compensation allowed them by law until the expiration of their respective terms of office.

State and Judicial Officers now in Office to take Oath to Support this Constitution

Sec. 30. All state and judicial officers heretofore elected, sworn, affirmed, or in office when this Constitution shall take effect, shall severally, within one month after such adoption, take and subscribe an oath, or affirmation, to support this Constitution.

General Assembly to Pass Laws Necessary to Enforce Constitution

Sec. 31. The General Assembly at its first session, or as soon as may be after the adoption of this Constitution, shall pass such laws as may be necessary to carry the same into full force and effect.

Ordinance Submitting Constitution to Vote of Electors Declared Valid

Sec. 32. The ordinance passed by this Convention entitled " An Ordinance for submitting the amended Constitution of Pennsylvania to a vote of the electors thereof " shall be held to be valid for all the purposes thereof.

The Term " County Commissioners " to Include the Philadelphia Commissioners

Sec. 33. The words " County Commissioners," wherever used in this Constitution and in any ordinance accompanying the same, shall be held to include the Commissioners for the City of Philadelphia.

Date of Adoption by the Constitutional Convention — Signers

Adopted at Philadelphia, on the third day of November, in the year of our Lord one thousand eight hundred and seventy-three.

JOHN H. WALKER,

D. L. IMBRIE,   President.
  Ch. Clerk.

Filed in the Office of the Secretary of the Commonwealth, November 13, 1873.

M. S. QUAY,
Secretary of the Commonwealth.

AMENDMENTS TO THE CONSTITUTION OF PENNSYLVANIA

Amendment No. 1

On November 5, 1901, Section 1 of Article 8, by a vote of 214,798 for, and 45,601 against, was amended so as to read as follows:

Sec. 1. Every male citizen twenty-one years of age, possessing the following qualifications, shall be entitled to vote at all elections, subject however to such laws requiring and regulating the registration of electors as the General Assembly may enact:

1. He shall have been a citizen of the United States at least one month.

2. He shall have resided in the State one year (or, having previously been a qualified elector or native-born citizen of the State, he shall have removed therefrom and returned, then six months) immediately preceding the election.

3. He shall have resided in the election district where he shall offer to vote at least two months immediately preceding the election.

4. If twenty-two years of age and upwards, he shall have paid within two years a State or county tax, which shall have been assessed at least two months and paid at least one month before the election.

Amendment No. 2

On November 5, 1901, Section 4 of Article 8, by a vote of 194,053 for, and 41,203 against, was amended to read as follows:

Sec. 4. All elections by the citizens shall be by ballot or by such other method as may be prescribed by law: Provided, That secrecy in voting be preserved.

Amendment No. 3

On November 5, 1901, Section 7 of Article 8, by a vote of 180,521 for, and 48,634 against, was amended so as to read as follows:

Sec. 7. All laws regulating the holding of elections by the citizens or for the registration of electors shall be uniform throughout the State, but laws regulating and requiring the registration of electors may be enacted to apply to cities only: Provided, That such laws be uniform for cities of the same class.

AMENDMENTS TO THE CONSTITUTION OF PENNSYLVANIA — 1909 — WITH SCHEDULE

Amendment No. 1.

On November 2, 1909, Section 8 of Article 4, by a vote of 155,741 for, and 150,281 against, was amended so as to read as follows:

Sec. 8. He shall nominate and, by and with the advice and consent of two-thirds of all the members of the Senate, appoint a Secretary of the Commonwealth and an Attorney General during pleasure, a Superintendent of Public Instruction for four years, and such other officers of the Commonwealth as he is or may be authorized by the Constitution or by law to appoint ; he shall have power to fill all vacancies that may happen, in offices to which he may appoint, during the recess of the Senate, by granting commissions which shall expire at the end of their next session ; he shall have power to fill any vacancy that may happen, during the recess of the Senate, in the office of Auditor General, State Treasurer, Secretary of Internal Affairs or Superintendent of Public Instruction, in a judicial office, or in any other elective office which he is or may be authorized to fill; if the vacancy shall happen during the session of the Senate, the Governor shall nominate to the Senate, before their final adjournment, a proper person to fill said vacancy ; but in any such case of vacancy, in an elective office, a person shall be chosen to said office on the next election day appropriate to such office according to the provisions of this Constitution, unless the vacancy shall happen within two calendar months immediately preceding such election day, in which case the election for said office shall be held on the second succeeding election day appropriate to such office. In acting on executive nominations the Senate shall sit with open doors, and, in confirming or rejecting the nominations of the Governor, the vote shall be taken by yeas and nays and shall be entered on the journal.

Amendment No. 2.

On November 2, 1909, Section 21 of Article 4, by a vote of 164,352 for, and 142,385 against, was amended so as to read as follows :

Sec. 21. The terms of the Secretary of Internal Affairs, the Auditor General, and the State Treasurer shall each be four years ; and they shall be chosen by the qualified electors of the State at general elections ; but a State Treasurer, elected in the year one thousand nine hundred and nine, shall serve for three years, and his successors shall be elected at the general election in the year one thousand nine hundred and twelve, and in every fourth year thereafter. No person elected to the office of Auditor General or State Treasurer shall be capable of holding the same office for two consecutive terms.

Amendment No. 3.

On November 2, 1909, Section 11 of Article 5, by a vote of 162,689 for, and 141,203 against, was amended so as to read as follows :

Sec. 11. Except as otherwise provided in this Constitution, justices of the peace or aldermen shall be elected in the several wards, districts, boroughs or townships, by the qualified electors thereof, at the municipal election, in such manner as shall be directed by law, and shall be commissioned by the Governor for a term of six years. No township, ward, district or borough shall elect more than two justices of the peace or aldermen without the consent of a majority of the qualified electors within such township, ward or borough ; no person shall be elected to such office unless he shall have resided within the township, borough, ward or district for one year next preceding his election. In cities containing over fifty thousand inhabitants, not more than one alderman shall be elected in each ward or district.

Amendment No. 4.

On November 2, 1909, Section 12 of Article 5, by a vote of 157,958 for, and 142,335 against, was amended so as to read as follows :

Sec. 12. In Philadelphia there shall be established, for each thirty thousand inhabitants, one court, not of record, of police and civil causes, with jurisdiction not exceeding one hundred dollars ; such courts shall be held by magistrates whose term of office shall be six years, and they shall be elected on general ticket at the municipal election, by the qualified voters at large ; and in the election of the said magistrates no voter shall vote for more than two-thirds of the number of persons to be elected when more than one are to be chosen ; they shall be compensated only by fixed salaries, to be paid by said county ; and shall exercise such jurisdiction, civil and criminal, except as herein provided, as is now exercised by aldermen, subject to such changes, not involving an increase of civil jurisdiction or conferring political duties, as may be made by law. In Philadelphia the office of alderman is abolished.

Amendment No. 5.

On November 2, 1909, Section 2 of Article 8, by a vote of 168,874 for, and 140,837 against, was amended so as to read as follows :

Sec. 2. The general election shall be held biennially on the Tuesday next following the first Monday of November in each even-numbered year, but the General Assembly may by law fix a different day, two-thirds of all the members of each House consenting thereto : Provided, That such election shall always be held in an even-numbered year.

Amendment No. 6.

On November 2, 1909, Section 3 of Article 8, by a vote of 162,117 for, and 140,841 against, was amended so as to read as follows :

Sec. 3. All judges elected by the electors of the State at large may be elected at either a general or municipal election, as circumstances may require. All elections for judges of the courts for the several judicial districts, and for county, city, ward, borough, and township officers, for regular terms of service, shall be held on the municipal election day ; namely, the Tuesday next following the first Monday of November in each odd-numbered year, but the General Assembly may by law fix a different day, two-thirds of all the members of each House consenting thereto : Provided, That such election shall always be held in an odd-numbered year.

Amendment No. 7.

(On November 2, 1909, the proposed Amendment to Section 14 of Article 8, by a vote of 128,287 for, and 194,810 against, was defeated.)

Amendment No. 8.

On November 2, 1909, Section 1 of Article 12, by a vote of 160,499 for, and 140,303 against, was amended so as to read as follows :

Sec. 1. All officers whose selection is not provided for in this Constitution, shall be elected or appointed as may be directed by law : Provided, That elections of State officers shall be held on a general election day, and elections of local officers shall be held on a municipal election day, except when, in either case, special elections may be required to fill unexpired terms.

Amendment No. 9.

On November 2, 1909, Section 2 of Article 14, by a vote of 160,184 for, and 141,547 against, was amended so as to read as follows :

Sec. 2. County officers shall be elected at the municipal elections and shall hold their offices for the term of four years, beginning on the first Monday of January next after their election, and until their successors shall be duly qualified ; all vacancies not otherwise provided for, shall be filled in such manner as may be provided by law.

Amendment No. 10.

On November 2, 1909, Section 7 of Article 14, by a vote of 159,953 for, and 140, 476 against, was amended so as to read as follows :

Sec. 7. Three county commissioners and three county auditors shall be elected in each county where such officers are chosen, in the year one thousand nine hundred and eleven and every fourth year thereafter ; and in the election of said officers each qualified elector shall vote for no more than two persons, and the three persons having the highest number of votes shall be elected ; any casual vacancy in the office of county commissioner or county auditor shall be filled, by the court of common pleas of the county in which such vacancy shall occur, by the appointment of an elector of the proper county who shall have voted for the commissioner or auditor whose place is to be filled.

Schedule for the Amendments.

The Schedule to carry into operation the amendments voted for November 2, 1909, by a vote of 147,162 for, and 141,551 against, was adopted :

That no inconvenience may arise from the changes in the Constitution of the Commonwealth, and in order to carry the same into complete opera- tion, it is hereby declared that —

In the case of officers elected by the people, all terms of office fixed by act of Assembly at an odd number of years shall each be lengthened one year, but the Legislature may change the length of the term, provided the terms for which such officers are elected shall always be for an even number of years.

The above extension of official terms shall not affect officers elected at the general election of one thousand nine hundred and eight ; nor any city, ward, borough, township, or election division officers, whose terms of office, under existing law, end in the year one thousand nine hundred and ten.

In the year one thousand nine hundred and ten the municipal election shall be held on the third Tuesday of February as heretofore ; but all officers chosen at that election to an office the regular term of which is two years, and also all election officers and assessors chosen at that election, shall serve until the first Monday of December in the year one thousand nine hundred and eleven. All officers chosen at that election to offices the term of which is now four years, or is made four years by the operation of these amendments or this schedule, shall serve until the first Monday of December in the year one thousand nine hundred and thirteen. All justices of the peace, magistrates, and aldermen, chosen at that election, shall serve until the first Monday of December in the year one thousand nine hundred and fifteen. After the year nineteen hundred and ten, and until the Legislature shall otherwise provide, all terms of city, ward, borough, township, and election division officers shall begin on the first Monday of December in an odd-numbered year.

All city, ward, borough, and township officers holding office at the date of the approval of these amendments, whose terms of office may end in the year one thousand nine hundred and eleven, shall continue to hold their offices until the first Monday of December of that year.

All judges of the courts for the several judicial districts, and also all county officers, holding office at the date of the approval of these amendments, whose terms of office may end in the year one thousand nine hundred and eleven, shall continue to hold their offices until the first Monday of January, one thousand nine hundred and twelve.

Appendix II

———◆◇◆———

[THE CONSTITUTION OF THE UNITED STATES OF AMERICA.][1]

WE THE PEOPLE of the United States, in Order to form a more perfect ·Union, establish Justice, insure domestic Tranquility, provide for the common defence, promote the general Welfare, and secure the Blessings of Liberty to ourselves and our Posterity, do ordain and establish this CONSTITUTION for the United States of America.

ARTICLE. I.

SECTION. 1. All legislative Powers herein granted shall be vested in a Congress of the United States, which shall consist of a Senate and House of Representatives.

SECTION. 2. [1] The House of Representatives shall be composed of Members chosen every second Year by the People of the several States, and the Electors in each State shall have the Qualifications requisite for Electors of the most numerous Branch of the State Legislature.

[2] No Person shall be a Representative who shall not have attained to the Age of twenty five Years, and been seven Years a Citizen of the United States, and who shall not, when elected, be an Inhabitant of that State in which he shall be chosen.

[3] Representatives and direct Taxes shall be apportioned among the several States which may be included within this Union, according to their respective Numbers,[2] [which shall be determined by adding to the whole Number of free Persons, including those bound to Service for a Term of

---

[1] This text of the Constitution has been printed from the copy issued by the United States Department of State which bears the indorsement, "Compared with the original in the Department of State, April 13, 1891, and found to be correct." Those parts of the document in brackets [] are not in the original, or have been modified or superseded by amendments, or were temporary in their character.

[2] The apportionment under the census of 1900 is one representative to every 193,291.

Years, and excluding Indians not taxed, three fifths of all other Persons].[1]
The actual Enumeration shall be made within three Years after the first
Meeting of the Congress of the United States, and within every subsequent
Term of ten Years, in such Manner as they shall by Law direct. The Number of Representatives shall not exceed one for every thirty Thousand, but
each State shall have at Least one Representative ; [and until such enumeration shall be made, the State of New Hampshire shall be entitled to chuse
three, Massachusetts eight, Rhode-Island and Providence Plantations one,
Connecticut five, New-York six, New Jersey four, Pennsylvania eight, Delaware one, Maryland six, Virginia ten, North Carolina five, South Carolina
five, and Georgia three.]

[4] When vacancies happen in the Representation from any State, the
Executive Authority thereof shall issue Writs of Election to fill such Vacancies.

[5] The House of Representatives shall chuse their Speaker[2] and other
Officers ; and shall have the sole Power of Impeachment.

SECTION. 3. [1] The Senate of the United States shall be composed of two
Senators from each State, chosen by the Legislature thereof, for six Years ;
and each Senator shall have one Vote.

[2] Immediately after they shall be assembled in Consequence of the first
Election, they shall be divided as equally as may be into three Classes. The
Seats of the Senators of the first Class shall be vacated at the Expiration of
the second Year, of the second Class at the Expiration of the fourth Year,
and of the third Class at the Expiration of the sixth Year, so that one third
may be chosen every second Year ; and if Vacancies happen by Resignation,
or otherwise, during the Recess of the Legislature of any State, the Executive thereof may make temporary Appointments until the next Meeting of
the Legislature, which shall then fill such Vacancies.

[3] No Person shall be a Senator who shall not have attained to the Age
of thirty Years, and been nine Years a Citizen of the United States, and who
shall not, when elected, be an Inhabitant of that State for which he shall be
chosen.

[4] The Vice President of the United States shall be President of the
Senate, but shall have no Vote, unless they be equally divided.

[5] The Senate shall chuse their other Officers, and also a President pro
tempore, in the Absence of the Vice President, or when he shall exercise
the Office of President of the United States.

[6] The Senate shall have the sole Power to try all Impeachments. When
sitting for that Purpose, they shall be on Oath or Affirmation. When the
President of the United States is tried, the Chief Justice shall preside : And

---

[1] The clause in brackets has been superseded by the thirteenth and fourteenth amendments.
[2] The Speaker is always one of the representatives ; the other officers are not.

no Person shall be convicted without the Concurrence of two thirds of the Members present.

[7] Judgment in Cases of Impeachment shall not extend further than to removal from Office, and disqualification to hold and enjoy any Office of honor, Trust or Profit under the United States: but the Party convicted shall nevertheless be liable and subject to Indictment, Trial, Judgment and Punishment, according to Law.

SECTION. 4. [1] The Times, Places and Manner of holding Elections for Senators and Representatives, shall be prescribed in each State by the Legislature thereof; but the Congress may at any time by Law make or alter such Regulations, except as to the Places of chusing Senators.

[2] The Congress shall assemble at least once in every Year, and such Meeting shall be on the first Monday in December, unless they shall by Law appoint a different Day.

SECTION. 5. [1] Each House shall be the Judge of the Elections, Returns and Qualifications of its own Members, and a Majority of each shall constitute a Quorum to do Business; but a smaller Number may adjourn from day to day, and may be authorized to compel the Attendance of absent Members, in such Manner, and under such Penalties as each House may provide.

[2] Each House may determine the Rules of its Proceedings, punish its Members for disorderly Behaviour, and, with the Concurrence of two thirds, expel a Member.

[3] Each House shall keep a Journal of its Proceedings, and from time to time publish the same, excepting such Parts as may in their Judgment require Secrecy; and the Yeas and Nays of the Members of either House on any question shall, at the Desire of one fifth of those Present, be entered on the Journal.

[4] Neither House, during the Session of Congress, shall, without the Consent of the other, adjourn for more than three days, nor to any other Place than that in which the two Houses shall be sitting.

SECTION. 6. [1] The Senators and Representatives shall receive a Compensation[1] for their Services, to be ascertained by Law, and paid out of the Treasury of the United States. They shall in all Cases, except Treason, Felony and Breach of the Peace, be privileged from Arrest during their Attendance at the Session of their respective Houses, and in going to and returning from the same; and for any Speech or Debate in either House, they shall not be questioned in any other Place.

[2] No Senator or Representative shall, during the Time for which he was elected, be appointed to any civil Office under the Authority of the United

---

[1] At present (1904) this is "$5000 per annum, with $125 annual allowance for stationery and newspapers, and a mileage allowance of twenty cents per mile of travel each way from their homes at each annual session."

States, which shall have been created, or the Emoluments whereof shall have been encreased during such time; and no Person holding any Office under the United States, shall be a Member of either House during his Continuance in Office.

SECTION. 7.   [1] All Bills for raising Revenue shall originate in the House of Representatives; but the Senate may propose or concur with Amendments as on other Bills.

[2] Every Bill which shall have passed the House of Representatives and the Senate, shall, before it become a Law, be presented to the President of the United States; if he approve he shall sign it, but if not he shall return it, with his Objections to that House in which it shall have originated, who shall enter the Objections at large on their Journal, and proceed to reconsider it.   If after such Reconsideration two thirds of that House shall agree to pass the Bill, it shall be sent, together with the Objections, to the other House, by which it shall likewise be reconsidered, and if approved by two thirds of that House, it shall become a Law.   But in all such Cases the Votes of both Houses shall be determined by yeas and Nays, and the Names of the Persons voting for and against the Bill shall be entered on the Journal of each House respectively.   If any Bill shall not be returned by the President within ten Days (Sundays excepted) after it shall have been presented to him, the Same shall be a Law, in like Manner as if he had signed it, unless the Congress by their Adjournment prevent its Return, in which Case it shall not be a Law.

[3] Every Order, Resolution, or Vote to which the Concurrence of the Senate and House of Representatives may be necessary (except on a question of Adjournment) shall be presented to the President of the United States; and before the same shall take Effect, shall be approved by him, or being disapproved by him, shall be repassed by two thirds of the Senate and House of Representatives, according to the Rules and Limitations prescribed in the Case of a Bill.

SECTION. 8.   [1] The Congress shall have Power To lay and collect Taxes, Duties, Imposts and Excises, to pay the Debts and provide for the common Defence and general Welfare of the United States; but all Duties, Imposts and Excises shall be uniform throughout the United States;

[2] To borrow Money on the credit of the United States;

[3] To regulate Commerce with foreign Nations, and among the several States, and with the Indian Tribes;

[4] To establish an uniform Rule of Naturalization, and uniform Laws on the subject of Bankruptcies throughout the United States;

[5] To coin Money, regulate the Value thereof, and of foreign Coin, and fix the Standard of Weights and Measures;

[6] To provide for the Punishment of counterfeiting the Securities and current Coin of the United States;

[7] To establish Post Offices and post Roads ;

[8] To promote the Progress of Science and useful Arts, by securing for limited Times to Authors and Inventors the exclusive Right to their respective Writings and Discoveries ;

[9] To constitute Tribunals inferior to the supreme Court ;

[10] To define and punish Piracies and Felonies committed on the high Seas, and Offences against the Law of Nations ;

[11] To declare War, grant Letters of Marque and Reprisal, and make Rules concerning Captures on Land and Water ;

[12] To raise and support Armies, but no Appropriation of Money to that Use shall be for a longer Term than two Years ;

[13] To provide and maintain a Navy ;

[14] To make Rules for the Government and Regulation of the land and naval Forces ;

[15] To provide for calling forth the Militia to execute the Laws of the Union, suppress Insurrections and repel Invasions ;

[16] To provide for organizing, arming, and disciplining, the Militia, and for governing such Part of them as may be employed in the Service of the United States, reserving to the States respectively, the Appointment of the Officers, and the Authority of training the Militia according to the discipline prescribed by Congress ;

[17] To exercise exclusive Legislation in all Cases whatsoever, over such District (not exceeding ten Miles square) as may, by Cession of particular States, and the Acceptance of Congress, become the Seat of the Government oi the United States, and to exercise like Authority over all Places purchased by the Consent of the Legislature of the State in which the Same shall be, for the Erection of Forts, Magazines, Arsenals, dock-Yards, and other needful Buildings ; — And

[18] To make all Laws which shall be necessary and proper for carrying into Execution the foregoing Powers, and all other Powers vested by this Constitution in the Government of the United States, or in any Department or Officer thereof.

SECTION. 9. [1] [The Migration or Importation of such Persons as any of the States now existing shall think proper to admit, shall not be prohibited by the Congress prior to the Year one thousand eight hundred and eight, but a Tax or duty may be imposed on such Importation, not exceeding ten dollars for each Person.] [1]

[2] The Privilege of the Writ of Habeas Corpus shall not be suspended, unless when in Cases of Rebellion or Invasion the public Safety may require it.

[3] No Bill of Attainder or ex post facto Law shall be passed.

[1] A temporary clause no longer in force.

[4] No Capitation, or other direct, Tax shall be laid, unless in Proportion to the Census or Enumeration herein before directed to be taken.

[5] No Tax or Duty shall be laid on Articles exported from any State.

[6] No Preference shall be given by any Regulation of Commerce or Revenue to the Ports of one State over those of another: nor shall Vessels bound to, or from, one State, be obliged to enter, clear, or pay Duties in another.

[7] No Money shall be drawn from the Treasury, but in Consequence of Appropriations made by Law; and a regular Statement and Account of the Receipts and Expenditures of all public Money shall be published from time to time.

[8] No Title of Nobility shall be granted by the United States: And no Person holding any Office of Profit or Trust under them, shall, without the Consent of the Congress, accept of any present, Emolument, Office, or Title, of any kind whatever, from any King, Prince, or foreign State.[1]

SECTION. 10. [1] No State shall enter into any Treaty, Alliance, or Confederation; grant Letters of Marque and Reprisal; coin Money; emit Bills of Credit; make any Thing but gold and silver Coin a Tender in Payment of Debts; pass any Bill of Attainder, ex post facto Law, or Law impairing the Obligation of Contracts, or grant any Title of Nobility.

[2] No State shall, without the Consent of the Congress, lay any Imposts or Duties on Imports or Exports, except what may be absolutely necessary for executing it's inspection Laws: and the net Produce of all Duties and Imposts, laid by any State on Imports or Exports, shall be for the Use of the Treasury of the United States; and all such Laws shall be subject to the Revision and Controul of the Congress.

[3] No State shall, without the Consent of Congress, lay any Duty of Tonnage, keep Troops, or Ships of War in time of Peace, enter into any Agreement or Compact with another State, or with a foreign Power, or engage in War, unless actually invaded, or in such imminent Danger as will not admit of delay.[2]

ARTICLE. II.

SECTION. 1. [1] The executive Power shall be vested in a President of the United States of America. He shall hold his Office during the Term of four Years, and, together with the Vice President, chosen for the same Term, be elected, as follows

[2] Each State shall appoint, in such Manner as the Legislature thereof may direct, a Number of Electors, equal to the whole Number of Senators

---

[1] The personal rights enumerated in Section 9, have been added to, and extended by, Amendments I.-X.

[2] The provisions of Section 10 have been modified and extended by Amendments XIII.-XV.

and Representatives to which the State may be entitled in the Congress: but no Senator or Representative, or Person holding an Office of Trust or Profit under the United States, shall be appointed an Elector.

[3] [The Electors shall meet in their respective States, and vote by Ballot for two Persons, of whom one at least shall not be an Inhabitant of the same State with themselves. And they shall make a List of all the Persons voted for, and of the Number of Votes for each; which List they shall sign and certify, and transmit sealed to the Seat of the Government of the United States, directed to the President of the Senate. The President of the Senate shall, in the Presence of the Senate and House of Representatives, open all the Certificates, and the Votes shall then be counted. The Person having the greatest Number of Votes shall be the President, if such Number be a Majority of the whole Number of Electors appointed; and if there be more than one who have such Majority, and have an equal Number of Votes, then the House of Representatives shall immediately chuse by Ballot one of them for President; and if no Person have a Majority, then from the five highest on the List the said House shall in like Manner chuse the President. But in chusing the President, the Votes shall be taken by States, the Representation from each State having one Vote; A quorum for this Purpose shall consist of a Member or Members from two thirds of the States, and a Majority of all the States shall be necessary to a Choice. In every Case, after the Choice of the President, the Person having the greatest Number of Votes of the Electors shall be the Vice President. But if there should remain two or more who have equal Votes, the Senate shall chuse from them by Ballot the Vice President.]¹

[4] The Congress may determine the Time of chusing the Electors, and the Day on which they shall give their Votes; which Day shall be the same throughout the United States.

[5] No Person except a natural born Citizen, or a Citizen of the United States, at the time of the Adoption of this Constitution, shall be eligible to the Office of President; neither shall any Person be eligible to that Office who shall not have attained to the Age of thirty five Years, and been fourteen Years a Resident within the United States.

[6] In Case of the Removal of the President from Office, or of his Death, Resignation, or Inability to discharge the Powers and Duties of the said Office, the Same shall devolve on the Vice President, and the Congress may by Law provide for the Case of Removal, Death, Resignation or Inability, both of the President and Vice President, declaring what Officer shall then act as President, and such Officer shall act accordingly, until the Disability be removed, or a President shall be elected.

¹ This clause has been superseded by Amendment XII.

[7] The President shall, at stated Times, receive for his Services, a Compensation, which shall neither be encreased nor diminished during the Period for which he shall have been elected, and he shall not receive within that Period any other Emolument from the United States, or any of them.

[8] Before he enter on the Execution of his Office, he shall take the following Oath or Affirmation : — "I do solemnly swear (or affirm) that I will faithfully execute the Office of President of the United States, and will to the best of my Ability, preserve, protect and defend the Constitution of the United States."

Section. 2. [1] The President shall be Commander in Chief of the Army and Navy of the United States, and of the Militia of the several States, when called into the actual Service of the United States ; he may require the Opinion, in writing, of the principal Officer in each of the executive Departments, upon any Subject relating to the Duties of their respective Offices, and he shall have Power to grant Reprieves and Pardons for Offences against the United States, except in Cases of Impeachment.

[2] He shall have Power, by and with the Advice and Consent of the Senate, to make Treaties, provided two thirds of the Senators present concur ; and he shall nominate, and by and with the Advice and Consent of the Senate, shall appoint Ambassadors, other public Ministers and Consuls, Judges of the supreme Court, and all other Officers of the United States, whose Appointments are not herein otherwise provided for, and which shall be established by Law : but the Congress may by Law vest the Appointment of such inferior Officers, as they think proper, in the President alone, in the Courts of Law, or in the Heads of Departments.

[3] The President shall have Power to fill up all Vacancies that may happen during the Recess of the Senate, by granting Commissions which shall expire at the End of their next Session.

Section. 3. [1] He shall from time to time give to the Congress Information of the State of the Union, and recommend to their Consideration such Measures as he shall judge necessary and expedient ; he may, on extraordinary Occasions, convene both Houses, or either of them, and in Case of Disagreement between them, with Respect to the Time of Adjournment, he may adjourn them to such Time as he shall think proper ; he shall receive Ambassadors and other public Ministers ; he shall take Care that the Laws be faithfully executed, and shall Commission all the Officers of the United States.

Section. 4. [1] The President, Vice President and all civil Officers of the United States, shall be removed from Office on Impeachment for, and Conviction of, Treason, Bribery, or other high Crimes and Misdemeanors.

ARTICLE. III.

SECTION. 1. [1] The judicial Power of the United States, shall be vested in one supreme Court, and in such inferior Courts as the Congress may from time to time ordain and establish. The Judges, both of the supreme and inferior Courts, shall hold their Offices during good Behaviour, and shall, at stated Times, receive for their Services, a Compensation, which shall not be diminished during their continuance in Office.

SECTION. 2. [1] The judicial Power shall extend to all cases, in Law and Equity, arising under this Constitution, the Laws of the United States, and Treaties made, or which shall be made, under their Authority ; — to all Cases affecting Ambassadors, other public Ministers and Consuls ; — to all Cases of admiralty and maritime Jurisdiction ; — to Controversies to which the United States shall be a Party ; — to Controversies between two or more States ; — between a State and Citizens of another State ;[1] between Citizens of different States, — between Citizens of the same State claiming Lands under Grants of different States, and between a State, or the Citizens thereof, and foreign States, Citizens or Subjects.

[2] In all Cases affecting Ambassadors, other public Ministers and Consuls, and those in which a State shall be Party, the supreme Court shall have original Jurisdiction. In all the other Cases before mentioned, the supreme Court shall have appellate Jurisdiction, both as to Law and Fact, with such Exceptions, and under such regulations as the Congress shall make.

[3] The Trial of all Crimes, except in Cases of Impeachment, shall be by Jury ; and such Trial shall be held in the State where the said Crimes shall have been committed ; but when not committed within any State, the Trial shall be at such Place or Places as the Congress may by Law have directed.

SECTION. 3. [1] Treason against the United States, shall consist only in levying War against them, or in adhering to their Enemies, giving them Aid and Comfort. No Person shall be convicted of Treason unless on the Testimony of two Witnesses to the same overt Act, or on Confession in open Court.

[2] The Congress shall have Power to declare the Punishment of Treason, but no Attainder of Treason shall work Corruption of Blood, or Forfeiture except during the Life of the Person attainted.

ARTICLE. IV.

SECTION. 1. [1] Full Faith and Credit shall be given in each State to the public Acts, Records, and judicial Proceedings of every other State. And

---

[1] Modified by Amendment XI.

the Congress may by general Laws prescribe the Manner in which such Acts, Records and Proceedings shall be proved, and the Effect thereof.

SECTION. 2. [1] The Citizens of each State shall be entitled to all Privileges and Immunities of Citizens in the several States.[1]

[2] A Person charged in any State with Treason, Felony, or other Crime, who shall flee from Justice, and be found in another State, shall on Demand of the executive Authority of the State from which he fled, be delivered up, to be removed to the State having Jurisdiction of the Crime.

[3] [No Person held to Service or Labour in one State, under the Laws thereof, escaping into another, shall, in Consequence of any Law or Regulation therein, be discharged from such Service or Labour, but shall be delivered up on Claim of the Party to whom such Service or Labour may be due.] [2]

SECTION. 3. [1] New States may be admitted by the Congress into this Union ; but no new State shall be formed or erected within the Jurisdiction of any other State ; nor any State be formed by the Junction of two or more States, or Parts of States, without the Consent of the Legislatures of the States concerned as well as of the Congress.

[2] The Congress shall have Power to dispose of and make all needful Rules and Regulations respecting the Territory or other Property belonging to the United States ; and nothing in this Constitution shall be so construed as to Prejudice any Claims of the United States, or of any particular State.

SECTION. 4. [1] The United States shall guarantee to every State in this Union a Republican Form of Government, and shall protect each of them against Invasion ; and on Application of the Legislature, or of the Executive (when the Legislature cannot be convened) against domestic Violence.

ARTICLE. V.

[1] The Congress, whenever two thirds of both Houses shall deem it necessary, shall propose Amendments to this Constitution, or, on the Application of the Legislatures of two thirds of the several States, shall call a Convention for proposing Amendments, which, in either Case, shall be valid to all Intents and Purposes, as Part of this Constitution, when ratified by the Legislatures of three fourths of the several States, or by Conventions in three fourths thereof, as the one or the other Mode of Ratification may be proposed by the Congress ; Provided that [no Amendment which may be made prior to the Year One thousand eight hundred and eight shall in any Manner affect the first and fourth Clauses in the Ninth Section of the first Article ; and that] [3] no State, without its Consent, shall be deprived of it's equal Suffrage in the Senate.

[1] Provisions extended by Amendment XIV.
[2] Superseded by Amendment XIII.
[3] Temporary in its nature.

ARTICLE. VI.

[1] All Debts contracted and Engagements entered into, before the Adoption of this Constitution, shall be as valid against the United States under this Constitution, as under the Confederation.

[2] This Constitution, and the Laws of the United States which shall be made in Pursuance thereof; and all Treaties made, or which shall be made, under the Authority of the United States, shall be the supreme Law of the Land; and the Judges in every State shall be bound thereby, any Thing in the Constitution or Laws of any State to the Contrary notwithstanding.

[3] The Senators and Representatives before mentioned, and the Members of the several State Legislatures, and all executive and judicial Officers, both of the United States and of the several States, shall be bound by Oath or Affirmation, to support this Constitution; but no religious Test shall ever be required as a Qualification to any Office or public Trust under the United States.

ARTICLE. VII.

[1] The Ratification of the Conventions of nine States, shall be sufficient for the Establishment of this Constitution between the States so ratifying the Same.

The Word, "the", being interlined between the seventh and eighth Lines of the first Page, The Word "Thirty" being partly written on an Erazure in the fifteenth Line of the first Page, The Words "is tried" being interlined between the thirty second and thirty third Lines of the first Page and the Word "the" being interlined between the forty third and forty fourth Lines of the second Page.

[NOTE BY PRINTER.—The interlined and rewritten words, mentioned in the above explanation, are in this edition, printed in their proper places in the text.]

DONE in Convention by the Unanimous Consent of the States present the Seventeenth Day of September in the Year of our Lord one thousand seven hundred and Eighty seven and of the Independance of the United States of America the Twelfth **In Witness** whereof We have hereunto subscribed our Names,

G⁰: WASHINGTON — *Presidt.*
and deputy from Virginia

Attest WILLIAM JACKSON *Secretary*

NEW HAMPSHIRE.
John Langdon
Nicholas Gilman

MASSACHUSETTS.
Nathaniel Gorham
Rufus King

CONNECTICUT.
Wm: Saml. Johnson
Roger Sherman

NEW YORK.
Alexander Hamilton

NEW JERSEY.
Wil: Livingston
David Brearley.
Wm. Paterson.
Jona: Dayton

PENNSYLVANIA.
B Franklin
Thomas Mifflin
Robt. Morris
Geo. Clymer
Thos. Fitz Simons
Jared Ingersoll
James Wilson
Gouv Morris

DELAWARE.
Geo: Read
Gunning Bedford jun
John Dickinson
Richard Bassett
Jaco: Broom

MARYLAND.
James McHenry
Dan of St Thos. Jenifer
Danl Carroll

VIRGINIA.
John Blair —
James Madison Jr.

NORTH CAROLINA.
Wm: Blount
Richd. Dobbs Spaight.
Hu Williamson

SOUTH CAROLINA.
J. Rutledge
Charles Cotesworth Pinckney
Charles Pinckney
Pierce Butler.

GEORGIA.
William Few
Abr Baldwin

ARTICLES

in Addition to, and Amendment of the Constitution of the United States of America, proposed by Congress and ratified by the Legislatures of the Several States, pursuant to the Fifth Article of the Constitution.

[ARTICLE I.]

Congress shall make no law respecting an establishment of religion, or prohibiting the free exercise thereof ; or abridging the freedom of speech, or of the press ; or the right of the people peaceably to assemble, and to petition the Government for a redress of grievances.

[ARTICLE II.]

A well regulated Militia, being necessary to the security of a free State, the right of the people to keep and bear Arms, shall not be infringed.

[ARTICLE III.]

No Soldier shall, in time of peace be quartered in any house, without the consent of the Owner, nor in time of war, but in a manner to be prescribed by law.

[ARTICLE IV.]

The right of the people to be secure in their persons, houses, papers, and effects, against unreasonable searches and seizures, shall not be violated, and no Warrants shall issue, but upon probable cause, supported by Oath or affirmation, and particularly describing the place to be searched, and the persons or things to be seized.

[ARTICLE V.]

No person shall be held to answer for a capital, or otherwise infamous crime, unless on a presentment or indictment of a Grand Jury, except in cases arising in the land or naval forces, or in the Militia, when in actual service in time of War or public danger ; nor shall any person be subject for the same offence to be twice put in jeopardy of life or limb ; nor shall be compelled in any Criminal Case to be a witness against himself, nor be deprived of life, liberty, or property, without due process of law ; nor shall private property be taken for public use, without just compensation.

[ARTICLE VI.]

In all criminal prosecutions, the accused shall enjoy the right to a speedy and public trial, by an impartial jury of the State and district wherein the crime shall have been committed, which district shall have been previously ascertained by law, and to be informed of the nature and cause of the accusation ; to be confronted with the witnesses against him ; to have compulsory process for obtaining Witnesses in his favor, and to have the Assistance of Counsel for his defence.

[ARTICLE VII.]

In suits at common law, where the value in controversy shall exceed twenty dollars, the right of trial by jury shall be preserved, and no fact tried by a jury shall be otherwise re-examined in any Court of the United States, than according to the rules of the common law.

[ARTICLE VIII.]

Excessive bail shall not be required, nor excessive fines imposed, nor cruel and unusual punishments inflicted.

[ARTICLE IX.]

The enumeration in the Constitution, of certain rights, shall not be construed to deny or disparage others retained by the people.

[ARTICLE X.][1]

The powers not delegated to the United States by the Constitution, nor prohibited by it to the States, are reserved to the States respectively, or to the people.

[ARTICLE XI.][2]

The Judicial power of the United States shall not be construed to extend to any suit in law or equity, commenced or prosecuted against one of the United States by Citizens of another State, or by Citizens or Subjects of any Foreign State.

[ARTICLE XII.][3]

The Electors shall meet in their respective states, and vote by ballot for President and Vice President, one of whom, at least, shall not be an inhabitant of the same state with themselves ; they shall name in their ballots the person voted for as President, and in distinct ballots the person voted for as Vice President, and they shall make distinct lists of all persons voted for as President, and of all persons voted for as Vice President, and of the number

[1] Amendments I.–X. were proclaimed to be in force December 15, 1791.
[2] Proclaimed to be in force January 8, 1798.
[3] Proclaimed to be in force September 25, 1804.

of votes for each, which lists they shall sign and certify, and transmit sealed to the seat of the government of the United States, directed to the President of the Senate ; — The President of the Senate shall, in presence of the Senate and House of Representatives, open all the certificates and the votes shall then be counted ; — The person having the greatest number of votes for President, shall be the President, if such number be a majority of the whole number of Electors appointed ; and if no person have such majority, then from the persons having the highest numbers not exceeding three on the list of those voted for as President, the House of Representatives shall choose immediately, by ballot, the President.   But in choosing the President, the votes shall be taken by states, the representation from each state having one vote ; a quorum for this purpose shall consist of a member or members from two-thirds of the states, and a majority of all the states shall be necessary to a choice.   And if the House of Representatives shall not choose a President whenever the right of choice shall devolve upon them, before the fourth day of March next following, then the Vice President shall act as President, as in the case of the death or other constitutional disability of the President. The person having the greatest number of votes as Vice President, shall be the Vice President, if such number be a majority of the whole number of Electors appointed, and if no person have a majority, then from the two highest numbers on the list, the Senate shall choose the Vice President ; a quorum for the purpose shall consist of two-thirds of the whole number of Senators, and a majority of the whole number shall be necessary to a choice. But no person constitutionally ineligible to the office of President shall be eligible to that of Vice President of the United States.

[ARTICLE XIII.] [1]

SECTION 1.   Neither slavery nor involuntary servitude, except as a punish-ment for crime whereof the party shall have been duly convicted, shall exist within the United States, or any place subject to their jurisdiction.

SECTION 2.   Congress shall have power to enforce this article by appro-priate legislation.

[ARTICLE XIV.] [2]

SECTION 1.   All persons born or naturalized in the United States, and sub-ject to the jurisdiction thereof, are citizens of the United States and of the State wherein they reside.   No State shall make or enforce any law which shall abridge the privileges or immunities of citizens of the United States ; nor shall any State deprive any person of life, liberty, or property, without

---

[1] Proclaimed to be in force December 18, 1865.
[2] Proclaimed to be in force July 28, 1868.

due process of law; nor deny to any person within its jurisdiction the equal protection of the laws.

SECTION 2. Representatives shall be apportioned among the several States according to their respective numbers, counting the whole number of persons in each State, excluding Indians not taxed. But when the right to vote at any election for the choice of electors for President and Vice President of the United States, Representatives in Congress, the Executive and Judicial officers of a State, or the members of the Legislature thereof, is denied to any of the male inhabitants of such State, being twenty-one years of age, and citizens of the United States, or in any way abridged, except for participation in rebellion, or other crime, the basis of representation therein shall be reduced in the proportion which the number of such male citizens shall bear to the whole number of male citizens twenty-one years of age in such State.

SECTION 3. No person shall be a Senator or Representative in Congress, or elector of President and Vice President, or hold any office, civil or military, under the United States, or under any State, who, having previously taken an oath, as a member of Congress, or as an officer of the United States, or as a member of any State legislature, or as an executive or judicial officer of any State, to support the Constitution of the United States, shall have engaged in insurrection or rebellion against the same, or given aid or comfort to the enemies thereof. But Congress may by a vote of two-thirds of each House, remove such disability.

SECTION 4. The validity of the public debt of the United States, authorized by law, including debts incurred for payment of pensions and bounties for services in suppressing insurrection or rebellion, shall not be questioned. But neither the United States nor any State shall assume or pay any debt or obligation incurred in aid of insurrection or rebellion against the United States, or any claim for the loss of emancipation of any slave; but all such debts, obligations and claims shall be held illegal and void.

SECTION 5. The Congress shall have power to enforce, by appropriate legislation, the provisions of this article.

[ARTICLE XV.] [1]

SECTION 1. The right of citizens of the United States to vote shall not be denied or abridged by the United States or by any State on account of race, color, or previous condition of servitude.

SECTION 2. The Congress shall have power to enforce this article by appropriate legislation.

[1] Proclaimed to be in force March 30, 1870.

INDEX

263

CPSIA information can be obtained
at www.ICGtesting.com
Printed in the USA
BVHW08s1031210918
528173BV00022B/1220/P

9 781528 453363